SIX GUYS FROM HACKENSACK

Coming Of Age In The Real New Jersey

GEORGE B. KIRSCH

INFINITY
PUBLISHING

Cover photo: Main Street, Hackensack, circa 1963,
Copyrighted by Pendor Natural Color @ www.pendorcolor.com.

Back cover photograph: The guys in 1994, aging by still young at heart.
From left: Richard, George, Barry Vasios, Kevin, Barry Cohen, Henry

ISBN 978-0-7414-7241-0 Paperback
ISBN 978-0-7414-7242-7 Hardcover
ISBN 978-0-7414-7243-4 eBook

Printed in the United States of America

Published March 2012

INFINITY PUBLISHING
1094 New DeHaven Street, Suite 100
West Conshohocken, PA 19428-2713
Toll-free (877) BUY BOOK
Local Phone (610) 941-9999
Fax (610) 941-9959
Info@buybooksontheweb.com
www.buybooksontheweb.com

TO THE MEMORY OF OUR PARENTS,
WITH GRATITUDE

PAULINE & HENRY CENICOLA

RITA & WILLIAM CLERMONT

GOLDIE & RUDY COHEN

ANNE & NATHAN KIRSCH

GERTRUDE & JACOB PRAGER

HAZEL & HAROLD VASIOS

Contents

Preface

This book is both a memoir of friendship and a social history of Hackensack, New Jersey during the post World War II era. Our group of six buddies met in elementary school in the early 1950s and graduated from high school in 1963. We remain friends to this day—largely because of the influence of our hometown and our shared experiences during our youth and adolescence. We are three Jews and three Gentiles who come from families that ranged from working class to professional. Our gang may not be unique, but it sure is unusual in our loyalty to one another over nearly six decades.

The six guys of the title were born in 1945, the cusp of the baby boom. We grew up during two of the most tumultuous and fascinating decades in American history. The events of those times profoundly impacted American domestic politics, international affairs, and popular culture. We knew the Cold War and the fear of nuclear annihilation, the polio epidemic and Dr. Salk, the civil rights movement, and the advent of shopping malls. From the conformity and prosperity of suburbia in the '50s we marched right into the sea change of the '60s—the escalation of the Vietnam War, the threat of the draft, the rise of Black Power and feminism, and the temptations of drugs, sex, popular music, and the counterculture.

I tell our stories in the context of an archetypal New Jersey community that underwent profound change after 1945. Hackensack was at the cutting edge of two new suburban trends. First was the town's diversity in social class, religion, ethnicity and race. Beginning early in the twentieth century, black, Italian, Polish, and Jewish newcomers migrated to Hackensack, joining longtime residents of Dutch, English, German and Irish ancestry. In the 1950s race relations and especially the desegregation of the elementary schools became major issues. Hackensack was also a trend-setter in the response of its business community to the opening of the first shopping centers in northern New Jersey in 1957. Prior to that, Hackensack's downtown business district, anchored by a classic Main Street right out of a "cruisin' the drag" *American Graffiti,* was the retail hub of Bergen County. The new malls devastated Main Street's downtown stores, put property values at risk, and thus jeopardized the financial standing of all the town's residents.

This book would not have been possible without the assistance of Henry Cenicola, Kevin Clermont, Barry Cohen, Richard Prager, and Barry Vasios. They have all been generous with their time and helpful with their constructive criticism and suggestions for revisions, but I am solely responsible for the content of this volume. The epilogue narrates brief biographical summaries of our professional accomplishments and families since 1972. I thank Erin Clermont for her encouragement, criticism, and thoughtful and thorough editing of the manuscript. Dan Collins and Doug Berman very kindly gave me their frank and helpful suggestions for revisions.

And I am grateful to those Hackensack veterans and close friends who granted permission for interviews and provided essential source material: Peter Boorjian, Walter Carroll, Seymour Chase, Kenny Dixon, Craig Jackson, Sylvia Lewis, Sidney Stein, Ruth Heiferman Taylor, Harold Vasios, and Kristine Vasios. Also helpful were Liz Mechmann, Jeff Horn, Fred Martens, Mark Kramer, Albert Dib, Barbara J. Gooding, Allan Petretti, Sharon Castanteen, and the staffs of the Johnson Public Library in Hackensack and the Hackensack Board of Education.

This book is dedicated to the memory of our parents. We benefited enormously from the financial security, family stability, and material comforts they provided, yet even more vitally from their unconditional love, encouragement, direction, and grounding in values that enabled us to have happy childhoods and live productive lives as adults. We also remember our grandparents and other ancestors who left Europe for the hope of better lives, first in the English colonies and later in the United States. They made it possible for us to chase after our own American dreams.

Prelude

I never thought that Susan, my wife of forty years, would be the first of our group to die. But ever since her mother passed away at fifty-five, she had begun to worry about her own chances for longevity. She had a maternal grandfather and a paternal grandmother who survived until their mid-nineties, I often reminded her, so it was likely she would live a long life and survive me.

That was not to be. In the late fall of 2005 she began to have some trouble speaking and swallowing. In November 2006 she was diagnosed with ALS, amyotrophic lateral sclerosis—Lou Gehrig's disease. After her neurologist told her the grim news she asked him how she would die. His answer was respiratory failure. That prediction came true in the early morning of August 3, 2008. When I awoke that Sunday at 5:50 a.m. she was not next to me in bed. I found her slumped over the toilet, unconscious, her body already turning cool. I called 911. The police and emergency squad came within a few minutes, but could not revive her. She had choked on some mucous trapped in her windpipe, and her heart had stopped. I called the funeral home and our son, Adam.

Her body lay on the bathroom floor for about an hour until two men arrived with a van to take it away. I kissed her cheek, one final time. I watched from a front window as the men loaded her remains into the rear of the vehicle. A jogger passed by and I wondered if he understood what he was witnessing.

My five closest friends came to Susan's funeral. They joined more than a hundred mourners who gathered at a Jewish chapel in Hackensack to pay their last respects. They were relatives, friends, colleagues, and even a few causal acquaintances. I treasured the attendance of all of them, but none more so than my Hackensack buddies.

Our group is six guys from Hackensack, plus our wives (minus two who dropped out via divorce, replaced with two second wives), eight children, two grandchildren (so far). Not a very large number of offspring for six marriages, but for us the quality of those sons and daughters counted much more than their quantity. My five friends and I met at Fanny Meyer Hillers elementary school on Longview Avenue in Hackensack in the early 1950s. We have stuck together since, sustaining our relationships long after our graduation from Hackensack High School in 1963.

Henry Cenicola, then residing in northern Bergen County, brought his wife, Betty, to Susan's funeral. Separated since 1995, they were still connected. His intense dedication to his career had served him quite well in the corporate world, even as it impacted his marriage. The lone Roman Catholic in our group, he was the only child of poor Italian immigrants who arrived at Ellis Island early in the twentieth century with hopes of a better life in America. Betty and his peers in business called him "Hank," but to us he

1

remained Henry. Modest, sociable, and friendly, he was extraordinarily generous to family and colleagues in need. A great story teller, he could enthrall his listeners for hours—sometimes to a fault.

Kevin Clermont's attendance meant the world to me, because I knew that he dislikes traveling, especially when he had to drive long distances alone. He left his home in the Cayuga Heights section of Ithaca, N.Y early in the morning for the four hour trip to Hackensack. Of French, German, and Irish descent, he and his family were lapsed Catholics who chose to have no affiliation with any denomination. His second wife, Emily, could not join him because she was caring for their six-year-old adopted Chinese daughter. He also has an adult daughter with his first wife, Pam. Kevin and I were intensely competitive in school, and he raised the academic bar very high for all of us. In our scholastic pursuits—though not in sports or social life—he set the gold standard. He had his eccentricities—he could be quite sarcastic—but that came from the dark Irish wit he inherited from his mother. Despite his great academic and professional achievements he has not sailed smoothly through life, as he has struggled with a series of chronic illnesses over the past few decades.

Barry Cohen also drove solo, departing from his new home on Cape Cod at the crack of dawn to arrive on time. His wife, Debbie, was unable to accompany him. The father of a daughter the same age as my son, he was the first of us to retire and begin collecting Social Security benefits. His family and mine were members of the Conservative Jewish synagogue in Hackensack. He was the last to gain admission to our group. We welcomed him into our inner circle of friends in school and bonded with Barry for life not so much for his academic achievements or professional accomplishments, but rather because of his character and personal qualities that go way beyond grade point averages, graduate degrees, and prestigious positions. We liked him because of his warm, caring, and friendly personality and his loyalty. We also respected the way that he coped with life's challenges, especially his struggles with a variety of medical problems, most probably caused by a lifetime of carrying too much extra poundage. Throughout his life's trials he has remained spirited, upbeat, and optimistic.

Richard Prager traveled the longest distance, flying in on very short notice from Ann Arbor, Michigan. He arrived in time for the funeral and stayed for the service at the cemetery and lunch with the other guys. He then returned to Newark airport for his flight home, spending perhaps only about six hours in New Jersey that day. I was touched by the special effort he made to pay his respects. Richard is also Jewish, but he and his family observed the Reform tradition of Judaism and were members of a temple in Teaneck. He has a son and a daughter with his first wife, whom he divorced after twelve years of marriage. His second spouse, Laurie, did not make the trip to Hackensack. Over the decades Richard's residence in the Midwest, busy schedule, and infrequent trips to New York City have kept him distant from the rest of us. Brilliantly successful but quite modest and compassionate, he is still one of our six guys, despite the geographical separation.

Barry Vasios arrived with his wife, Cheryl. The parents of two adult daughters, they were the only couple in our group to choose the city lifestyle over a return to suburbia or a move to a small town. Although Barry's family heritage was three-quarters WASP—his mother was a member of the Daughters of the American Revolution—he had always identified more with his Greek lineage through his father and paternal grandfather. The best athlete and the most charismatic of us, he had long ago abandoned both competitive sports and strenuous exercise. His long hours at work and active participation in raising and educating his children left him very little leisure time for other pursuits—except for his love of history. Prosperous at the age of sixty-three, he still planned to work for several more years in a pressure-packed position in Manhattan before he would retire.

On a late winter Saturday afternoon in early March 2009 I stood on the sunny terrace of an apartment on the sixteenth floor of an elegant high-rise perched on the side of a steep hill. Susan had passed away seven months earlier, and our son Adam, twenty-seven, had started a new job in California. It was time for me to sell our house in Glen Ridge. Thomas Wolfe famously wrote "You Can't Go Home Again," but I wasn't so sure. This apartment was on Overlook Avenue in Hackensack.

Just a few hundred feet behind me to the west, on Prospect Avenue, was the former site of Richard's house. A half-century ago we often gathered there, dreaming about girls, talking about school and Boy Scout hikes and camping trips, and playing basketball on the backyard driveway, with the backboard and hoop nailed to the front of the garage. But that dwelling and dozens of others had long since been bulldozed away, giving ground to massive buildings with doormen, luxury apartments, swimming pools, health clubs, and parking garages. Richard's father, a doctor, had moved his family and medical practice to the first high-rise on Prospect Avenue, a half mile to the north. Looking to the east, I had a spectacular view of the skyline of Manhattan, ten miles away. Directly below me were Hackensack High School and its parking lots and athletic fields.

Two hours earlier I had joined Barry Vasios to visit Harold, his ninety-one-year-old father, in his room in a rehabilitation center a few blocks to the north on Prospect Avenue. Harold was recovering from a brain operation to remove a clot. In a few weeks he would be discharged to live with nursing care back in his house, a mile and a half to the south.

After lunch Barry and I went to his dad's house, where Barry grew up. I gazed out a window at the side lot where we used to play ball, pretending we were Mickey Mantle, Duke Snider, Willie Mays, Ted Williams, Stan Musial. . . .We went into the den, lined with bookcases decorated with family photographs. There was a picture of Harold in his army uniform, and

Barry reminisced about his dad's stories of his service during World War II. We shared a few moments of silence and then went our separate ways.

A few minutes later I was standing with my real estate agent back at the apartment, weighing the reasons for returning to my hometown nearly fifty years after moving away. I would be close to my brother and sister-in-law, who had settled in Hackensack to raise their three daughters and now were partners in their own law firm there. I would be midway between my friends in Glen Ridge and Montclair and my job in the Riverdale section of the northwest Bronx. I would save twenty minutes each way commuting to work. The cooperative apartments in the luxurious buildings along Prospect Avenue were much less expensive than the comparable units in Montclair, Glen Ridge, or Manhattan. But most of all, my heart told me it was time to come home.

So I prepared my one hundred-year-old, six bedroom twelve-room Queen Anne house in Glen Ridge for sale. Emptying a house that held decades of personal possessions and memories was physically and emotionally exhausting. I cleaned it all out and packed up my stuff for moving to Hackensack. I hired workmen to patch the leaking slate roof, renovate and redecorate several rooms, excavate and dispose of the old underground 1000 gallon oil tank, clean, paint, and waterproof the basement, and remove the asbestos from heating pipes. I gave away or threw out my wife's clothing and dozens of boxes of her college and graduate school notes and professional books; sorted and stored her patient files from her practice as a clinical psychologist, trashed my son's childhood toys; and junked huge quantities of assorted household and garage debris. I chose the furniture that I would take to my new digs and put the rest on Ridgewood Avenue, where scavengers in cars, trucks, and vans scooped all of it up within a few hours. In mid-August I moved to Hackensack; six weeks later my attorney (my sister-in-law) closed the sale of my house.

My son Adam had frequently kidded me about my affection for the small city with a funny name that was often ridiculed by comedians and songwriters—most recently, by Billy Joel. "Dad," my son would say, "for you all roads lead back to Hackensack." And now I knew he was right.

1. A House in Hackensack

If I could have chosen the best place to grow up in the 1950s, I could have done worse. My father, Nathan S. Kirsch, could have kept his family on Lydig Avenue in the northeast Bronx, or perhaps he could have taken us north to Westchester or east to Long Island, following the paths commonly taken by Jews of my parents' generation in search of middle-class security. But shortly after World War II chance or fate dictated a New Jersey destination when my dad's sisters helped him buy Archie Rose's Dress Shop on Main Street in Hackensack. In 1948 we moved to a house on Heath Place in the "Garden Suburbs" development of new homes and apartments built on the former site of the Hackensack Golf Club.

It was a fresh start in life for my parents after they had struggled through the trials of the Great Depression and World War II, and even for Dan, my six-year-old brother, who had to start first grade in a new school. But our uprooting did not matter much to me, at age three. For my dad it meant beginning a journey that would lead him to local prominence as a successful merchant, lawyer, city prosecutor, and municipal court judge. Born in 1917, he was the second son and seventh child of Jewish immigrants, Rebecca Leiter and Benjamin Kirsch. His mother was born in Russia, near Minsk, in 1886. She emigrated with her family when she was four, partly because of religious persecution and partly because her father was conscripted into the Russian army and refused to serve. My paternal grandfather, also a native of Russia, moved to New York City and became a tailor.

My dad had a rough childhood, because his father had an alcohol problem and abandoned his family. His mother was overwhelmed with the responsibility of taking care of nine children. My father was quite a storyteller, and as we listened to his tales Dan and I sometimes had a hard time separating fact from fiction, but it appears that his mom greatly depended upon a Jewish "Big Brothers" charitable organization. At one point things got so bad that Dad was put up for adoption, but a few of his sisters prevented that from happening. He told us that during his boyhood he spent a lot of time on the streets and riding the subways. He didn't take school seriously until around ninth grade, when a kindly Irish teacher saw some academic potential in him and motivated him to make something of himself.

At James Monroe High School in the Bronx he became enraptured by my mother, a young English teacher, Anne G. Rizack. Seven years his elder, she was born in 1910, the third daughter and youngest child of Eli Rizack and Bertha Lossin. The Rizacks came from a small town near Minsk in Russia. Her father was a leather tanner and later worked in a men's clothing store after immigrating to New York City around 1905. Her mother ran a store in Russia before coming to America. A precocious and brilliant student, Anne skipped several grades, sailed through high school, and earned an undergraduate degree from Hunter College and a Masters from Columbia. She enjoyed teaching at Monroe at a time when it was one of the best high schools in New York City.

The tenth anniversary issue of the school newspaper, the *Monroe Doctrine,* published in June 1935, lists my dad as managing editor and my mother as faculty adviser. He was seventeen; she was twenty-four. I was a teenager before I found out that my mother was so much older than my father and also his high school teacher. Perhaps it seemed scandalous to family members when they first fell in love; it certainly came as a shock to me learning of their courtship. But now, after reading his love letters to her more than seventy years later, I can understand why he was so attracted to a young woman who was passionate about literature and who could so easily cast a spell over students. They married in 1938.

My father did well enough at Monroe to be admitted to the City College of New York (CCNY) and graduated in 1939. He alternated his course work with part-time jobs in department stores. (He was fond of amusing my brother and me with tales about using different names to gain employment selling shoes in rival stores). During World War II he was not drafted until the spring of 1945, partly because he had a young son to support—Dan had been born in August 1942. My father began his basic training at Camp Rucker in Alabama. In June he wrote to relatives: "We are simulating combat conditions in the Pacific islands, and by this time, I've learned enough to kill almost all the Japs I'll meet, whether I have to shoot them with my good and faithful M-1 rifle, my carbine automatic, my Browning lightweight machine gun, hand grenades, or in hand-to-hand fighting with bayonet, or using commando tactics, not to say anything of my M1A9 bazooka. In our problems of warfare we use all of these."

He never saw combat, because he scored high enough on an Army intelligence test to qualify for the Army Specialized Training Program. In mid-July he got the good news of his transfer to a foreign language school at the University of Chicago, where he was stationed in a bunker in a football stadium, later named Soldiers' Field. He had no idea that he was living very near scientists recruited for the Manhattan Project, who were developing the atomic bomb. Beginning in early August he studied Japanese to prepare for the planned American invasion and occupation of Japan that fall. But that attack never occurred, thanks to Present Harry Truman's decision to drop atomic bombs on Hiroshima and Nagasaki on August 6 and 9. Japan surrendered on Dan's third birthday, and I was born two weeks later.

When I discuss Truman's approval of the nuclear destruction of Japanese cities with my students I always tell them that Truman made the right call. The war ended, perhaps sparing my father's life, and he was discharged soon afterward, in early September. I grew up with a loving father who lived a long and fruitful life. But for historical balance in my college courses I also review the revisionist arguments that criticize Truman's decision. After all, there was much more at stake than the survival of an obscure Army private from the Bronx who was studying Japanese in Chicago. But still, the way the war ended worked for me.

During the immediate postwar years, veterans and their wives created a huge market for suburban home builders. On Long Island William Levitt was busy revolutionizing the housing industry with his system of mass producing inexpensive homes. In Bergen County, Fred Ingannamort was using more conventional methods to construct affordable garden apartments and bungalow, Cape Cod, and colonial-style houses. In February 1947 his company ran newspaper advertisements that showcased "Federal Housing Authority Approved Homes" in Dumont, priced at $9,990, with a down payment of $990 and a monthly charge of $63. GIs were guaranteed a month's head start in purchasing these houses, with the promise that "after thirty days, unsold homes—if any—will be made available to the general public."

In November Ingannamort announced plans for three developments in Bergen County, including the construction of a 264 apartment community and ninety-five homes (priced from $16,900 to $30,000) for sale in 1948 in the "Garden Suburbs" section of Hackensack, between Central Avenue and Passaic Street. Twenty years earlier Bernarr MacFadden, a physical culture celebrity, had purchased the property from the Hackensack Golf Club. (A half-century later I wondered whether I was destined to become a golf historian because of the site of my childhood home.) MacFadden added utilities to the land and sold it to Ingannamort's company. The real estate section of the October 24, 1948 issue of the *New York Times* reported recent house sales to my father and our neighbors on Heath Place and Maple Hill Drive. Prices were listed as ranging from $14,990 to $27,500—reflecting some bargaining and discounting in final sales. My dad paid $17,500 for our house on Heath Place. Unlike the Levittown model, which had two bedrooms, a living room, kitchen, and an unfinished second floor, our model had an unfinished full basement, living room, dining room, kitchen, and three bedrooms upstairs.

My father's investment in a store in Hackensack turned out to be an excellent career move for him, but it was much tougher on my mother. She was a New York City lover from her early girlhood, and in many ways she was a misfit as a suburban housewife and working woman. When we moved to Hackensack she used her contacts to get a transfer from James Monroe High School in the north Bronx to Julia Richmond High School on the East Side of Manhattan. She was determined to maintain her career as a New York City teacher, even if it meant getting out of bed early to take an intercity bus to the Port Authority Bus Terminal and then another bus or taxi to Julia Richmond. She never learned how to drive a car. She was devoted to the students in her English and Journalism classes and loved the stimulation provided by colleagues in Julia Richmond's English department. For years after her retirement a few of her former students and colleagues would travel to Hackensack or our summer home on Fire Island to visit her.

"For Enduring Grandeur, Brick Colonial Homes" read the headline that streamed above this house for sale by Ingannamort Homes in the *New York Times* of August 22, 1948. Potential buyers were assured that the total price and modest monthly payments "were within your means." My parents purchased one of these homes, on Heath Place in the "Garden Suburbs" development, which the ad described as "immediately adjoining the finest residential section of Hackensack—an extremely desirable neighborhood." Courtesy of Perry Inganamort, Inganamort Realty.

The Hackensack we moved to in 1948 was in the early stages of a series of changes that would profoundly alter life in the town. The city's colonial origins go back to the 1600s, when The Netherlands claimed ownership of what is now New York and New Jersey on the basis of voyages of exploration begun by Henry Hudson in 1609. In the 1620s the Dutch government began colonization of the region, naming it "New Netherland" and enabling immigrants from England, Scotland, and Scandinavia to found agricultural villages in what is now Bergen County. In 1664 the Dutch yielded control of its settlements after English forces conquered New Amsterdam at the lower end of Manhattan across the Hudson River. England's King Charles II then deeded what is now New Jersey to his brother James, Duke of York. James in turn granted that colony to two fellow English nobles, Lord John Berkeley and Sir George Carteret. In 1667 a legislative council divided the colony into East Jersey and West Jersey. The following year planters from the West Indian island of Barbadoes obtained more than 5,000 acres of East Jersey. This territory, which included lands that lay between the Hackensack and Passaic Rivers, became known as New Barbadoes.

The newcomers from the West Indies and European immigrants shared the land and traded with its original inhabitants, Lenni-Lenape Indians of the "Ackingsah-sack" tribe. In 1690 they negotiated a peace treaty with its chief, Oratam. Three years later New Jersey's colonial government established the New Barbadoes Township on land that lay between the Hackensack and Passaic Rivers. It also formed the Village of Hackensack from adjacent territory that extended east from the Hackensack River to the Hudson River. Through a series of acts passed during the late nineteenth century, the New Jersey legislature subdivided New Barbadoes Township into many smaller townships, culminating in an 1896 law that combined New Barbadoes and Hackensack into one entity, much reduced in size from colonial days. Boundaries were fixed as they exist today, at the Hackensack River to the east and the borders of the adjacent communities of River Edge, Maywood, Hasbrouck Heights, and South Hackensack to the north, west, and south. The town's official name remained "New Barbadoes" until 1921, when the town's citizens voted to honor the land's indigenous Indians and their chief Oratam by formally naming the city "Hackensack" and including Oratam's image in its official seal.

Celebratory local histories of Hackensack record with pride its colonial origins and Revolutionary War heritage. Works published to commemorate Hackensack's 300th anniversary highlight Hackensack's most historic and hallowed ground—The Green--the site of the First Reformed Dutch Church, built in 1685-86 and later called the `Church on the Green'. The Green is now a small park at the southern end of Main Street, a few yards north of the Bergen County Courthouse. In mid-November 1776, General George Washington briefly established headquarters for the Continental Army on The Green at the Mansion House, home of Peter Zabriskie. His troops encamped there for a few days before Washington ordered them to resume their retreat across New Jersey, thereby abandoning the town to the British. A monument on The Green memorializes Brigadier General Enoch Poor, an early Revolutionary War hero who served with Washington and the Marquis de LaFayette, and who distinguished himself at the Battles of Saratoga, NY and Monmouth, NJ. He died of disease in 1780 at the age of 44; his remains are interred in the old cemetery adjacent to the Church on the Green.

One has to consult more scholarly studies for narratives of less heroic incidents in Hackensack, including an early slave revolt. In May 1741 villagers accused a group of black slaves of burning seven barns. According to *The New York Weekly Journal* of May 11, 1741, residents saved an eighth building and captured a "Negro Man" with "several Strong Circumstances [appearing] against him." Suspicious fires in New York City that season made the people in Hackensack even more alarmed. A few weeks later three black men were convicted of arson and were burned alive at the stake.

From the late 1800s through the first decades of the 1900s Hackensack grew into a thriving small city, due largely to improved transportation and industrial development. The construction of railroads with connections to New York City made Hackensack one of northern New Jersey's first commuting suburbs, and they also attracted manufacturing to

9

the town. Although Hackensack never rivaled Newark, Paterson, or Passaic as a major East Coast industrial city, it did attract smaller companies, which opened textile, slipper, wallpaper, brick and other factories. The town's increasingly diversified economy also included Italian contractors who clustered in the south end. Wealthy families built grand homes on the hilly sections of Prospect and Summit Avenues, as well as on Anderson and upper Union Streets and Clinton Place. The city's population increased by a third during the boom times of the 1920s, as black migrants from the southern United States and European immigrants from Ireland, Germany, Italy, Greece, Poland, Russia, and other nations sought employment in the homes of affluent families, in shops, and in small factories. The town maintained a slower but still steady pace of growth during the difficult decades of the Great Depression and World War II. The 1950 U.S. Census counted 29,219 persons in Hackensack (up 11.2% from 1940), including 10.9% listed as "nonwhite." (Presumably most of these were African American, since there were very few Asian or Hispanic people in town at that time.) The median family household income was $3,845; 83.9% of males and 37.1% of females were employed in the labor force (defined as age fourteen and older)

At mid-twentieth century Hackensack was a bustling suburb with a downtown business district that was at the peak of prosperity. As the county seat, Hackensack was the site of the impressive Bergen Courthouse. Designed by James Reilly Gordon in the American Renaissance style and completed in 1912, it anchored Main Street at its southern end. The town preserved the adjacent historic village green, First Reformed Church, and cemetery that dated back to colonial and Revolutionary War times.

Main Street extended from the courthouse nearly two miles to the north. At the lower end, dozens of small clothing stores, law offices, banks, luncheonettes, and five and dime shops lined both sides—some with less than ten feet of frontage. In the middle of Main Street were the landmark People's Trust bank headquarters, the Johnson Public Library, the YMCA, and the Fox and Oritani (named after Chief Oratam) movie theaters. The upper end featured newer or recently renovated larger department stores, including Arnold Constable, Sears Roebuck, and Packard Bamberger's. Shoppers from all over Bergen, Passaic, Essex, and other northern New Jersey counties crowded its discount and upscale retail stores, especially during the December holiday season.

In 1950 Hackensack was well known as a New York City suburb, a county seat, and a premier shopping district, but it was also distinctive for its ethnic, religious, racial, and social class diversity. By the early 1900s a German neighborhood had appeared on Hudson Street and a cluster of Irish newcomers on Union Street north of Essex Street was known as "Little Dublin." Italians established a strong presence on Vreeland Avenue, extending a few blocks north to Essex Street. One-fifth of the city's population was foreign-born in 1920. By mid-century new waves of Italians,

Poles, Irish, Greeks, Armenians, Jews, and blacks had migrated to the town, joining descendants of earlier Dutch, English, and German settlers who inhabited more affluent neighborhoods. These stretched north from Passaic Street in the "Fairmount" neighborhood to Route 4, and west of Summit Avenue through the new "Garden Suburbs" to the Maywood border. Sprinkled in these areas were many Irish and a few Greeks, Jews, Armenians, and others who had attained middle-class status. The wealthiest lived in a few palatial estates or large homes on upper Summit Avenue or Prospect Avenue.

Black residents constituted the majority in the center of town, especially along Central Avenue, First, Clay and Berry Streets, and Railroad Avenue. That community traced its roots back to southern migrants who traveled north to Hackensack in the early 1900s to find work as domestics in private white households and as laborers in factories. E. Frederic Morrow, an African American who became senior White House advisor to President Dwight D. Eisenhower, wrote a memoir of his youth in Hackensack during the 1920s in which he recalled vivid incidents of racism. Conditions for black people in Hackensack had improved only slightly by the 1950s. Racial segregation in the schools, movie theaters, restaurants, social clubs, saloons, and cemeteries remained customary. In response blacks formed their own social and religious centers, especially at the Mount Olive Baptist Church on James and First Streets (later on Central Avenue), and the New Hope Baptist Church, at Berdan Place and First Street. Traditionally the black population had voted Republican and had not been particularly active in demanding equal rights. As the civil rights movement gained momentum nationwide after World War II, Hackensack's black clergy and civic leaders had a golden opportunity to lobby for desegregation in the school system (especially at the elementary level) and for better jobs in municipal government and the public and private sectors. It remained to be seen how militant and effective they would be.

Italians dominated Hackensack's First Ward—the south end of town below the Bergen County Courthouse, down Hudson Street. They were first- and second-generation newcomers, mostly from Naples and surrounding villages. Many of the men worked in Hackensack's brickyards and nearby paper mills in Bogota and Ridgefield Park. The most talented, ambitious, and well-connected founded construction companies, initially relying on the brute strength of their fellow countrymen, using rudimentary pickaxes, wheelbarrows, shovels, and carts. A few of these contractors specialized in building and paving driveways, streets, and sewer systems, earning revenues for projects ordered by authority of Hackensack's City Council. Other Italian businessmen opened pizza parlors and restaurants. Their wives often supplemented family incomes by working as seamstresses. The Church of the Immaculate Conception (St. Mary's) on Vreeland near the southern border of the town; St. Francis Church on Lodi Street; and St. Anthony of Padua Episcopal Church, also on Lodi Street, were the religious and social centers of the Italian community. Their priests celebrated Sunday and holiday masses and presided over baptisms, confirmations, weddings, and funerals. Several miles to the north Holy Trinity Church served the Irish Roman Catholic residents, whose ancestors had arrived in Hackensack in 1861.

The Neapolitan Italian southern end of town was also home to a growing number of Poles, many of whom also worked in local brickyards or factories. Early in the 1900s a few dozen Polish families who had been attending mass at St. Mary's began traveling to Passaic. A priest at Passaic's predominantly Polish St. Joseph's parish helped them organize and construct a church of their own in Hackensack. In 1909 they dedicated their new building on lower Hudson Street, also named St. Joseph's.

The Jewish population around 1950 was much smaller than the Hackensack Italian community, numbering a few hundred families who were dispersed in the central, northern and western sections of the city. Their presence in town dated back to the late nineteenth century, when a few Jews from Eastern Europe settled near the southern ends of State and Main Streets. In 1908 eleven families purchased a lot at State and Meyer Streets in what was then a Jewish section of the city and founded a conservative synagogue, the Hackensack Hebrew Institute (HHI). Over the next decade they gathered for worship and observance of Jewish holidays at Plager's furniture store, the old Armory Hall at the corner of Main and Mercer Streets, and the Odd Fellows Hall and German Hall, both on Main Street. In mid-1918 the thirty-five families of the congregation launched a fundraising drive for their new building, which opened for services in 1920 as the first synagogue in Bergen County.

After World War II hundreds of thousands of Jews left the tenements and apartment buildings of New York's five boroughs for the greener pastures of suburbia. In many Bergen County communities Orthodox, Conservative, and Reform Jews founded congregations and built synagogues and temples. In Hackensack the HHI already served the needs of the few Orthodox and the more numerous Conservative Jews, including Barry Cohen's family and my own. Those who preferred Reform Judaism, including Richard Prager's parents, joined a temple in the neighboring town of Teaneck.

Suburban towns that had previously been overwhelmingly Protestant and closed to Hebrews (through restricted covenants in deeds) had become more tolerant and even welcoming to both Catholics and Jews. The Jewish newcomers were pleased that previously restricted places were now opening up, but they also worried about the risk of full assimilation into mainstream American society. Therefore, joining a synagogue or temple was often driven more by sociological than religious motivations. As a minority they felt they needed to maintain Jewish rituals, traditions, holidays, and customs. This entailed teaching their children Hebrew and celebrating family weddings and bar and bat mitzvahs. The preservation and transmission of Judaism, support for the new state of Israel, and social reform (including civil rights for black people) became more vital to suburban Jews than the study of the Torah and theological questions.

The HHI was both a religious and social center, but for recreation, entertainment, and educational events Jews would also congregate at the Young Men's Hebrew Association (YMHA) on Essex Street. The "Y," the Jewish answer to the Christian YMCA, was a popular community center with an indoor swimming pool, gymnasium, handball courts, locker room and showers, and facilities for meetings, concerts, and special events. Beginning around the age of eight, Jewish children would go to our "Y" for dances, movies, roller skating, swimming, and basketball games among ourselves or against teams from other Bergen County Jewish community centers.

Jews of course love to eat, and the Famous Deli seemed like a small piece of Manhattan's Lower East Side that magically appeared on Main Street. It was always a treat when my dad took us there or brought home corned beef, pastrami, or even tongue sandwiches on rye bread with mustard, with lots of coleslaw and sour pickles, which we would wash down with Dr. Brown's cream soda or root beer. I can't believe I actually used to eat the tongue of a cow—today it seems disgusting--and the last time I ordered calf's liver was twenty years ago. Hebrew school, services at the synagogue, basketball at the "Y," and corned beef sandwiches—that sums up my life as a Jew during the 1950s.

2. Junior Leaders

In 2009, just after I moved back to Hackensack, I drove south on Prospect Avenue past Essex Street, turned left and arrived at Longview Avenue. At the crest of a steep hill and aptly named, it offers a fine view of Manhattan. I had come to visit my elementary school, Fanny Meyers Hillers. The front of the red brick building looks much the same as it appears in pictures taken when it opened in 1927 and when my friends and I were pupils here in the 1950s. The interior of the school has been renovated, and a multi-story wing was attached to its north side in 2003. A sign on the right front lawn identifies it as "The Academy on the Hill." As the children filed out at dismissal, Hispanics seem to outnumber whites, and there are many more black kids than in my day—when there were virtually none. Today, as sixty years ago, its playground is still asphalt, a facility one might expect to find at an urban school in Newark, Paterson, or Passaic, but not in a suburb like Hackensack. But at least we used to have a patch of woods below the blacktop that spread down the slope to Polifly Road. Today only a few trees remain, leading to a small community park with a basketball court, two tennis courts, and playground equipment at the bottom of the hill.

In 1950 the Cenicola family moved to Parker Avenue so that their only child, Henry, could attend kindergarten at this school, then called Longview. In September his mother dressed him in shorts for his first day. In the classroom he sat down next to Kevin because he was also wearing shorts. Just a few months earlier the Clermont family had moved into an apartment complex on Arcadia Road. (That street's name soon became a joke to residents, because it was lined on both sides with drab two-story brick buildings that looked more like housing for factory workers than postwar "garden" apartments.) When Kevin told his mother (Rita) that he was not supposed to wear shorts to school, she replied that he should tell his teacher that his shorts were from Saks Fifth Avenue. Mrs. Hillers passed away in the middle of that year, and the Board of Education named the school after her in honor of her forty-one years of teaching and service. (Her husband's membership on the Board didn't hurt her chances for such a memorial.) Two years later Henry and Kevin had a second-grade teacher who had trouble maintaining order in her classroom. She taped a girl's mouth to shut her up and tied Henry to his chair after he repeatedly ran around the room. Soon thereafter she had a nervous breakdown. Henry concluded that he, Kevin, and their classmates "killed one teacher and drove another to the loony bin."

Before kindergarten I had a few miserable days in nursery school. Homesick, I cried all day and my mother took me out, even though it meant forfeiting tuition money my parents could ill afford to lose. One year later I had a happier debut in kindergarten at the Fairmount School in the northern end of town. But in 1951, because of overcrowding there, the Board of Education and the Superintendent of Schools transferred all children from the "Garden Suburbs" section who were five to eleven years old to the Hillers school.

I flourished over the next six years at Hillers. I had a caring, wonderful first-grade teacher who helped me get off to a good start, and I survived a terrifying second-grade instructor who gave me nightmares. Fortunately, my third-grade teacher was a kind and nurturing woman. We began each day by proclaiming our patriotism by reciting the Pledge of Allegiance. Next we reaffirmed our faith in God by reading a few short passages from a Bible story or a psalm. In December of that year (1953) the New Jersey Supreme Court banned the distribution of the King James version of the New Testament (with parts of the Old Testament) by the Gideons International in public schools, on the grounds that the passages were sectarian and thus violated the principle of separation of church and state in both the U.S. and New Jersey constitutions. But that decision did not ban the actual practice of Bible reading or reciting the Lord's Prayer in public classrooms. My teacher then asked each of us to bring a religious text to school that our parents approved. My mother gave me a Golden Bible of Old Testament stories to use, which pleased my teacher.

Bible reading and school prayers in New Jersey schools remained legal until our senior year in high school, but the actual practice depended entirely on the policy of our respective homeroom teachers. At State Junior High School, Barry Cohen and Henry had a woman who was a strict disciplinarian and a devout Christian. She insisted that each school day begin with a student recitation of a psalm. One of their classmates was a Jewish student who resented the practice. Each time it was his turn to read he would choose the shortest psalm and race through it in a few seconds. Occasionally a few of his classmates followed his example, mainly to irritate her. She also tormented a girl whose parents were agnostics, and who refused to read from the Bible. In 1963 these religious exercises in public schools ceased when the U.S. Supreme Court ruled them unconstitutional because they constituted an establishment of religion. The recitation of the Pledge of Allegiance remained mandatory.

Barry Vasios also attended kindergarten at the Fairmount School, since in 1950 his family still lived on Clinton Place in the northern part of Hackensack. In June 1951 they moved to his grandfather's house on Parker Avenue., so Barry completed the last few weeks of kindergarten at Hillers. That fall, in first grade, he met Henry, Kevin, and Barry Cohen. He became friends with Richie in second grade, just after the Pragers moved to town, and with me a year or two later. Barry has fond memories of most of his elementary school teachers, except for his third grade instructor. She refused to allow her pupils to go to the gym for recreation. When one of them asked permission to go to gym, she replied: "Jim is dead." Barry had an independent side that he displayed in sixth grade, when his teacher required all students to read a good newspaper. Barry picked the *Daily News*, mostly because he liked its sports section. She disapproved of that journal. But when the rest of us selected the *New York Times,* Barry switched to the *Herald Tribune.*

Three of the guys were in the same third-grade class at Hillers School, 1953-54. Richard, in tie, bottom left; Barry Cohen, third row from left, second desk from rear; Barry Vasios, in plaid shirt by the blackboard. Since the teacher wanted to eliminate the problem of two Barrys in her class, she held a contest to determine which of them would be known by his middle name. But both were already using their middle names. So when Barry Cohen lost the competition, the teacher began calling him Donald, his first name.

We all took our turn in the limelight when we performed in Hillers school productions. I wrote a few very short plays (with the help of my parents) that were inspired by television programs. I invariably chose Ruth Heiferman as the female lead, often casting her as a teacher who wore horn-rimmed glasses. Perhaps I picked that role for Ruth because she was so smart, but she was also very cute. (I did not learn until much later that she was also very shy.) She was also in my Sunday school class at the Hackensack Hebrew Institute. As we advanced through grade school I had a crush on her, as did most of my buddies, so there was a running competition to see which of us would win her heart.

Henry's unforgettable moment came as a member of the school chorus and glee club in our fifth-grade Christmas pageant. He was the third King in the scene in which the three royal Wise Men visit the baby Jesus in Bethlehem. After the first and second Kings sang their lines, Henry proclaimed: "The third wise man brings myrrh." But just at that moment, a pupil sitting in the audience near an isle, stood up and heaved his lunch onto the wood floor. Kids started screaming, everyone was yelling, but Henry soldiered on with "the third wise man brings myrrh." Years later he recalled: "No one gave a damn about my solo; it was like a fire in the auditorium." The boy later apologized to him.

Early each summer we gathered at Riverside (later renamed Foschini) Park on the Fourth of July to watch Hackensack's fireworks festival—an annual patriotic ritual that reminded the citizens of the city's colonial heritage and historic role in the Revolutionary War. The colorful skyrockets that lit up the evening sky provided a stirring climax to the town's twelve hour celebration of America's birthday. It began at 9:30a.m. at the high school athletic field with the Hackensack track and field "Olympics," and continued in the afternoon with an annual baseball game between the town's firemen and policemen. Evening events started at 7:00P.M. at Foschini Park with the traditional watermelon and pie-eating contests and sack, wheelbarrow, three-legged, and backward crab races.

We enjoyed watching the fireworks show but were more excited when we purchased illegal firecrackers from older boys in our neighborhoods. Somehow they had obtained them from sources "in the South." We tried to keep the small explosives and larger ashcans, cherry bombs, and the really scary M-80s secret from our parents, who warned us that we risked losing an eye or a finger or worse from firecrackers. But that did not stop us from igniting the smaller ones on the sidewalks. The closest I came to being a juvenile delinquent was when a couple of boys and I tried to blow up a bird bath with an ashcan in some old lady's backyard. Luckily, it did not work.

Kevin demonstrated his knowledge of the powerful M-80 to his father during one of the summer picnics the Clermont family regularly took with his uncle "Bubby" and Aunt Marion at a Bergen County park just off the Palisades Interstate Parkway. Kevin told his dad and his uncle that if an M-80 was lit and then flushed down a toilet, it could destroy the plumbing in the bathroom. His dad ridiculed that claim, so Kevin persuaded him to try an experiment. They took the large pot they used to boil corn on the picnic, filled it with water, and then tied a rock to the M-80 so it would sink. They set the pot in the middle of an empty park road. Kevin lit the M-80 and tossed it and the attached rock into the pot. Then they all ran to hide behind some boulders. A few seconds later they witnessed an unbelievably huge and loud explosion. The rock shot eighty feet into the air, the water scattered all around the site, and the metal pot split on the ground, flat as a pancake. Incredibly, the flattened pot picked up the imprint of the road. Kevin proved his point and the remnants of the pot hung in his house for the next few years.

In the winter we enjoyed sledding on the hills of Hackensack, roller skating indoors at the Roller Rink at the corner of First and Atlantic Streets or at the YMHA on Essex Street, and ice skating at Zabriskie's Pond, at Hackensack's northern border with River Edge. In those days that part of the town (Fifth Ward) was still quite rural. There was no official supervision of ice skating on Zabriskie's Pond—no posted signs or system of flags that informed the public about whether the ice was hard and thick enough for safe skating. You had to rely on word of mouth and the judgment of parents to prevent you from falling through the ice.

Throughout the year we hung out at each others' homes, playing poker for pennies, nickels, and dimes. We would also bowl at alleys that still employed boys to reset pins by hand, or go to more modern lanes at the giant new Bowler City on the Midtown Bridge approach to Bogota.

At lunch time or after school our favorite retreat was Breslow's, a luncheonette near the corner of Essex Street and Prospect Avenue, which was owned and operated by Dave and Irv Breslow, who had inherited it from their parents. When my friends and I stopped by Dave was always behind the counter—he was there twelve hours a day, including weekends. His customers were neighborhood regulars, kids, and doctors, nurses, and orderlies from Hackensack Hospital, a few blocks away.

Skating at Zabriskie's Pond: Kevin with his dad, Bill Clermont.

At Breslow's my buddies and I bought Topps baseball cards (wrapped with bubblegum), wiffle bats and balls, candy, and food. After school or on weekends if I had some extra money at hand—say fifty cents or a dollar—I would treat myself to a burger or a sandwich, and a soda (nickel for a small Coke; a dime for a large coke or vanilla or chocolate egg cream) or milkshake. During sixth grade Henry and Barry Cohen ate lunch there nearly every day. But first they would spend a few minutes as student monitors— "Junior Leaders"—at their assigned street corner posts. Barry would arrive first and save Henry a seat, and they would usually each order a small beefsteak rather than a hamburger, so they could be sure that they were getting a fresh cooked piece of meat.

Kevin also used to hang out at Breslow's, that is, when he had free time away from the daily piano practice his mother mandated for him under the delusion he had some musical talent. In many ways Kevin would turn out to be the most gifted of all of us, but certainly not as a pianist or master of any other instrument. A highlight (or lowlight) of Kevin's Hillers career was his lead role in a school play about the life of Mozart. Unfortunately, despite his lessons, his skills were not advanced enough for him to actually play the piano in the drama. He had no sense of rhythm, no aptitude for music, and in general hated playing the piano. Kevin quit after his music teacher told his mother he did not seem to be progressing and that perhaps she could find better ways to spend her money.

During our last two years at Hillers we were all Junior Leaders, members of the Junior Patrol that enforced safety rules that prohibited us from running on sidewalks or stairs, riding bikes dangerously, walking on private property, or just plain misbehaving. We were all proud of our spotless white belts and colored strips of felt that signified meritorious service in this student police force. But our belts were also a source of anxiety, because they had to be properly cleaned each week. Kevin recalls the trauma his sister Erin suffered one morning after their mother washed her belt, but did not leave time for it to dry. So Rita stuck the belt into the oven, but kept it in there too long and burned it. Erin's terror about the punishment she might face made such an impression on Kevin that he dreaded the day he would be "called up to serve."

In retrospect, the Junior Leaders were a pint-sized proto-fascist organization that helped the principal and the teachers maintain discipline and law and order inside and outside of school. According to an article in the June 1957 "first and last edition" of the school newspaper, the *Hillers Herald*, Junior Leaders existed "for the protection of all the children" and was "of great help to Hillers school by preventing accidents outside and inside of school." But the editor did concede that "some children think that the Junior Leaders pick on them." In fact, one time Barry Vasios chased a younger boy he viewed as a troublemaker all the way home. We were just a bunch of bright kids trying to be good citizens, even if it meant tormenting our classmates by barking orders to them, like "Please walk two abreast," or "Please keep off the grass."

In sixth grade Richie was appointed Chief of the Junior Leaders, a high honor. He was in charge of inspecting his troops and reporting violations of our dress code and rules of personal conduct. He had struggled with reading and writing skills during his time in kindergarten and first grade at PS 181 in Brooklyn and in second grade in Hillers. He found it easier to write words backwards than forwards, showing some early evidence of a mild case of dyslexia. Tutoring remedied his problems, and his academic improvement along with his leadership qualities greatly impressed the principal and his teachers. They rewarded him with the highest ranking position in the Junior Leaders, just four years after he arrived in town. Today Rich concedes that the organization resulted in "autocratic approaches by little kids who did not know what they were doing."

In sixth grade I was appointed class president, which meant that most Fridays I presided over student government meetings. My most anxious moments came at the graduation ceremony in June 1957, when I was in charge of part of the program. In rehearsal for that event Henry and Caren Warshawski practiced a clarinet duet and a song that included the lyric "fresh as the air with new mown hay." Henry joked that the line should end with "new mown farts." He recalls that I turned him in to the school principal, Mr. Young, for using bad language in school. (You could tell what a role model I was in those days.) Mr. Young wrote a note home to Henry's father (whom he had taught decades earlier). Henry could have lost the note en route to his house, but instead dutifully delivered the message to his father and took the medicine. His dad was not happy that he had to take a day off from work to explain to Young that his son was really a good boy and a good student. At graduation I struggled through a weak trumpet solo of "Twinkle, Twinkle, Little Star," and Henry and Caren also performed. I then delivered some bumbling remarks welcoming the parents and guests before I introduced the Superintendent of Schools, Hobart De Puyt.

In a list of "Junior Superlatives" for that year the *Hillers Herald* cites me as "most popular," Henry as "best dancer," and Barry Vasios as "best looking." It also recognizes Barry Cohen ("sportsmanship") and Richie ("contributed most"). Kevin was not mentioned. As we got our report cards and finished our last day at Hillers we looked forward to another summer of fun. But we were also anxious about starting seventh grade downtown, one block from Main Street, at the already infamous State Street Junior High School.

During our years at Hillers school all of us except Barry Cohen joined a hallowed boyhood institution: scouting. Cub Scouts and Boy Scouts seemed a lot like school, with their codes of conduct, regimens, merit badges, and advancement in rank. We were in different dens as Cub Scouts, and Kevin's dad became a "den mother" because no woman volunteered. When we were eleven we all signed up for Boy Scout Troop 11, which met one evening a week in the basement of the Second Reformed Church. Our scoutmaster was a friendly but somewhat eccentric middle-aged bachelor whom we all respected and trusted as a father figure and leader. The only thing that was peculiar about him was that he dabbled in hypnosis with a few scouts. I never let him try it out on me.

In those days I had no knowledge of the origins of the Scouting movement in Great Britain, its introduction into the United States, or its primary goal, which was to inculcate positive character values in boys. Early in the twentieth century civic leaders and clergymen realized that because of industrialization and urbanization fewer children were growing up on farms or in small towns, where their parents, teachers, and ministers had raised them to be hard-working, law abiding, reverent, and patriotic citizens. They feared that in the modern cities and suburbs evil forces threatened to corrupt the youth. Thus they invented such institutions as the YMCA and YMHA, summer camps, adult-sponsored sports like Little League Baseball and the Boys Scouts of America.

Cub Scout Pack 19, which met at the Reformed Church on Prospect Ave. Kevin is the short one, center front; Henry to his right, and Barry Vasios holding the American flag.

As I look over my worn copy of the eleventh printing of the Fifth Edition of the *Handbook For Boys* (first published in 1910), I see a striking resemblance between the Scout Oath (or Promise), the Scout Law, and Benjamin Franklin's list of virtues and system of moral bookkeeping that he recounts in his *Autobiography*. We memorized the Scout Oath, which I can still recite today: "On my honor I will do my best: `To do my duty to God and my country, and to obey the Scout Law; to help other people at all times; to keep myself physically strong, mentally awake, and morally straight.'" Back then I wondered what it meant to be "mentally awake" and especially "morally straight." The handbook's explanation of "mentally awake" refers to being alert and perhaps helping the police capture dangerous criminals, like the Hardy Boys. But the section on "morally straight" is not as clear. It discusses religious teachings, the Ten Commandments, and in particular God's laws "Not to steal, not to lie, not to abuse your body." Did that mean that a boy should not "abuse" his body by masturbating?

Today, more than fifty years after I first learned the Scout Law, I can also still rattle it off from memory: "A scout is Trustworthy, Loyal, Helpful, Friendly, Courteous, Kind, Obedient, Cheerful, Thrifty, Brave, Clean, and Reverent." Here is Franklin's "List of Virtues": Temperance, Silence, Order, Resolution, Frugality, Industry, Sincerity, Justice, Moderation, Cleanliness, Tranquility, Chastity, Humility." There is a fair degree of overlap, although the Scout Law was written for adolescents, while Franklin compiled his code primarily for adults. Franklin carried on a lot about morality but he did not especially value "reverence." He did list "chastity" (although he did not practice what he preached). But citing that virtue would not have been proper in a code written for teenage boys in the 1950's.

In the summer of 1956, just before our eleventh birthdays, we were eligible to complete a very demanding series of hikes in Indiana and Kentucky on the Lincoln trails. My parents (especially my overprotective Jewish mother) thought that I was too young for the trip and refused permission. Richie also stayed home, perhaps because his (Jewish) mother consulted with my mom and also concluded that Richie was not old enough to go. But Barry Vasios, Kevin, and Henry all participated. In Indiana they endured some extreme heat, compounded by the barrenness of the treeless landscape. The trails in Kentucky were easier, but the guys were alarmed when the scoutmaster suffered what appeared to be a heart attack. Barry ran to try to find assistance, but it turned out that he had just become ill.

Troop 11 provided an ideal activity for boyhood and adolescent bonding, as well as an early exposure to adulthood—especially as a few of us secretly experimented with cigarettes (bad idea) and snuck issues of *Playboy* magazine into our tents on camping trips. Scouting taught me some of the facts of life quite distinct from sex, especially when I botched my first attempt at earning a merit badge in campfire cooking and returned home distraught. I was upset because I did not have much prior experience with disappointment and failure; at Hillers my school assignments were not particularly challenging and I was accustomed to earning high marks. Thus my poor performance on my cooking test came as a kind of a shock. One year later in summer camp I was more mature and finally earned the cooking merit badge, although this time I received some critical assistance from Barry Vasios and Richie, who ate some rather raw baked potatoes for me that day.

The freezing winter camping trips, long spring hikes, and sweltering summer camps toughened us up, and the time spent in the woods taught us more about nature than we gained through our everyday lives in suburbia. I especially enjoyed the long autumn hikes up the New Jersey Palisades along the western bank of the Hudson River. My only experience with firearms came during these years in the rifle range adjacent to our basement meeting hall. Today it seems remarkable that we were allowed to shoot down there (even though we used small rifles and tiny ammunition), considering the danger of one of us being hit with a stray bullet while changing or checking the paper targets. Scout camp each August for one or two weeks provided me with my first extended separation from my family. In 1956 I got sick in camp and spent a few days in the infirmary, watching the telecast of the Republican Party nominating President Dwight David Eisenhower for his second term.

As the oldest of us, Barry Vasios was the first to attend summer Scout camp, and the older boys initiated him by painting a red "R" on his forehead. They also made him do silly and stupid errands, like ordering him to go down to the trading post and ask for "one hundred feet of shoreline," or "one hundred feet of skyline." More upsetting was a hazing incident when a few of the older scouts took Barry down to the latrine pits in the ground with holes cut in boards above. They grabbed Barry by the legs and held his head over the hole, a few feet above the excrement.

The following year at camp Barry, now a veteran, continued the tradition of hazing, trying to ensure that Kevin and Henry experienced the same rituals he had endured the prior summer. (Kevin now describes the treatment as "physical and mental abuse.") First, when he and another boy, Kevin, and Henry were all enrolled in a merit badge course on weather, he and his co-conspirator forced Kevin and Henry to go down to the Nature Lodge every day to take the required readings in wind direction, temperature, and humidity. He and several older boys also repeated the latrine hazing by grabbing their legs and threatening to stick their heads through the holes in the outhouses. A half-century later, Kevin had not forgotten these incidents. To amuse his colleagues he enjoyed recounting a few of these Boy Scout stories about his old Hackensack buddy Barry. On one occasion he invited Barry to be an honored guest at a luncheon. Afterward, when Kevin introduced Barry to one of his female colleagues, she laughed as she remarked: "Oh, you're the guy who held Kevin's head over the latrine!" Barry was mortified that Kevin had shared those stories, but for Kevin it was just joking around and perhaps a little bit of payback.

Kevin had another unpleasant experience at summer camp one year that had nothing to do with Barry. For scouts who wanted to earn the reptile study merit badge the camp had a snake pit facility—a bathtub sunk into the ground—for sunning the reptiles during the daytime. To prevent their escape the snakes were confined overnight in a tiny chicken-wire domed cage. Since the staff built the cage too small, it was difficult to get the reptiles in and out of it. They selected Kevin and Steve Wexler (the shortest scouts) to remove the snakes from the cage and place them in the snake pit each morning and then pluck them out of the pit (bending over at the waist) and put them back into the cage each evening. So each night Kevin couldn't sleep thinking about those serpents and what awaited him the next morning.

Barry and Henry were both honored by being selected for the elite Order of the Arrow. That privilege required that they dress as Indians, wearing only a jockstrap and towel as a loincloth, and walk a trail shoeless as they led the scout troop down to the shoreline of a lake. No easy feat, since the trail was loaded with horse manure from an earlier equestrian party. They also had to sleep alone in the woods overnight, and the next day they had to remain silent and do a public service task—removing leaves from under the mess hall. Richie recalls sitting across a table during Henry's day of silence knowing that if Henry muttered a word any of us could take out our pocket knife and put a notch in his arrow.

Hackensack's Boy Scout troop 11, 1958, summer jamboree. Kevin: front row, second from left; Richie, Henry, and George: second row, first, third and fifth from left. Barry Vasios is standing in third row, second from right. Note creative spelling in sign.

Most of us reached the rank of Life Scout, but we all quit after turning fourteen before any one of us became an Eagle Scout. As we entered Hackensack High School in the fall of 1960 it was simply not cool to be a Boy Scout. We were eager to join the in crowd of athletes (jocks) and popular kids, and we did not want to risk ridicule if we were spotted wearing our scout uniforms. Kevin was just two merit badges short of fulfilling the requirements for Eagle Scout, not counting an Eagle project. His mother was convinced he would never recover from not becoming an Eagle Scout, but he chose to go with the group.

Thirty-five years later, when my son Adam was a member of Troop 55 in Glen Ridge, New Jersey, he had the benefit of half a dozen close friends who decided to remain active in scouting up through their junior year in high school. I was happy to help his scoutmaster until Adam made it clear when he was about thirteen that he did not need or want me around anymore on his hikes or camping trips. Adam's Eagle Scout project involved collecting and recycling used eyeglasses for needy people with poor eyesight. At his awards ceremony I was very proud of his accomplishments and I regretted that my friends and I had never completed the requirements for Eagle Scout.

Our elementary school years coincided with the advent of television as a pillar of popular culture in the United States, as it revolutionized family life. The Cenicolas did not own a television set until Henry was in the fifth or sixth grade, but he might well have been the first of us to watch the tube daily. In 1949, when he was four, his family lived on Williams Avenue in the largely Italian southern end of Hackensack. They were tenants renting rooms in a two-family house owned by his uncle and godfather Johnny Arrabito, who operated a milk and dairy distribution business. That year Arrabito purchased the first television set in the neighborhood, which featured a tiny screen—perhaps 5 inches by 8 inches—and a magnifying convex lens on the front of the tube that enlarged the images. The new product was a huge hit. Children flocked to the Arrabito house in the afternoon to sit on the porch and enjoy *Junior Frolics* cartoons, followed by *The Howdy Doody Show*, with the marionette title character, Buffalo Bob, Clarabelle the Clown, and a host of puppets. The crowd of kids grew so large that Arrabito had to limit them to only four per day. Henry and his cousin John Jr. responded to a *Howdy Doody Show* offer and received an invitation to sit in the "Peanut Gallery"—onstage bleachers with seats for about forty fans. But on the day they were on the air John cried the whole time, so he and Henry were not called upon to participate in the fun on camera.

Barry Vasios's maternal grandfather bought the first television set for Barry's family in 1949 when they lived on Clinton Place, shortly after it became widely available to the American public. The Clermonts and the Cohens waited four more years before they allowed the tube into their homes. When Kevin's parents finally purchased a twelve-inch set, they kept it in their bedroom because his mother thought that a TV in the living room was "common." They also strictly regulated the hours that Kevin and his sister Erin could watch programs on their own, though they were permitted to view Sid Caesar with them. A family friend, Ben Murphy, was a singer in the show. Trying to find Ben on the 12-inch screen was a fun game, kind of a forerunner to "Where's Waldo."

We all loved Howdy Doody, the puppet show *Kukla, Fran and Ollie*, Don Herbert's children's science series, *Watch Mr. Wizard*, and Jack Barry's interactive Saturday morning program, *Winky Dink and You.* For that popular program, viewers purchased a plastic sheet to place over the television screen. The *Winky Dink* cartoon character would then prompt the kids to draw or write lines or characters to advance or complete the story. Unfortunately, sometimes the children would simply write on the screen itself, or alternatively, forget to remove the plastic piece. In that event the picture would appear darker, with a grayish green tint from the sheet.. Within a few years most of our families were regular viewers of the variety shows hosted by Jack Benny (*Jack Benny Program*), Milton Berle (*Texaco Star Theater*), Sid Caesar (*Your Show of Shows*), and Ed Sullivan (*Toast of the Town*), along with *The Life of Riley*, *The Phil Silvers Show*, (originally entitled *You'll Never Get Rich*) featuring Silvers as Sargent Bilko, and later the long-running, groundbreaking western, *Gunsmoke.*

It was a major event in my house when my dad purchased our first television set, sometime in late 1950 or early 1951. My mother initially opposed its entry into our living room, but I suspect she relented because she realized it would help her mother adapt to the shock of moving with us from the Bronx to Hackensack. I would lie on the floor next to my grandmother's chair, watching Garry Moore's afternoon talk show. Grandma Bertha, an immigrant who arrived in this country in the early 1900s as a young mother, still struggled with the English language after nearly a half-century of life in the Bronx. But she could understand what was said on the tube. Thus she passed her final years in suburban New Jersey, entertained by Moore, Groucho Marx, Milton Berle, Jack Benny, Gertrude Berg, and other Jewish entertainers she had enjoyed on radio and who were now making the transition to the small screen. For news she still relied on the Yiddish daily newspaper, *The Forward*, which my parents ordered for home delivery each weekday. But for amusement she loved TV, even though she never fully understood how the pictures arrived in our living room. At times she seemed to believe that the characters on the screen could also see us—just as if they were actors on a theater's stage.

I was soon addicted to television, even as my mother kept after me to read. In addition to the kids' programs I enjoyed family sitcoms, westerns, comedy, variety, quiz and game shows, reruns of Hollywood films, news broadcasts—and especially sports. My passion for athletics no doubt began in my living room, as I watched Yankee games on WPIX (channel 11) and the Giants and Dodgers on WOR (channel 9). Dodger telecasts were especially memorable because of Happy Felton's Knothole Gang (one of Barry

Cohen's favorites). I was also hooked on college football. When I was very young (perhaps six or seven) I became so excited while viewing a Saturday afternoon game that I tackled Grandma, causing her to fall. When my mother returned from shopping I confessed; she then scolded me after my grandmother had assured her she was fine and had taken care not to hurt me when she fell. I also watched telecasts of games played by the New York Giants and the New York Knickerbockers, though the National Football League and the National Basketball Association were still years away from gaining huge television audiences. My friends also watched a lot of sports on television.

When I was eight I actually made a cameo appearance on an NBC program on art. My mother imagined (quite wrongly) that my brother and I had artistic talent. Many days over several summers she took us into Manhattan for art lessons. Since she did not drive, it was not an easy commute. We had to take a train to Secaucus, a bus through the Lincoln Tunnel, and then a taxicab to the art school. One Saturday my teacher arranged for her students to be guests on Ben Grauer's program. My dad tried to record the episode with our family's 8-millimeter camera, but when the film was developed its quality was so poor I could barely be seen.

As a youngster I gained my earliest impressions of mainstream American family life from viewing *The Adventures of Ozzie and Harriet*, *Leave it to Beaver*, and *Father Knows Best*. The parents, kids, and neighbors would get into some kind of minor trouble that was happily resolved by the end of thirty minutes. There were never any plot lines that involved sex, drugs, alcohol, or psychological crises. There were no disturbing heated arguments; certainly nothing like those that raged in my house all too frequently. (These resulted from the stress of my parents' careers, marital tensions, and family battles among our relatives.) Unlike my mother, who commuted into New York City every weekday to teach in a public high school, none of the television moms held a regular paying job—although they "worked" very hard at keeping the family functioning smoothly. I knew that the main point of *I Love Lucy* was to showcase the comedic talent of Lucille Ball, and not to portray a typical American family. A Cuban bandleader like Desi Arnaz was a far cry from the WASP fathers on the other shows, but it was obvious he was in the script only as a foil to his dizzy but lovable wife. *The Goldbergs*, however, was something entirely different—an ethnic sitcom about a Jewish family in the Bronx, who after a few seasons moved to the suburbs. Their story closely paralleled my own family's experiences, especially in those episodes that explored the consequences of a Jewish family's attempt to assimilate into the world of middle-class Protestant America. By its very nature *The Goldbergs* was both more relevant to my family life and also more likely to treat serious social and cultural issues.

Ten per cent of Hackensack's population was black in the 1950s, but my neighborhood was all white and my school had only a few minority students. Thus my only significant exposure to black culture came through the media—especially radio and television. *Amos and Andy* simply reinforced traditional stereotypes of "colored people" as happy-go-lucky folks who had a lot of fun as they interacted with each other and tried to minimize the indignities inflicted upon them by white people. There was also Jack Benny's butler Rochester, who was his loyal straight man, and the program *Beulah*, which featured an Aunt Jemima type family maid who helped a white family navigate through life. There were never any blacks in print ads for General Motors automobiles or in radio or television commercials for laundry detergent, deodorant, toothpaste, or any other product marketed to the white middle class. The advertising men must have concluded either that black people would buy products targeted at white consumers as a matter of course or that they would purchase items made exclusively for the "Negro" population. Or maybe black men and women were simply invisible to them.

Each July my parents enrolled Dan and me in Candy Mountain Day Camp in Rockland County. Summer camps had been popular among New York City's Jewish families since the early twentieth century, and they continued to patronize them even after their postwar migration to the suburbs. Jewish parents chose day camps like Candy Mountain because they could not afford the sleepaway variety or they did not want their children to spend up to eight weeks away from home. My folks did not have the extra cash to ship their sons off to the Catskills or Adirondacks. While I was commuting an hour by bus each way to Candy Mountain, my future wife Susan (who grew up in the more affluent town of Great Neck on the north shore of Long Island) was enjoying her summers at Camp Che-Na-Wah, 100 miles north of Albany.

At Candy Mountain I played softball, swam, tried archery and arts and crafts, rode old broken-down horses, learned to cook over a campfire, gained some knowledge of the woods and nature, and made a new set of friends. A few were even from faraway Brooklyn, kids who spent the summers with relatives in Bergen or Rockland Counties. A highlight of each summer was our camp sleepover under the stars, which meant a few hours of shuteye, predawn prowling around the grounds and disturbing our counselors' sleep, followed by exhaustion the next day.

One summer in July I came down with the mumps, which was miserable for me as well as my brother. Our family doctor put a quarantine notice on our front door, thereby barring Dan from going to Candy Mountain. After I recovered Dan was still confined to our home quarters for another week, as a preventive measure. To this day he has not forgiven me for spoiling his summer camp that year. Since my parents could not afford to pay the cost of the full eight weeks of camp we stayed home in August, whiling away the dog days playing baseball or board games with our friends, reading, or watching Gary Moore with Grandma. Summertime also brought regular early evening visits from the Good Humor ice-cream truck. Dan and I would listen for the bell and race to the street to buy chocolate and vanilla cups and pops.

George reading a book about wildlife in the Nature Lodge, Candy Mountain Day Camp, New City, NY.

Later on Dan went off to Buck's Rock sleepaway camp in Connecticut, so for a month or so I'd be the only child in the Kirsch household—a preview of what my life would be like when he went off to college. Dan's camp combined work with activities in art, sculpture, theatre, writing, though few sports. Dan watched a cow give birth. He also miraculously survived a lightning strike on his cabin which left him stunned but otherwise unscathed. Buck's Rock offered him his first introduction to the sport of fencing. Those lessons provided him with the fundamentals that later helped him earn "All America" fencing honors at Harvard.

Nearly four decades later, my son Adam attended Buck's Rock. It is still an ideal choice for adolescents who prefer the arts or writing or computers to traditional team sports. During his two summers there Adam spent most of his time welding sculptures out of scraps of heavy metal. His masterpiece was a large model artillery tank that we transported to our backyard in Glen Ridge, where it stood for fifteen years—a curiosity item for neighbors.

On the hottest August days I enjoyed swimming with my friends at the Arcola pool, a few miles away on Passaic Street in Paramus. We took the public bus to get there. I took my cousin Elizabeth (Beth) there a few times, when she and Aunt Sarah (my mom's sister) were visiting, on vacation from their home in Colorado. We amused ourselves by trying to master jumping and diving off the high (ten foot) board, without much success, but it was a great way to pass the time during the waning days of summer.

There was also a public pool in Hackensack that was much closer to home, but my parents forbid me and Dan from going there. They feared that we might contract polio and become paralyzed for life. I was inoculated with the Salk polio vaccine in 1955, after a few months delay in its distribution to our schools, so it was highly unlikely that I or my brother would be stricken with polio. Later I realized that the real reason we couldn't go to that pool was their anxiety over increasing demands by the town's black residents for equal access to it. Although my parents were liberal on racial issues, they were also cautious about confrontations and perhaps did not want their sons to participate in any desegregation incidents. Or deep down perhaps they simply did not want us to swim with black people. In any case the Hackensack Swimming Club closed its doors shortly thereafter. Many residents believed that was the result of pressure applied by blacks for the pool's desegregation.

My parents also took Dan and me on summer trips to the Catskills and winter automobile excursions to Florida. In February 1954 we journeyed out West to visit Aunt Sarah and her children. That adventure gave me my first view of the Rocky Mountains, Grand Canyon, Painted Desert, and other wonders of nature. A few of my friends took more modest summer trips. Kevin's family spent two weeks each summer camping near the ocean in Montauk, at the eastern end of Long Island. Barry Vasios journeyed to Point Pleasant at the Jersey Shore. Richie's parents rented a beach house on Long Beach Island, also on the Jersey Shore. Barry Cohen and Henry mostly hung out at friends' houses, playing marathon wiffle ball tournaments.

When I was around eleven I came home from camp one warm July afternoon agitated with some questions about sex. Perhaps I had been embarrassed by my ignorance when I listened to campmates talk about the subject, or maybe

George on vacation with his parents, Anne and Nate Kirsch, at Lake George, NY, early 1950s.

I was just distracted by the sight of female counselors and older girl campers in bathing suits and didn't understand it. In any case, my parents responded to my innocent inquiries by driving me to a bookstore in the new Bergen Mall shopping center. There they bought me a short book written for young adolescents that had all the answers about the birds and the bees. It included anatomical depictions of male and female reproductive organs, and a text that described how a man inserted his penis into a woman's vagina. It proclaimed that intercourse between husband and wife was "normal, natural, and right." Its illustration of love-making featured a balding, hefty middle-age man lying on top of a fleshy, smiling middle-aged woman (who bore no resemblance to the girls of my dreams in *Playboy*.) I suppose I learned some stuff from the book, but it was not clear how its lessons might be applied by a boy who was aroused by girls at camp and at school who were developing large breasts.

I do not recall a single conversation about sex with my father; perhaps he figured that I would learn what I needed to know from books, magazines, conversations with my friends, and trial-and-error experiments. Around eighth grade, Kevin's dad began a talk with him about the facts of life. Kevin remembers being ignorant of such matters until his older sister, Erin, gave him a pamphlet to read on the topic, titled *Facts of Life and Love for Teenagers*. His dad was just as uncomfortable as Kevin was at the moment. Kevin brought the talk to an end with "It's okay Dad, Erin gave me a book to read." Sighs of relief all around.

At Candy Mountain my curiosity about sex (or more accurately, naked girls) led me and a few of my friends to sneak in back of the girls locker room, where a hole in the wall afforded a glimpse of flesh of prepubescent campers and voluptuous counselors. Unbeknownst to me, one of the staff had caught me in the act, but he waited until a farewell luncheon on the last day of camp to reveal my transgression to the assembled staff and children. He made a joke out of it. I don't think he told my parents, but I was still mortified.

We also learned as much as we could about female anatomy from the "dirty" or "nudie" magazines. Henry had sources from cousins in Hasbrouck Heights who would give him material that "made *Playboy* look like the Scriptures." He also lived very close to Carmen's Barber Shop on Essex Street. He would go there for a haircut on Saturday mornings when Carmen was most busy with adult men. Carmen would say: "I can take you later, but you'll have to wait." Of course that was exactly what Henry wanted— extra time to stare at the pictures of naked women. Barry Cohen also patronized Carmen's shop, but on weekdays after school. He would also peak at the "girlie" magazines, but being shy, modestly concealed them inside a newspaper.

3. White and Black

Long before my friends and I were born, Hackensack already had a diverse mix of social classes and ethnic, racial, and religious communities. Naturally, social biases and tensions lay beneath the surface of daily interactions among Italians, Poles, Jews, blacks, Greeks, and residents of Dutch, English, and German ancestry, but relations among its citizens were reasonably civil and tolerant if not always cordial.. The most prominent ethnic neighborhoods were the Italian and Polish sections in the south end of the city and an African American concentration in the town's center. There was no single large cluster of Jews, but most lived in the northern and western wards, including my own postwar "Garden Suburbs" development of small houses and modest two-story apartments near the Maywood border. While there was some anti-Semitism in Hackensack, the town's Christian majority did not seem to be too threatened or upset by the growing number of Hebrews.

The worlds of blacks and whites were separate but definitely not equal. The nationwide civil rights movement was just beginning to disturb the customary patterns of racial segregation in Hackensack. Public schools were nominally integrated above the sixth grade and the city's police and fire departments had several black employees. But the black community mostly kept its distance from the white world. Its religious and social life was grounded in the Baptist Mt. Olive and New Hope churches, where congregants gathered on Sundays for morning and afternoon services, with ample time available for conversations about family, politics, and other news of the week. These churches were critical centers for disseminating information and gossip and for debating current events. Their ministers were just beginning to assume a more active role in protesting municipal plans (such as urban renewal projects) that threatened to have an adverse impact on black residents in the Central Ward. Hackensack's African-American community also had a substantial number of black licensed professionals—doctors, dentists, and lawyers. There were others, well trained in specialized medical fields, whose certifications were delayed by discriminatory state legislation.

For recreation and relaxation black men gathered on playgrounds and in stores, pharmacies, pool halls, and bars operated by African Americans—especially Leon's, the Club Twenty, and the Seventy-Two Club. Blacks knew they were generally not welcome in the Italian and Polish neighborhoods and were scarcely seen on the all-white but ethnically mixed blocks where my buddies and I lived. An exception was their patronage of the Fair Tavern and Black Mike's in the Italian southern end of town.

In 1953 Hackensack's Board of Education implemented a combined school redistricting and desegregation program that resulted in my reassignment from Fairmount School in the northern end of town to Fanny

Meyer Hillers School in the southwestern section. The Board drafted the plan to alleviate crowding at Fairmount and also to remedy the vexing problem of racial segregation in Hackensack's elementary schools. When my family moved to Hackensack in 1948 the town's school system was in transition from the austerity of the Great Depression and World War II to the more liberal spending of the baby boom era. The hard economic times of the 1930s and the war emergency and military draft of the early 1940s significantly reduced school enrollments, which declined from 5,450 to 4,228 (23 percent) between 1937 and 1946. As a result, in 1947 the Board of Education prepared a consolidation plan that proposed merging the elementary grades at State Street into the Union Street and Fairmount schools; moving the seventh grades of the Broadway and Jackson Avenue schools into State Street Junior High School; and combining the Jackson Avenue and Broadway schools into the Broadway school. But after the mayor and City Council objected to the closing of the Jackson Avenue building the proposed plan was tabled.

Three years later real estate developers were building and selling hundreds of new homes and garden apartments for families with young children, like my own. As the town's population expanded north and west, the number of pupils in the public schools between 1946 and 1952 increased by 15 percent, to 4,879. Now the challenge was not consolidation, but rather expanding and/or building new facilities. The deterioration and closure of Union Street School in the center of Hackensack compounded the crisis. Superintendent Hobart De Puyt and the Board of Education then convinced the City Council that the town should build a new elementary school on Beech Street, across First Street from Hackensack High School.

The growing population in the northern and western regions of Hackensack and the construction of the Beech Street School in the center of town provided De Puyt and the Board of Education with the opportunity to implement the redistricting plan. In our town the vast majority of young black students attended School Number 5, located in the former high school at the corner of First and High Streets. Although Hackensack's black community was not as yet applying great pressure on the administration to desegregate the elementary schools, De Puyt and the Board members were fully aware of the civil rights movement in the nation. De Puyt resolved to take a proactive approach to the problem in Hackensack, even before the landmark Supreme Court decision of Brown v. Board of Education of Topeka, Kansas in 1954. (Desegregation of the secondary schools was not an issue, since both State Street Junior High School and Hackensack High School had enrolled students of all races for decades).The timing seemed to be auspicious. De Puyt and the Board of Education appeared to be in the vanguard of the U.S. campaign to desegregate public education.

Or maybe not. The new redistricting plan that school officials announced in the late spring of 1953 aimed at a more racially balanced enrollment in the new Beech Street School, but not in the other elementary schools. Even though the scheme was hardly revolutionary, it still caused an uproar among parents who lived north of Passaic Street but south of Anderson Street, because it assigned the white children who lived on those blocks to Beech Street. The majority of the students in that new building would certainly be black after the city closed School Number 5. Moreover, the boundary lines that defined the new elementary school districts essentially maintained the Hillers and Fairmount schools as all-white. The minutes of the Board of Education meeting at which the De Puyt and the Board formally presented their redistricting proposals suggest that the citizens who opposed the scheme were reluctant to voice their objections in terms of race—the 800-pound gorilla in the room. A petition signed by 250 parents residing in the region most affected by the redistricting plan stressed the traffic hazards that their youngsters would encounter walking to and from the Beech Street School, along with the inequitable and illogical requirement that they attend a school that was more distant from their homes than the neighborhood Fairmount School.

A supporter of the plan dismissed the safety factor, however, labeling the parental protests as a "mere smokescreen for snobbery." Other proponents thought that it represented a reasonable solution to the twin tasks of alleviating overcrowding and advancing racial integration of the schools. One woman expressed the hope that the Board of Education "will not permit such arguments based on fear of change for social reasons to influence you in your decision to make an equitable distribution of the school population." But she also revealed that her family was not directly affected when she added: "Frankly, if I could live in the southern perimeter area of the Fairmount School district, I would welcome the proposed change as an opportunity to further my children's education by moving them from a homogenous school to a school in which they could see American Democracy at work and not merely read about it." Sylvia Lewis, my future classmate in high school and college, recalls that a neighbor's mother came to her door with a petition urging white parents to press the Board of Education to create an integrated school. One year later De Puyt acknowledged that "the greatest objection to the opening of the new Beech Street School was the problem of racial discrimination." He claimed that "this opposition was eliminated after the school was organized."

In November 1953, School Number 5 closed and its pupils switched to the new, centrally located Beech Street School. Sylvia Lewis spent kindergarten and first grade at Hillers, but after her family moved to Hamilton Place, she transferred to Fairmount. The new plan then reassigned her to Beech Street. There she recalls "no discernable difference between Beech Street and Fairmount when it came to the quality of the teachers or what they taught." But today she feels that "it did seem a bit strange to me that my Beech Street homeroom was predominantly black but my classes were mainly white." She asks today:: "Did the teachers divide us by race or by some long-forgotten test?" Looking back, Sylvia believes she benefited from her contact with black students, which the redistricting plan made possible. Kristine Vasios, Barry's cousin, agrees. She attended Hillers School from kindergarten through second grade, was transferred to Beech Street when it opened, and returned to Hillers for fifth and sixth grade after her family moved to Coolidge Place. She recalls no significant racial problems at Beech Street. Quite the contrary. She invited black classmates to her home and was the only white person at a birthday party on Railroad Avenue in the heart of the Central Ward. The two years she spent at Beech Street, she says, enabled her to feel comfortable decades later as a graduate student in Ohio, when she was the only white employee of a community center she managed in a minority neighborhood. But while the redistricting plan achieved its objectives at the Beech Street School, it did not have much of an impact on the Hackensack school system as a whole.

As far as I was concerned, the system seemed to be segregated, because there were very few black students at Hillers. I was in the second or third grade when I first sat down beside a black classmate, but I was oblivious to why their numbers in my school were so low, given Hackensack's substantial black population. I was too busy playing punch ball, learning arithmetic, and following the exploits of Dick, Jane, and Spot to care about sociological problems. I knew nothing about school district lines, and how effectively they could still shield seven-year-olds from black kids, whom many white parents in town viewed as a "bad influence" on their offspring. My rather dim awareness of the civil rights movement derived mostly from my love of baseball and familiarity with Jackie Robinson, the Brooklyn Dodgers, and a few other black ballplayers.

. During the mid-1950s, when I was still in grade school and my brother Dan was attending State Street Junior High, the National Association for the Advancement of Colored People (NAACP) and other civil rights organizations intensified their demands for equal opportunities in education, public accommodations, and employment. In Hackensack racial relations between whites and blacks remained relatively calm if not warmly cordial, but there were some subtle and more overt forms of racism. There was also increasing discontent among the town's black residents over the indignities they endured on a daily basis. For example, at a Board of Education public meeting on May 10, 1954, students who were selected to participate as Youth Day Board members complained about the lack of social events, especially school dances, in the high school. An administrator replied: "It is difficult to hold dances because of racial differences." He explained that "the High School had leaned backwards to avoid racial discrimination, but the fact that they have no discrimination is due to this precautionary measure." He then cited one case: "There was a track meet and a queen was supposed to have been chosen, but they had to reject the idea because there would have been a great deal of comment if one of the colored trackmen had been permitted to kiss the queen."

A proposal for the construction of a swimming pool at Hackensack High School and demands for equal access to the public Hackensack Swimming Pool on River Street and the Arcola Pool in Paramus also revealed the depth of racial prejudice in town during this period. At a Board of Education meeting in mid-May 1954, an official suggested that Board members were reluctant to install a swimming pool at the high school for the same reason they shied away from scheduling school dances—to avoid personal contact between the races that might generate public opposition. The same prejudice blocked the construction of a pool at the high school for another decade and also doomed the Hackensack Swimming Pool, even though at the time polio fears were generally given as the reason for its closing.

In September 1957 my buddies and I began seventh grade at State Street Junior High School. Except for Barry Vasios and Henry we all had older siblings who had gone there without too much trauma, but the school was still somewhat scary. First, the building was foreboding. Its institutional gray concrete exterior was not nearly as warm or welcoming as the redbrick walls of the Hillers School. Second, our transportation was now via public bus rather than by foot or carpool. Third, and perhaps most important, we encountered two groups of students who were intimidating to a bunch of middle-class white kids from the genteel, nurturing, preppie environment of Hillers school. These were the African-Americans from the center of town, and the rough crowd from the south end, who were mostly Italian. We were to experience much anxiety—make that outright fear—as we interacted with them in homeroom, in the cafeteria, in gym or shop classes, or on the playground during recess before and after school. It helped that we had already gotten to know a few of the black and Italian boys from our days playing Little League baseball. It was also fortunate that there were a few newcomers from the neighboring town of Rochelle Park who were even more clueless and vulnerable than we were. Henry's Italian friends and relatives from the south end also provided some protection for him and indirectly for the rest of us.

State Street Junior High School exposed us to a degree of profanity far beyond the few four letter words we boys had heard on ball fields or through our Little League or Boy Scout experiences. At State Street the lavatory inscriptions were much more graphic than any word some sixth-grader had dared to etch on the Hillers boys' room walls. Many of the girls, including Kevin's older sister Erin, first learned the meaning of the off-color vocabulary (and the accompanying jokes) from the Italian girls in seventh grade. Erin also joined in pocket book fights on the asphalt playground during recess in which her white classmates swung their large bags at each other.

In homeroom and in required classes like shop we sat alongside older students of both races who had been "left back" in elementary or junior high school. They were repeating grades, marking time until they turned sixteen and could legally quit school and get working papers that would qualify them to earn money. We heard rumors that some had spent time in "reform school" (whatever that meant) and even that one boy had returned to State Street after serving some time for rape. One of our seventh-grade classmates actually drove his car to school before dropping out to become a pin setter at a local bowling alley—one of the few that did not yet have the machines that would soon make his vocation a relic of the past. There were also a few heroine addicts, most of whom were white. Adults labeled our rougher classmates "juvenile delinquents;" we called them "hoods" and tried to stay as far away from them as possible. Though Ruth Heiferman was not fearful at State Street School, she was intrigued by the older boys hanging around until they were old enough to drop out. At school social events she viewed their invitations to dance with her as an exciting taboo, but because they were two or three years older, she opted out.

Seventh grade also marked our first extended association with black students as classmates. It was a revelation. While the majority of them were no trouble at all, there were several who were disruptive. Occasionally one of them came to school dead drunk; and a few treated teachers with bitterness and disrespect alien to our elementary school's Spartan discipline. Erin was shocked when an older black boy slapped a speech teacher. Periodically there were playground fights. One time a particularly brazen seventeen-year-old charged the vice principal with a broken milk bottle. Occasionally boy-girl relationships bordered on the obscene; I knew something about sex by then, but it was still shocking to hear stories about black girls who got pregnant and dropped out of school. The black boys were intimidating, especially to a short innocent Jewish kid who got good grades but was woefully lacking in street smarts.

Erin recalled a scary confrontation with an older handsome black boy. He became enraged at her after she taunted him about a comic book he had concealed from their teacher. He rolled it up, stuck it into her mouth, and tried to shove it down her throat. More humiliated than scared, she did not report the incident, perhaps because (she now concludes with chagrin) he was good-looking and "a tortured soul." Ruth remembers taunts and sassy remarks from black girls in the locker room before or after gym class or intramural sports. But there were no physical attacks, and she did not feel intimidated by them.

The sum total of these experiences effectively shattered the make-believe world of Hillers elementary school for me and my friends. As we matured and played baseball and basketball we got to know a few black classmates as teammates in eighth and ninth grade. But even though these were the years of Martin Luther King Jr. and the civil rights movement, the racial and social chasm between blacks and us and our families was still wide. That was even true for my liberal parents. But most of my relatives on my father's side were racists, as were many citizens of Hackensack.

We struck up friendships with black classmates who performed academically at our level, or were teammates in Little League who could protect us from the more hostile element. We got to know John Anderson, who was from a black middle-class family. He was bright and serious enough about his studies to be placed in the "star" or tracked classes in English and Mathematics. But we knew that he was shunned and threatened by the tougher black kids who resented anyone of their race who hung out with white people. Barry Vasios befriended an African American girl by helping her with her homework. She was an older, tall girl who seemed to have a crush on him. One day an Italian kid (one of Henry's cousins) and another tough boy jumped on Barry and started to beat him up. The black girl interceded and took the two bullies apart, thereby saving Barry's butt.

We were oblivious to the routine encounters with racism our black classmates experienced. We had met Craig Jackson in Little League and got to know him better in junior high school. His family's roots in Hackensack extended back to his grandfather's arrival in 1911—further back that any of our family members, except for Barry Vasios's Dutch ancestors. Yet I doubt he ever felt as welcome in town as we did. He was not free to go anywhere he wished. It was only safe for him to walk from his home on Third Street up the steep hill to Prospect and Summit Avenues on Halloween, or when he was seeking work shoveling snow or raking leaves. If he wanted to play touch football or baseball in a pickup game on the Civic Center field in my neighborhood he would walk along the train tracks—otherwise the police would stop him and steer him back to the black part of town. Walter Carroll, another black classmate, who decades later served on the Hackensack Board of Education, was frequently stopped by police in Maywood or Rochelle Park whenever he visited high school friends who lived in those all-white towns.

Racial restrictions in Hackensack public accommodations persisted into the 1950s. On Main Street several restaurants would not serve black people. If they sat down they would not be asked to leave, which was against the law, but the waitresses would simply ignore them, or make them wait to be served until all the white customers had eaten. When Walter Carroll was a boy he and his older sister were refused service at Woolworth's. During that time the store also had a section reserved for blacks near the doughnut machine. Until the mid-1950s the movie theaters had separate sections for black patrons. Moreover, Jackson, Carroll, and other African Americans were banned from the Hackensack and Arcola swimming pools. The were also barred from the YMCA pool, even though they enjoyed all other privileges there and black churches helped raise money for the Y's new building (with a pool) on Main Street.

Relations between Italians and blacks in Hackensack during this period were mixed. On Main Street Italian teenagers or young men sometimes taunted or threatened blacks, but they backed down when those kids returned with older brothers or friends. Yet there were also many close friendships between black and Italian classmates, especially those forged on the football gridiron or the baseball field. In one notorious incident, a group of Hispanic newcomers threatened to take over the Union Street park, and black and Italian high school students banded together to force the Latinos to retreat. The police showed up just in time to break up what could have been an ugly and violent showdown.

In September 1957, as we began our own initiation into an integrated junior high school, the political fallout of the civil rights movement began to reach Hackensack. That month witnessed the battle between the federal government and Governor Orval Faubus over the integration of Little Rock Central High School. President Eisenhower authorized the deployment of the 101st Airborne and federalized the Arkansas National Guard to safeguard nine Negro students as they began high school. The Republican candidate for Governor of New Jersey, Malcolm S. Forbes, tried to capitalize on Eisenhower's action by urging Hackensack's black voters to support his candidacy and other Republican nominees in that fall's elections. In an address to a predominately black audience of about two hundred people at the Hackensack YMHA, Forbes stated: "Your all-out efforts in behalf of a Republican victory are an obligation you have to Negroes and to other citizens concerned with civil rights throughout the nation." He added: "If you didn't think highly of the Republican candidate for Governor and other local candidates, I think even then you would still have a desire to use this means to show how you are backing the rights of those nine children [in Little Rock] to go to school."

Many in Hackensack's black community were probably already well disposed to the Republicans, since one of their own held a key post in the inner circle of Eisenhower's advisors. In 1955 Everett Frederick Morrow had been appointed to a high-level position in the Special Projects Group, which included the Council of Foreign Economic Policy and the offices of the special assistants on disarmament and foreign policy and public works planning. He became the first black man to hold a position of that rank in the Executive branch. His sister, Nellie K. Parker, became the first black woman to teach in the Hackensack public schools and was later honored when a new elementary school built one block from my childhood home was named after her. Hackensack's black leadership remained mostly Republican, but there were signs that black voters in the central ward were increasingly switching to the Democratic column.

When we entered Hackensack High School in the fall of 1960 we gained new friends from students who had completed junior high at the Fairmount School in the north end of town. A smaller contingent of newcomers commuted a few miles from Emerson, which did not yet have a high school. They were all white. We knew a few of the Fairmount boys from Little League or as opponents of State Street's ninth grade basketball team. We added a few of them to our core group of friends. At lunch time, as was the case at State Street, self segregation by race, ethnic group, or social cliques governed seating in the cafeteria. We rarely if ever sat at a table with black students.

Only a few of the 28 black students in our class were enrolled in the College Prep curriculum. We were friendly with several of the leading black athletes and some of the others who were enrolled in the general or commercial curriculums. The vast majority of the black teenagers were no trouble to the teachers, principal or other administrators, but a few ran afoul of school discipline or even the law. During the early 1960s two incidents occurred that further crystallized the racial bias of white staff and students. A football dance ended in a race riot ignited by a black boy, and a largely African American audience ruined a talent show when a chorus of boos and laughter forced a female cello player off the stage. Many students condemned the blacks' behavior as barbarous—as indeed it was. Although only a few were responsible for these episodes, many white people viewed the teenagers' behavior as further evidence that all blacks were inherently disrespectful or even criminals at heart. But this era also marked the rise of the civil rights movement, and my parents and I subscribed to the theory that pent-up rage over mistreatment by whites underlay the black students' misconduct and their ridicule of whites.

My parents also believed that environmental factors and a legacy of racism and not any inherent intellectual inferiority explained black students' record of underachievement in school. My friends and I were placed in College Prep courses that were reserved for the best academic students. There were very few African Americans in those classes, which tended to reinforce the viewpoint shared by most teachers, guidance counselors, administrators, and parents that blacks were not as bright as whites. The bias of the guidance counselors was critical, because with the exception of only a few cases they actively discouraged black students from electing the college preparatory curriculum. Instead, they directed ("tracked") them into commercial or general courses. That practice did not make much difference for most of the minority pupils. That group included Walter Carroll, who at the time had little interest in higher education. Craig Jackson's football skills earned him a dozen scholarship offers, but he dripped out of Fiske after only one year. (Much later in life he earned a B.S. in Business Administration from Nyack College in New York, graduating Summa Cum Laude in 2011).

It is not surprising that the school guidance counselors did not recognize the talents of black students who might have benefited from some timely encouragement, because most of them were inept. (My friends and I worried that they would mess up our college applications). Unfortunately, as Craig Jackson later explained to me, the guidance staff members were "prisoners of their own culture." They were not sympathetic or supportive because they were not raised in Hackensack and thus had little familiarity with its black population. They also lacked adequate contact with the black teachers, who also could have done more to identify and encourage those black students who possessed enough talent and initiative to pursue a college education. Yet despite these obstacles and discouragements, at least ten of the 28 black graduates of my class continued their education at a college or nursing school. Two-thirds of the thirty-five black graduates of Jackson's class of 1964 attended either college or trade school. Among this group were the most gifted black male athletes. Jackson and a few others were able to earn sports scholarships to colleges, thanks to the reputation of the football team's legendary coach, Thomas Della Torre. Perhaps the most famous athlete of our era was Billy Harris. A member of my brother's graduating class, he later excelled on the gridiron for the University of Colorado.

The civil rights revolution motivated minority female students enrolled in the commercial (secretarial) curriculum to demand equal opportunity in the workforce, but sometimes the high school's teachers and guidance counselors sabotaged their jobs searches. In 1958 the Hackensack Board of Education heard a grievance filed by two black girls who were seeking entry-level secretarial or clerical positions in business. They accused their teacher (the wife of a member of the Board of Education) of trying to steer them into domestic work, mainly by repeatedly delaying giving them job information until the deadlines for applying to those positions had passed. They argued that white female graduates "were sent out in plenty of time to apply for positions, while they were sent to only one place to apply (and this only because of their constant insistence)." They also reported that as a last resort their teacher had finally recommended them for a position at the Metropolitan Life Insurance Company in Manhattan, even though there were comparable job openings available in Hackensack.

Out of our graduating class of 396 students, 28 (7 percent) were black. The 1960 federal census listed Hackensack's nonwhite population as 13.6 percent. Even if one allows for a few Hispanic and Asian people in this category, the black population of our town was significantly underrepresented among high school graduates. Furthermore, the proportion of black students who completed high school remained virtually identical to the 7.5 percent (36 out of 478) of my brother's class of 1960, despite the increasing emphasis on education provided by leaders of the civil rights movement both nationwide and locally. In 1965 the trend turned upward as 10.5 percent of black students (48 out of 455) earned high school diplomas. Five years later the percentage dipped down to 8.9 percent (51 out of 576), but that statistic is misleading because the class of 1970 included s new cohort from Maywood, which sent only white pupils to HHS.

Would full integration of all of Hackensack's elementary schools (including Hillers) have made any significant difference in enhancing the prospects of black students and reducing racial prejudice in the 1950s and early 1960s? At the time I believed that such a policy would have been helpful, and I wrote an essay on that subject in an English composition class in college. Today my arguments in that paper seem simplistic and naïve. Of course, back then I had no idea of the experiences of black people, either in the country as a whole or in Hackensack, or what my black classmates really thought about the white kids in school. The guys and I felt that we got along well with them, and on a superficial level that was probably true, especially with those who were or who had been teammates in sports. On the surface they seemed to respect us, but occasionally we would pick up hints of hostility or resentment. Later in the sixties, in college and graduate school, I would learn about black culture and nationalism, and that African Americans did not necessarily want to be or act like white people. A half-century later I can only imagine the feelings that lay behind the surface of our seemingly cordial day-to-day interactions.

Craig Jackson later explained to me how his family and many of his peers coped with the racism of that era:

> You knew racism was there, but you were also trained at home as to what to expect. Things are going to happen and nine times out of ten, you had no real vehicle of fighting it in a short period of time. It was a long battle to fight which you would probably not win. So except for the most resentful parts that dealt with your humanity as a whole, you had to disregard [the racism]; you just move on, as most [blacks] do today.

Walter Carroll, Craig Jackson, and many black residents of Hackensack experienced the effects of racial prejudice during their childhood and adolescence, but they had some white friends and think in retrospect that we all got along pretty well. That was also true of Hackensack's black community as a whole for that time period. Accommodating white prejudice, the black population segregated itself and was content for the time being to accept partial integration and second-class citizenship. But that would soon change, as the next decade would witness more racial tension and confrontations.

As for my friends and me, we came to realize that we were fortunate to have grown up in a suburb that was so diverse for its time in race, ethnicity, and social class. We all learned how to deal with many different types of people and how to cope and survive. But of course since we were white we were still privileged. We could and did have the best of both worlds.

Anti-Semitism was also part of the cultural landscape of Hackensack during the 1950s, though to a much lesser degree than racial tensions. Moreover, since our town was part of the larger New York City metropolitan region, its Christian majority was more familiar with Jewish people and therefore more tolerant than the inhabitants of more rural or isolated sections of the United States. However, private golf and tennis clubs did not accept either Jews or blacks as members. In Hackensack the Oritani Field Club on River Street was restricted to white Gentiles, but players of any race or religion could compete in regional tennis tournaments it sponsored. (It was the site of Arthur Ashe's victory in the Eastern Clay Court Championships in 1961.) Although I experienced very little prejudice against Jews as a boy, once while playing baseball at the local Civic Center field I was shocked by remarks by some rough neighborhood kids. I heard a few of them loudly praise Hitler, expressing regret he had not killed all of the Jews, and that he had not turned all of their incinerated bodies into lampshades or soap. After that I tried to stay away from them if I could.

Even though my mother's family was Orthodox we did not strictly observe all of the religious customs. Perhaps that was because my father did not have much religious training as a boy, which was understandable given his dysfunctional family. He did not learn basic Hebrew until after his mother died, when he decided to honor her memory by attending services a few mornings a week to recite the Kaddish (mourner's prayer) for her. Looking back, it seems puzzling that during the early 1950s my parents permitted Dan and me to observe some of the secular Christmas rituals. We never had a tree (Hanukkah bush), but we hung stockings on a desk (our house did not have a fireplace). One Christmas Eve my father assembled a set of Lionel trains in our living room after we went to bed, delighting us on Christmas morning. I loved to play with those trains—especially the locomotive that produced puffs of smoke with its white pills, and the lumber, cattle, and milk cars. When my son Adam was nine years old, I brought them down from our attic and laid them out on the sun porch. But either I waited too long, or perhaps model trains no longer held any magic for his generation. He lost interest after a few weeks, much preferring his video games.

Barry Cohen and Richard Prager, the other Jews among the six guys, share family histories very similar to my own. Barry's paternal grandparents, Simon and Yetta Cohen, came to the United States from Russia around 1900, fleeing the tsarist pogroms against the Jews. They settled in New York's Lower East side of Manhattan, but sometime before 1910 they moved to Hackensack. Friends already living there convinced them that Hackensack was cleaner and safer than Manhattan, and also that the town needed a good European tailor. Simon Cohen opened a tailor shop on Anderson Street that lasted for nearly forty years. He owned a home on State Street near the Hackensack Hebrew Institute, of which he was a founding member. His son Rudy (Barry's father) was born in Manhattan in 1905 and was a graduate of Hackensack High School. In 1939 he married Goldie Rosenberg, the daughter of Lithuanian Jews who emigrated to the U.S. around 1900 and settled in Passaic. Rudy Cohen worked at Wright Brothers, building war planes.

In 1941 Rudy and Goldie opened a leather goods store in Passaic in which they sold luggage, handbags, wallets, portfolios, attaché cases, and other items. During the 1950s Rudy and Goldie and their sons Robert (born in 1941) and Barry (born in 1945) lived in an apartment on Beech Street near Hackensack High School. Every Saturday Goldie and her sons would take the 44 bus to Passaic. She would help out in the store, and Barry and his brother would spend the afternoon at the movies. When Bob got to be fourteen Rudy and Goldie would drive together to Passaic on Saturday mornings, trusting him to look after Barry at home. When Bob enrolled in college at

Rutgers Goldie started working as a bookkeeper at Tuscan Dairies for extra income.

Barry Cohen was the last to join our group. His first name was actually Donald, but he preferred his middle name. Affectionately known as "Pudge" because of his extra poundage, Barry had above average athletic ability and a deadly outside shot in our pickup basketball games. He had a ruddy complexion and was about my height of five feet seven inches. He was a hard worker who took his school assignments very seriously. We welcomed him into our inner circle because of his sunny disposition and engaging personality. I got to know him through Hebrew school and the YMHA basketball team, and one summer during our junior high years he bonded with Steve Wexler and Henry through daily wiffle ball games. Sometime during the early winter of ninth grade I invited Barry to a card game at either my house or Richie's. Someone (perhaps it was Kevin) suggested that we initiate him into our gang. We were a pretty tame and innocent bunch of adolescents and knew nothing about serious hazing (like consuming gallons of alcohol or water). It was pretty cold outside and there was snow on the ground, so we ordered him to take his shirt off and run around the house seven times. He gladly complied.

Richard Prager's family illustrates another variation on the theme of the migration of central and eastern European Jews to the United States during the early 1900s. His paternal grandfather was trained as a watchmaker in Vienna, Austria, and emigrated here via Ellis Island around 1907. He settled in Keyport, New Jersey, and opened Prager's Jewelry Store on Front Street, which his family operated until the 1980s. Richard's maternal grandparents came to America from the same community, Bialystok, Poland, between 1908 and 1912. Richard's father, Jacob, excelled at Keyport High School, entered Columbia College at the age of sixteen, and earned a medical degree from Columbia's College of Physicians and Surgeons. He completed an internship and residencies at Brooklyn Jewish and Kings County hospitals and began his medical career in hospital administration in Philadelphia and Brooklyn, eventually becoming the administrator of what is now Maimonides Hospital in Brooklyn. In 1952 he moved his family to a house on Prospect Avenue in Hackensack, starting an internal medicine practice in its front rooms. Richard's mother, Gertrude Slote, was a graduate of Adelphi University on Long Island. The Pragers' daughter, Claire, was born in 1941; Richard arrived in 1945. Gertrude was a homemaker—the only one of our moms who lived the more conventional life of a suburban housewife.

When I was still at Hillers I attended Hebrew school at the Hackensack Hebrew Institute on State Street in preparation for my bar mitzvah, which would be held when I turned thirteen. Stephen Wexler, Jerry Solomon, Barry Cohen, and I studied Hebrew, the liturgy for services, and Judaism two afternoons a week and Sunday mornings. Our synagogue was affiliated with Conservative Judaism, which at that time encouraged girls to study Hebrew and Jewish traditions and customs, but did not allow them to celebrate their bat mitzvahs. My instructors, rabbi, and cantor were mostly bearded old men who seemed like characters from nineteenth-century eastern European Jewish ghettoes. Although they were fairly strict, they did allow us some recreation during breaks. We were required to attend most Saturday services during the year that preceded our bar mitzvah, and of course, the High Holy Day services on Rosh Hashanah and Yom Kippur. On those days we took long breaks outside the sanctuary, especially during early October when World Series games were still broadcast in the afternoons. As Reformed Jews, Richard's parents joined Temple Beth Emeth in Teaneck. They enrolled him in Sunday school and also one afternoon a week in the temple's Hebrew school, which was based in the YMHA in Hackensack because Beth Emeth lacked sufficient space for classrooms in its small building in Teaneck.

In 1958 we completed our training and performed well enough at our bar mitzvahs to please our proud parents and families. I thoroughly enjoyed being the center of attention on the day of my bar mitzvah, and especially during the afternoon party under a big tent in our backyard. Richie's bar mitzvah bash at the Steak Pit was more posh than mine or Barry Cohen's, which was held in the social hall in the basement of our synagogue. The only other bar mitzvah celebration among our classmates that surpassed Richie's was Daniel Brent's affair. His parents treated us and about a half dozen other boys to a Saturday early evening dinner at Sardi's restaurant in Manhattan, followed by a Broadway show—*West Side Story*.

My bar mitzvah pretty much ended my formal education in Judaism, although our family continued to observe the High Holy days, Hanukkah, and Passover. The same was true of Barry Cohen, Steve Wexler, and most of our Hebrew School classmates. Richard, however, continued to attend Sunday school at his Reform temple through his confirmation in tenth grade. He also served as an assistant in Sunday school through high school.

My first encounters with death occurred during these years, as I lost both of my grandmothers. (My grandfathers died years before I was born.) Bertha Rizack, who lived with us after we moved to Hackensack, became sick with peripheral circulation problems and gangrene that nearly necessitated amputation of one of her feet. She had difficulty climbing the stairs to her bedroom, but she enjoyed watching television and sitting on the front stairs of our house—we had no front porch--in good weather. As I approached adolescence in the mid-1950s perhaps she sensed I no longer required her care, and thus she had fulfilled her last family obligation. Or perhaps her mind drifted back to her own girlhood in Russia and the life and family she left behind when she immigrated to the United States in the early 1900s. During the winter of 1958 she was confined to her bed, and then, late on a Friday afternoon in early March, my father called an ambulance to take her to Hackensack Hospital. I held the front door as the paramedics brought her on a cot down the stairs, but as I looked into her eyes I knew that she was already gone. A few minutes later my mother called me from the hospital, hysterical, telling me the sad news and blaming the doctors for the loss of her mother. But later she confided that during the final days of my grandmother's life she had consoled her daughter, telling her that it was time she joined her own mother whom she had left behind in Eastern Europe a half-century earlier. I grieved for her and loved her for taking care of me when I was very young, but selfishly I was also upset that her passing prevented me from attending a school dance that Friday evening and playing in a YMHA basketball game on Sunday.

My father's mother, Rebecca Kirsch, departed the world nine months later under much different circumstances. We were at a family Hanukkah celebration in early December at her apartment on the West Side of Manhattan when she was stricken with a bad headache while she was cooking. My father and a few of his sisters got her to lie down on her bed and called a doctor. She died a few minutes later, the victim of a stroke. My brother recalls that after she was pronounced dead one of our cousins took us downtown to the movie theaters on Forty-Second Street to get us out of the apartment while the grownups made the funeral arrangements. He has a dim recollection of passing by sex shops, but I have no memory of any of that. Maybe they left me back in the apartment because they thought I was too young. A few days later our father purchased a family plot in a Jewish cemetery in Bergen County, using the first space to bury his mother. Four decades later my parents were laid to rest in adjacent graves, right next to Barry Cohen's family plot.

Around this time I became more aware of troubles within my father's large family. He had seven sisters and a mysterious "black sheep" brother, Irving, who had disappeared many years before. I heard rumors that Irving had gotten in trouble with the law and had called to ask Dad for help. My father probably had the means to offer him some assistance, but I sense that he was unwilling to do so. My two favorite aunts on my father's side were Mabel (wife of Abner Klipstein, a press agent), and the youngest and wildest one, Olga. She occasionally stayed at our house on weekend and loved to play ball with me and my friends. Sometimes she drove us to football games. Two of my older aunts, Dorothy and Estelle, married rich men (and when their husbands died married other rich men) and lived in upscale Tenafly. They were sweet to me but often tormented my mother, for they were quite content to be housewives and looked down upon any woman who worked. They apparently felt threatened by my mother's education and career. They also sensed and resented her contempt for their lifestyle and lack of culture. Then there was my aunt Martha, who with her husband ran a third-rate hotel in the Borscht Belt in the Catskills. I loved our infrequent visits there in the summer, even though I sometimes had to share a small bed with Dan.

Especially troublesome to me was Aunt Lillian, who was raising my cousin Kenny. He and I were both born in 1945. His mother, Aunt Rose, had died giving birth to him, and her sister Lillian had agreed to adopt him. Lillian, like her elder sisters, had the knack of finding and marrying wealthy Jewish men. But unfortunately she also had a destructive gambling habit and lost hundreds of thousands of dollars in Las Vegas, Lake Tahoe, and other venues where she found the action she craved. Her lifestyle was not exactly ideal for nurturing Kenny. As he grew into adolescence his behavior at home and school became more and more erratic and irresponsible. Lillian's solution was to shower him with fancy clothes, watches, jewelry, and eventually expensive cars. After Lillian married her second husband, Herbert Rosener, the family relocated to San Francisco, where he owned a chain of movie theaters and other real estate.

As I prepared for my bar mitzvah in 1958, Lillian asked my father if he could help arrange some minimal training for Kenny so he could also experience that rite of passage. But I think that her real goal was to have a big party (which did take place—at the Plaza Hotel). Around that time, Kenny made several trips to Hackensack and got to know some of my friends. At some point Lillian asked my father if Kenny could live with us for a longer period, not only for his bar mitzvah preparation, but for his high school years as well, to help straighten him out. When my parents discussed that possibility with me and Dan, I was very upset, because I did not want to include Kenny in my inner circle of friends. I also did not want to share our family's resources and my parents' attention with him. It was a great relief when my parents decided it was not feasible to incorporate Kenny in our family. So Lillian then shipped him off to a boarding school in Milford, Connecticut, where he performed poorly and got into much trouble over the next few years. In the end, he never graduated from college, and around 1980 he drove his Maserati into a bridge abutment and killed himself. I still feel some guilt over my opposition to taking Kenny into our family. But who knows whether that would have turned his life around.

4. The Ravens

During our three years at State Street my friends and I founded our own gang. But we were not tough teenagers who defended our territory against raids by rival bands of ethnic groups, like the Sharks and the Jets from *West Side Story*, which was then in the midst of its long run on Broadway. We were middle-class suburban white kids. Academic focus, a passion for sports, and half a dozen years of shared experiences, not ethnic pride, bound us together. We spent so much time together that we became part of each other's families—almost like brothers.

Our parents were also granting us more independence. We could now take the #35 bus to the Port Authority Terminal in Midtown Manhattan, unaccompanied by an adult. We were now free to go to college basketball games at Madison Square Garden, then on Eighth Avenue and Fiftieth Street, especially the Holiday Festival Tournament during Christmas vacation. Or we would walk a few more blocks to Broadway to see newly released movies. For more adventurous excitement we would take the subway down to Eighth Street in Greenwich Village to check out the record stores, funky clothing shops, and theaters that screened the latest erotic Swedish or French art films. Kevin and I liked to shop for the latest albums and watch art movies that were hard to find in suburbia. A Francophile from an early age, he introduced us to French foreign films, especially those that featured the nude Brigitte Bardot.

In ninth grade, college admission began to loom larger on our radar screens. Since both of my parents were college graduates, I took it for granted that I would also continue my education after high school. The same was true for Richard, but since his dad was a physician he was also thinking about a medical degree. The other four guys would be the first in their families to go to college. We knew that even though we would complete ninth grade at State Street, our marks for that year would count on our Hackensack High transcripts.

Barry Vasios and I spent a lot of time together after we both were chosen to play on the eighth and ninth grade State Street basketball squads. As I got to know Barry better, I was bemused by his self-identification as a Greek-American, although I knew that he was also quite proud of his WASP genealogy (mostly through his mother's ancestors). Years later he told me why his Greek ancestry was so important to him, even though three of his four grandparents were descended from English, Dutch, or French Huguenot stock. He explained that as a child he discovered that in American society people were often categorized by their last name. New acquaintances often inquired about the spelling of "Vasios." Next they usually asked: "What kind of a name is that?" Barry would reply "Greek." He was not comfortable saying: "Greek, but I am really only a quarter Greek." Barry inherited his pride in his Greek heritage from his dad, who had experienced ethnic taunting as a child even though his mother was of English descent. As he grew older Barry was sensitive to any perceived ethnic slights directed at him. Also, Barry and his brother were not members of a Greek Orthodox church or other Greek organization. Thus they did not benefit from the same kind of support from a wider ethnic community that the Italian population provided for Henry or Jewish culture gave me, Barry Cohen, and Richard. Barry also observed that the only advantage he gained from his last name came from misplaced and misguided ethnic stereotyping.

Barry Vasios's paternal grandfather, Spiro (or Sam), was born in the Peloponnese region of Greece and immigrated to the United States through Ellis Island in 1906. His travels took him to Michigan, where he met Ruth Sofia Martin in a luncheonette in Bay City. Spiro Vasios spoke only Greek; Ruth knew only English, but as his son Harold recalled: "Somehow they fell in love." The couple married and moved to Lincoln, Nebraska around 1914 where they ran a shoeshine and hat cleaning store. They then relocated back east to Paterson, New Jersey, where Harold was born on Marshall Street in 1917. His father opened the same kind of businesses, first in Paterson, and later at 163 Main Street in Hackensack, next to the Lyric Theater. In 1924 the Vasios family moved from Paterson to Hackensack, where Harold attended School #5 on First Street, State Street School, and Hackensack High School.

On Barry's maternal side he is pure WASP. His mother, Hazel, traced her lineage to Dutch immigrants named Ackerman, who in 1643 journeyed from Holland to its colony of New Netherland. As a descendant of both the Ackerman and Demarest families Hazel qualified for and became an active member of the Daughters of the American Revolution and the Ackerman Descendants, 1776. Her father, Albert Mellor Bratt, was born in England, near Liverpool. He came with his family to the United States around 1888, lived in New York City for a few years, and then purchased building lots in Hackensack's First Ward. Hazel Bratt was born in Hackensack in 1919, attended the Union Street, Longview Avenue, and State Street schools, and Hackensack High School, where she met Harold Vasios. Although she and Harold both graduated in 1936, Hazel was two years younger because she had skipped two grades. She completed one year at Donovan Business School on Banta Place, and then was hired as a teller at the Hackensack Mutual Savings and Loan. Perhaps it was Harold's sports prowess that first caught Hazel's eye—in high school he was a star varsity athlete on the football and baseball teams, captain of the basketball squad, and a member of Northern New Jersey Interscholastic League championship teams in basketball and baseball.

After graduation Harold worked as a clerk in the Juvenile Division of the Bergen County Probation Department, and in February 1941 he enlisted in the U.S. Army (ten months before Pearl Harbor). He completed basic training in Virginia and was assigned to Alaska. He became quite ill and received a medical discharge in 1943 without ever seeing combat. He and Hazel married in 1943. The newlyweds first lived at 275 Beech Street in

Hackensack, and then moved to an apartment at 64 Clinton Place. Barry was born there on May 1, 1945. His brother, James, arrived on March 13, 1950. The Vasios family then relocated to a new house on a plot of land given to them by Hazel's father, Albert Bratt, on Simons Avenue.

Barry's paternal grandfather was raised in the Greek Orthodox tradition. After his marriage he remained Greek Orthodox, but he permitted his wife to raise their children as Protestants. From childhood Barry's mother, Hazel, had been a member of Hackensack's historic Dutch Reformed Church on the Green. After she and Harold were married they joined the Second Reformed Church on Anderson Street. Barry's parents enrolled him in its religious school, and he was confirmed there at the age of thirteen.

I frequently visited the Clermont household as well. Kevin's mother, Rita, was a vibrant, cheerful woman who was very proud of her Irish heritage—especially its music. I enjoyed listening to the Clancy Brothers with her. Kevin's sister, Erin, had grown into a slim, black haired beauty who had deepened her relationships with her aunt Jo (and through her), Gypsy Rose Lee and Tennessee Williams. She seemed to us to be quite "avant garde," artsy, and bohemian (this was the '50s, after all). She also made it clear that she wanted nothing to do with her younger brother and his friends. Erin and her partner-in-crime, Marion, had switched from their previous pastime of picking on Kevin (treatment which he later labeled sadistic), to a new policy of simply ignoring him and us.

All of us loved spending time with Kevin's father, Bill. We knew him as a coach of Kevin's Little League team, the Ratner Rockets. As a young man he had been skilled enough on the diamond to compete as a ringer for the New York Athletic Club's baseball team. An avid golfer, he, his brother Al ("Bubby" to the kids), and several friends played early Sunday morning rounds at the lush semiprivate daily-fee Rivervale course in northern Bergen County. It was a big deal for me when Bill invited me to play eighteen holes with him and Kevin. I also enjoyed their family dog, a West Highland white terrier named Chester, who was very lovable and playful except during thunderstorms, when she became terrified and hid under a couch or bed.

Unlike my parents, neither Rita nor Bill Clermont had a college education, but both were nonetheless very smart and opinionated. They did not seem to put much pressure on their son to be a high achiever in school. They did not have to, since Kevin was more self-motivated. Kevin knew that his father disliked his job as an aeronautical engineer—even though it gave him status as a professional—and that he regretted he had never gone to college. Bill often told his children that he "missed the boat." That advice no doubt had a profound impact on Kevin, but his mother Rita's experience as an orphan likely also contributed to his perfectionism. Living her childhood as a ward of the state made her extremely status conscious and eager for her children to succeed. So with a father who thought he had "missed the boat" and a mother who was trying to overcome her lowly origins, Kevin was programmed (whether he knew it or not) to succeed. During his years at State Street he kept a low profile, concentrating on his studies. We called him "Mick," because of his Irish heritage. He was still the shortest of our group and one of the smallest students in our class, so even though he was a good athlete he could not yet excel in school sports. But although his delayed physical development was somewhat of a liability at State Street, his brilliant intellect, keen wit, and good looks were assets. He had fine facial features and wavy dark blond hair. The girls thought he was one of the cutest boys in our class.

Kevin's family history is more diverse than the rest of our group, encompassing lineage from France, Germany, and Ireland. His paternal grandfather, Albert Joseph Clermont, was a carpenter and a contractor, a descendant of seventeenth-century French emigrants who settled in Trois Rivieres, Quebec, and then came to the United States in the nineteenth century. His wife, Christina Frederica Weltz, of German descent, was born in Manhattan. Albert and Christina were married in 1905 in the Bronx. Their youngest child (of six), William ("Bill"), Kevin's father, was born in the northeast Bronx in 1915. Bill graduated from Yonkers High School in 1933, worked at the Brick Row Book Shop, and then taught himself the fundamentals of engineering. He landed a good position without the benefit of an undergraduate degree because his cousin was an executive at Bendix Aviation. As an employee for a defense contractor he received a deferment from the draft and thus had no military service during World War II. Earlier he had tried to enlist but was classified 4-F due to poor eyesight.

On his mother's side, Kevin is all Irish. His maternal grandfather, Thomas Healy, was born in 1888 in a tiny village in County Clare. One of the younger of fourteen children of a teacher, he arrived at Ellis Island in 1910. Within a year of landing he married Mary Hayes (a passenger on the same ship) in 1911 in New York City. Thomas and Mary had five children: Mary Josephine (called Jo), a girl who died as an infant, Rita (Kevin's mother), Francis, and Tommy. Rita was born in 1915 in Manhattan. (Everyone called her Rita, but her birth certificate records Ruth as her first name.) Although Thomas was a baker in Ireland, in America he could only find work in manual labor and as a stableman, trucker's helper, and warehouse porter. After her marriage Mary became a janitress. She died in poverty and in squalid conditions on September 26, 1922, leaving four children to be cared for by their father. Neither Thomas nor Mary became an American citizen.

Thomas was unable to cope. Other relatives were unwilling or unable to care for his children. The Manhattan Department of Public Welfare committed Rita and her siblings to the Mount St. Michael's Orphanage near Greenridge on Staten Island. After Thomas's death of lobar pneumonia in 1925 the four Healy children became true orphans. Rita was seven years old when she moved into Mount St. Michael's and spent nearly ten difficult years there. She was confirmed in September 1926, graduated from St. Michael's

School in 1928, and earned a diploma from St. Peter's High School in New Brighton, Staten Island, in 1932. Shortly thereafter she was discharged from the orphanage, beginning her adult life in the midst of the Great Depression at the age of seventeen, with her Aunt Delia taking responsibility for her. She secured a clerical position at Equitable Life Insurance and rented a room in Yonkers in a cousin's house. There she met William Clermont and within a month they were engaged. She returned to St. Michael's for her marriage to her "Billy" in 1938.

Rita's older sister, Jo, had somehow managed to get herself discharged from the orphanage at the age of thirteen, less than one year after her father died. While her siblings were still in that institution she kept the family together. With an apartment and a job during the 1930s she became a surrogate mother to her younger siblings after they left St. Michael's. A strong-willed woman who worked for a while for the Theater Guild, she formed close friendships with a number of show business celebrities, including Gypsy Rose Lee.

During the late 1930s and 1940s Billy and Rita lived in a variety of apartments in Manhattan, Queens, and New Jersey, including Gypsy Rose Lee's townhouse on East 63 Street. Erin was born in 1943 in Women's Hospital (later St. Luke's) in Manhattan. After the war the family moved to Woodside, a heavily Irish neighborhood in Queens. Kevin was born in Physicians Hospital in Jackson Heights in 1945. In 1949 the Clermont family moved to a house in Mahwah, NJ, for a brief but failed experiment in "off the grid" bohemian living. Six months later they moved to 44 Arcadia Road in Hackensack. In May 1955 the Clermonts bought a house at 87 Rowland Ave., where Erin and Kevin finally got their own rooms.

During Kevin's early childhood the Clermont family frequently visited Gypsy Rose Lee's townhouse, which was also the headquarters of her burlesque company. Well-endowed strippers got fitted there for G-strings, pasties, and other scanty attire of their trade, thereby providing Kevin with his first peeks at naked women. Erin and Kevin often played with Gypsy's son Eric, who was one year older than Kevin. Gypsy always brought Kevin and Erin gifts after she returned from world tours.

Through Aunt Jo the Clermonts also became friendly with Celeste Holm and Tennessee Williams. As Holm's personal assistant Jo made sure her sister's family was invited to Holm's parties. Kevin also played with her son Danny, both at her Central Park West duplex apartment and in Kevin's garden apartment in Hackensack. The boys were the same age, but unfortunately, Danny had a nasty temperament. Their play dates ended when Danny threw a wastebasket at Kevin's head. Jo had become friendly with Williams when she worked at the Theatre Guild. Throughout the 1950s he appreciated the monthly trips by Jo and Rita to visit his sister Rose, who was confined to a psychiatric institution in Tarrytown, New York. Williams avidly followed Kevin's scholastic achievements throughout his high school and college years. Through Aunt Jo, Kevin had another link to a literary luminary.

A dear friend of Jo's, Elaine Anderson, had married John Steinbeck, and Jo asked him to inscribe a copy of *The Red Pony* to Kevin. He still has the book.

Kevin's parents had been baptized and were nominally Roman Catholics, but they had long since rejected any allegiance to the Catholic Church. Despite their anticlericalism, they felt an obligation to provide some kind of religious training for their children, so they placed Kevin and Erin in the hands of the Methodist church, apparently because Erin's Brownie friend attended services there. Kevin was about five years old. Erin soon left the Methodist church to join her new best friend in a Presbyterian congregation. For the next seven years or so Kevin's parents dropped him off at the Methodist Sunday School every week, and returned a few hours later to pick him up. Overall Kevin's religious experience was not integrated at all into his family life. He later recalled that when he was at Sunday school "I never felt so lonely in my life." Kevin's lasting impression of religion was that it was a "tremendous source of loneliness and depression." By the time we reached junior high Kevin had joined a Unitarian church, which he viewed as intellectual and liberal, with antiwar and antinuclear sermons. Kevin recalls no sense of community to keep him there, however. Today he believes that if you follow the Unitarian way of thinking, you have to conclude that there is no point in attending church at all.

When we entered State Street Junior High School my friends and I were too preoccupied with adjusting to our new environment to worry about college admissions. The academic work was not particularly challenging until ninth grade. Seventh grade was a year of transition into more independence. Eighth grade was just a waste of time, except for Miss Pindar's science class. She was a very demanding teacher who insisted that we hand in corrected homework and reports with no mistakes. Kevin remembers the frustration of recopying work to meet her standards, and attributes his perfectionism in part to her strict style of teaching and the anxiety it generated in him.

In ninth grade our schoolwork got more serious, since our grades would now count on our high school transcripts and college applications. Thanks to my mother's influence, I elected to take French rather than Latin, which most of my peers selected. But we were together for the other subjects, including first-year algebra, science, social studies, and English. In mathematics we were among the first students in the nation to follow an experimental approach developed by the Illinois Committee on School Mathematics, beginning with basic algebra. The method proved to be annoying to Kevin and myself, especially since it was also applied in a few of our high school courses. The "New Math" put more emphasis on mathematical concepts rather than memorization of formulas. It was designed to make math more engaging to students, but it could also be very frustrating to those of us who were used to mastering a set of specific instructions to solve problems.

While the rest of our group made a smooth transition from Hillers to State Street and remained conscientious about our school assignments, Henry appeared disinterested in academic achievement, choosing to hang out with the south end crowd. While most of his southern Italian relatives tended to be short and stocky, he had grown tall and skinny. So we called him "Worm." Witty, engaging, and friendly to all, he was extremely popular and seemed to know practically everyone in Hackensack's Italian community. He was not blessed with much innate athletic ability, and his lack of coordination led to a few minor incidents that caused some injuries. After a few of these mishaps (like running into a fence in a Little League game) we viewed him as an accident waiting to happen.

Henry was the only Italian Roman Catholic among the guys, and the only one whose parents were first-generation immigrants. In 1908, his father, Enrico (Henry) Giuseppi Cenicola, passed through Ellis Island at the age of two, in the care of his paternal grandfather, Giuseppi. Although both were natives of Ceprano, a town south of Rome, they had moved to Naples before sailing to New York City. They settled in a largely Neapolitan neighborhood on Hudson Street, and later moved to Lodi and River Streets. Enrico attended elementary school in Hackensack and earned an eighth-grade diploma before dropping out of school after the death of his father.

Henry's mother, Palmina (Pauline) Carmella Buonomo, was born in 1910 in a small village near Sarento in Italy. She was raised by her grandparents (whom she thought were her real parents), because her mother died giving birth to her. Soon thereafter her father, Pietro, departed for the United States. By 1922 Pietro had prospered enough in his construction business to purchase a first-class ticket for Pauline's passage to America. When Pauline was told the truth about her situation she promptly ran away and hid on a neighbor's farm before she finally agreed to come to the States. One year later, when Pauline was thirteen, Pietro sent her to work in the silk mills of Paterson, without any U.S. schooling and with little command of the English language.

Enrico Cenicola and Pauline Buonomo met in a night-school class in Hackensack in the mid-1930s. He was not quite thirty years; she was four years younger. One evening Enrico asked Pauline if he could walk her home after class. She agreed, but when they arrived a few minutes late at her home (perhaps because they stopped for a soda), Pietro was furious at Enrico for not asking permission in advance to accompany his daughter. Enrico must have eventually gained Pietro's respect and confidence, because he and Pauline were married in 1939. Enrico then got a job in a boiler construction factory in Bogota, where he broke his leg. That injury got him an exemption from military service during World War II. Henry arrived in the world in 1945, exactly one week after the surrender of Japan. During the late 1940s Henry's parents rented an apartment in a house on Williams Avenue owned by Pauline's stepsister at the southern-most tip of Hackensack. Next, they relocated to a house on Parker Avenue in order to enroll their son in the

Longview (soon to be renamed) Hillers School. Shortly thereafter they moved again to an apartment on the corner of Essex and Prospect Avenue.

It was by no means preordained that Henry would go to college. First-generation Italians traditionally placed loyalty to family vocations and businesses ahead of educational opportunities for their sons. In addition, his father had only an eighth-grade diploma, and his mother only a few years of night school. Thus Henry did not benefit from the same kind of parental guidance that the rest of us received, particularly concerning preparation for college. After a lackluster performance in seventh grade and a minimal effort the next year, he experienced a life-changing moment. He credits an English teacher, Miss Ferrara, with helping him to get back on the path that would ultimately lead to membership in the national junior and senior high honor societies and ultimately a college degree. One day, after Henry barely escaped receiving a failing grade for a marking period in Ferrara's English class, she asked him to stay after school. She told him that decades earlier Henry's father had been one of her pupils, but after his own father died he was compelled to drop out after completing the eighth grade. As a young woman Ferrara had urged Henry's father to stay in school or at least attend night classes, because he had performed well in class. Now she told Henry that he had the potential to be a good student; that he should apply himself; and that he should do it for his dad.

Henry then went home and asked his father to verify Ferrara's story. It was one of the rare occasions when Henry and his dad talked about personal matters. Teary-eyed, Enrico told his son that Miss Ferrara's tale was true. After that, Henry still maintained his friendships with his Italian family and friends, but he resolved to study harder. We will never know how Henry's life might have unfolded if Miss Ferrara had not seen something special in him as an eighth-grader.

Being one of Henry's his closest friends benefited me, since I got invited to parties and Friday night Catholic Youth Organization dances in the basement of his church. No one seemed to care that I was Jewish, and my parents did not forbid me from partying on Shabbat. At the beginning we danced to ballads of Pat Boone, the Everly Brothers, Bobby Darin, the jitterbug tunes of Danny and the Juniors, the doo-wop style of the Coasters, Rays, and the Platters, but that all gave way to the new sounds of Elvis Presley, Chuck Berry, Jerry Lee Lewis, and the ill-fated Sam Cooke and Buddy Holly. The Italian girls were quite sexy and enticing, and not as intimidating as their Jewish counterparts. Kevin remembers strong feelings of yearning and titillation at those dances. I also loved the annual Italian religious festivals with their great food and rides. I discovered many similarities between Italian and Jewish cultures, especially in family relationships and wedding celebrations. This early experience with Catholic culture later helped me to feel comfortable with my colleagues and students at Manhattan College, a Catholic (albeit primarily Irish) institution.

At State Street we also participated in a few extracurricular activities in music and journalism. I played the trumpet (poorly) in the concert band and worked as an editor on the school newspaper, *The Statement*. Our band director was not particularly gifted or inspiring, and our public performances bordered on the brink of humiliating. Once we got completely lost during a piece, but he kept waving his arms until we all got to the last note, though not at the same time. My Aunt Olga was then still married to a musician who played trumpet in Broadway musical orchestras. He was kind enough to give me instructional books for practice to improve my tonguing technique. But alas, it turned out that my upper lip was too weak for me to ever become an accomplished trumpeter. I would have been much better off if I had switched to the clarinet or another woodwind instrument.

Writing editorial and news stories was more satisfying. Since my mother taught journalism at Julia Richmond High School in New York City she was pleased with my interest in that field and offered much encouragement and praise. I disappointed her in ninth grade, however, when I broke the rules on a trip to the Columbia University Scholastic Press Association's convention. Perhaps because I thought of myself as a sophisticated New Yorker who knew his way around town, I persuaded a few friends to leave the meeting for a few hours for a side trip by public bus to visit my Aunt Mabel and her two young sons in her apartment on the Upper West Side. She was startled to see us, as we arrived unannounced, and I am sure she wondered whether we had permission. We did not, of course, and when we returned to Columbia the moderator scolded us for missing a few sessions. I could have been suspended for this adventure, but because I was an honor student the principal gave me a pass.

As my friendships with Barry Vasios, Kevin and Henry strengthened, I also grew closer to Richie, as we then called him, Barry Cohen, and Stephen Wexler. They all called me "Ben" or "Benner" (after my middle name, Benson). We called Richie "Turtle" because of his body shape—just before the growth spurt that transformed him into a six-foot, dark haired, handsome guy. We called his physician father "Jolly Jake" (behind his back, of course). He often drove us to ball games or scouting events. Richie's backyard was our favorite venue for pickup basketball, touch football, and soccer games, partly because of the hoop on the garage, but also because his house was in the center of town. His fancy bar mitzvah party, held at the upscale Sid Allen's Steak Pit on Route 4, was the site of the official founding of our gang. At that celebration the guys all received cool black oblong hats. In our English class we had read some poetry and short stories of Edgar Allen Poe. We especially enjoyed "The Raven." So in 1958 we became "The Ravens."

When Stephen Wexler joined our inner circle in junior high the Ravens morphed into "the Magnificent Seven." (In high school the girls in our class started calling us "the Fellas.") Steve's father, Oscar, was a non-practicing lawyer who worked for the Veterans Administration in Newark; his mother, Millie, was a welcoming, warm hearted housewife. Steve's nickname was simply "Wex." After Kevin's growth spurt in the ninth grade Steve became the shortest of our group. Too small for varsity sports, he more than held his own in our sandlot games. On vacation days and during the long summers he hosted marathon wiffle ball tournaments at his house. The fourth Jewish member of the Ravens, Steve was smart, gifted in math, intense, hard working, and ambitious. He was more overtly materialistic than the rest of us and the first to hold an after school job. He and Kevin had an ongoing academic rivalry. As tension increased between them Steve remained friendly with Henry, me, and Barry Cohen, but distanced himself from Kevin and Barry Vasios.

In June 1960, as the presidential campaign heated up for the summer Democratic and Republican nominating conventions, my friends and I graduated from State Street Junior High School at the less than palatial Fox Theater on Main Street. Henry, Barry Cohen, Stephen Wexler and I were in the band and seated in the orchestra pit. The ceremony honored Barry Vasios, who received the American Legion Award for "courage, honor, leadership, patriotism, scholarship, and service," and Richard, the recipient of the Philip C. Staib Award for good character and community service. I recall being disappointed that I did not receive any special recognition. I was also surprised that the school's administration did not honor Kevin, since in my view he had clearly distinguished himself as the brightest and most dedicated student in our grade. But being slighted did not seem to bother him at all. As a reward for our hard work my parents treated Kevin and me to an afternoon at Freedomland, a U.S. history-themed amusement park in Baychester in the northeast Bronx.

During the following summer, Kevin and I got to meet the Kingston Trio, thanks to my uncle, Abner Klipstein, who was press agent for the Forest Hills musical festival in Queens. Kevin had introduced me to the folk singing of the super-preppy group—Dave Guard, Bob Shane, and Nick Reynolds—who were then at the peak of their popularity. We traveled by bus and subway from Hackensack to the Forest Hills tennis stadium in Queens. In honor of this occasion I had worn a wool sports jacket and was sweltering in the summer heat and humidity. After the concert my uncle arranged for us to meet the three singers. Dave Guard asked me why I was wearing such a warm jacket. I was speechless, and just started to sweat more. Kevin told Nick Reynolds that although he was thrilled to meet him, Reynolds should also be glad to meet him, since Kevin owned every one of the group's albums. Reynolds responded: "You must be a glutton for punishment." We could only spend a few minutes with the celebrities, however, since we had to catch the last bus back to Hackensack that evening. We had a grand time.

5. Main Street vs The Mall

When my father bought Archie Rose's dress shop on Main Street in Hackensack he had good reason to be optimistic about his business prospects. Bergen County was just beginning its post-World War II boom, as home construction and factory building fueled a major increase in consumer spending. The George Washington Bridge had opened in October 1931, but the Great Depression and the war had delayed the bridge's full impact on the suburbanization of northern New Jersey. Twenty years later Hackensack was at the brink of a new era of growth and prosperity. In 1950 its retail sales rose to a record high of just over $88 million. The town's residents constituted only about 5 percent of Bergen County's total population, but its merchants grossed about 21 percent of the county's total retail sales. A research study ranked Hackensack's Main Street fourth in the nation among comparable town business districts. Cars carrying holiday shoppers jammed both Anderson and Main Streets during the 1951 Christmas season. In early June 1955, the *Bergen Evening Record* published a nostalgic piece, "Bustling Main Street Far Cry From Old Days," that transported the reader back fifty-five years to the two-mile long "elm-lined dusty thoroughfare of 1900." The writer reminisced: "There are not too many who remember those wonderful days when there was no such thing as chambers of commerce, traffic lights, and glittering chromium store fronts, when one could get drugs in a drugstore and there were neighborhood grocery stores instead of huge supermarkets."

Business in Hackensack was booming, but under the surface there were signs of trouble ahead, even before the opening of the new shopping centers in Paramus in 1957. The sales figures for the 1950s are deceiving, for they obscure the relative decline in Hackensack's share of Bergen County's gross receipts. The city's record sales in 1957 were five times greater than twenty years earlier and $52.5 million above the sales reported in the 1948, but its proportion of all county business actually declined nearly 40 per cent over the previous twenty years and 33 1/3 per cent since 1948. Bergen County's rapidly growing population explains the big jump in total receipts, but it also provided opportunities for merchants in dozens of other suburbs to lure shoppers away from Hackensack.

During the 1950s Hackensack's central business district featured several characteristics that distinguished its downtown from those of cities of comparable size. First, it was more linear, in that the vast majority of retail and service shops, grocery stores, law offices, banks, restaurants, and department stores were concentrated on only one major avenue—Main Street. Very few were located on cross streets and parallel roads—River, Moore, and State Streets. (There was one perpendicular spur—a strip of stores on Anderson Street that ran west from Main Street for a few blocks.) Second, numerous small establishments, including some with less than ten

59

feet of frontage, occupied the lower end of Main Street. That was the result of a pre-World War II escalation of property values that prompted realtors to subdivide all available space. Third, there was a lot of vacant land behind these small stores. When the town fathers plotted out the downtown area the depth of lots fronting on Main Street was fixed at 150 feet or more. But since the average shop or office was only around 90 or 100 feet deep, their action created abundant room in back for future parking needs.

Traveling north on Main Street, among the most notable structures were the People's Trust Company's headquarters, erected in 1926 and the tallest building in Bergen County for almost forty years, and the Fox and Oritani movie theaters. The department stores and specialty shops at the upper end of Main Street catered to a more upscale clientele. In late October 1950 Oppenheim Collins opened its tenth store at the northeast corner of Main and Berry Street, selling a wide assortment of women's wear, accessories, children's clothing, and shoes. It also housed a beauty parlor and soon competed with the nearby Arnold Constable for the more affluent female customers. A few blocks away, at the northern end of Main at Anderson Street, stood the Sears, Roebuck and Company building, with its distinctive art deco tower. When Sears opened in 1932 as the largest department store in Bergen County, its payroll of 350 employees primed the pump of the town and county economy during the depths of the Depression. In 1957 the challenge was not hard times, but rather competition from the new malls. As it celebrated its twenty-fifth anniversary Sears announced its intention to compete aggressively with the flagship retail businesses that anchored the upstart Paramus shopping centers. Farther to the north the three-story Packard-Bamberger's, adjoining buildings, and parking lots sprawled over twelve acres. The owner, Frank W. Packard, sold everything from toothpaste to fresh meat, boy's dungarees, women's lingerie, automobile tires, television sets, washing machines, phonograph records, furniture, and wine. A modern version of the old general store of the past, the complex also included a barber shop, beauty salon, and restaurant. Packard claimed that his department store drew up to 50,000 customers a week and grossed around $20 million in 1954, with a higher figure expected for 1955.

Hackensack's Main Street was also a social hub of Bergen County, especially for teenagers on Saturdays. We paid less than a dollar for double feature films at the Fox and Oritani theaters, then went out for soda or ice cream. During the fall, cheerleaders, band members, and any high school student with a car would blast their horns as they drove up and down Main Street before every home and away football game, returning in the late afternoon whenever the Hackensack High Comets were victorious (which was quite often). On school nights some kids would tell their parents that they needed the car to go downtown to work on a term paper at the Johnson Public Library. Instead they wound up driving up and down Main Street. As the Beach Boys sang, "Seems she forgot all about the library that she told her old man now." Kevin's older sister Erin and her friends loved to "cruise the drag" with rock and roll blaring out of the radio. Starting at the Courthouse at the south end, they'd shout out friendly off-color salutations to "Charlene," a flamboyant, tough transvestite who replied in kind with indecent retorts, waves, and laughs. A few years later when the Ravens finally got "wheels," we actually did go to the library to study and work on research projects.

My dad's business, Roses Dress Shop, was moderately profitable, but our family's modest middle-class standard of living depended heavily on my mother's schoolteacher salary. I spent many Saturday afternoons at Roses making a nuisance of myself, aggravating the salesgirls who were trying to sell dresses to customers. When I was about nine or ten my dad told me that Mickey Mantle's wife had shopped at Roses. That was thrilling news to me, for I was still a Yankee fan in those days, and he was my first sports hero.

My father was active in the Hackensack Chamber of Commerce. He had to be, for he and his fellow merchants were bracing for the competition they expected from the new shopping centers that were scheduled to open in 1957 in Paramus. The R.H. Macy Company was building Garden State Plaza on 150 acres at the intersections of Routes 4 and 17 and the soon-to-be completed Garden State Parkway. Its premier shopping attraction was a 340,000-square-foot branch of L. Bamberger & Company (a division of Macy). At its perimeter were 5,500 parking spaces (with room for a total of 11,000). Less than one mile away, the Allied Stores Corporation invested $40 million to construct Bergen Mall at the junction of Forest Avenue and Route 4. The 320,000-square-foot Stern's department store stood at its center. Bergen Mall occupied 106 acres and could accommodate up to 8,500 automobiles.

Although the developers claimed that they intended to build upon and perfect the concept of downtown shopping for the benefit of consumers, they seemed to pose a gigantic threat to the Main Street businesses. But while the flagship department stores were expected to thrive, it was by no means certain that the smaller specialty shops in the new malls would also be profitable. They would thrive, survive, or go out of business depending on how many customers they could tap from the mall traffic generated by the large department stores. Some businessman, including Frank W. Packard, predicted that higher rents, increased advertising costs, and other expenses that reduced profits would force many of the smaller units in the malls to close. However, Packard did not anticipate the successful application of percentage leases. Under the new arrangements, a store owner guaranteed a minimum rent and agreed to pay more if his sales exceeded his expectations. Through that device, the managers of Garden State Plaza and Bergen Mall could count on a basic level of rental income while reducing the risk for reluctant tenants. When their projections for future sales growth were realized, the store owners were willing and able to pay the increased rents, and all parties benefited.

The new malls also generated more rental income for landlords and more retail sales for merchants by adding office buildings. Companies that leased space for professional services or business operations discovered that it was easier to hire and retain personnel. Their employees benefited from the convenience of shopping at nearby stores during their lunch hours or after work. Thus the office buildings produced more profits for the store owners. The malls were beginning to resemble mixed commercial, professional, and retail downtown business districts, but with less hassle over traffic jams and parking.

While Garden State Plaza was not the first regional shopping center in the nation or even in the East—those honors belonged to Country Club Plaza in Kansas City, Missouri, Northgate in Seattle, Shoppers World in Framingham, Massachusetts, and the Cross-County complex in Yonkers, New York—it was the first of its kind in suburban New Jersey. More important, Garden State Plaza would offer the ideal combination of one-stop comparison shopping and ample parking, unlike Hackensack's Main Street, where customers still had to move their cars several times to complete a day of shopping.

A large display advertisement in the special Garden State Plaza section of the *Bergen Evening Record* celebrated the mainstream view of the typical American consumer family. A husband, wife, and their young children (two girls and a boy) are loading large packages into their open convertible automobile. The slogan above the illustration identifies them as "The Family that Made the Garden State Plaza Come True." The text explains: "Without this family. . .and hundreds of thousands of others, all on wheels. . .New Jersey's largest shopping center would still be a dream. But because drive-in shopping is now your way of shopping, we're here." It invited all to come to opening day on Wednesday, May 1, where they would see "a dream city for shoppers come true." They could "stroll through air-conditioned stores where you can buy everything from Band-Aids to broadloom, cookies to cashmere." They could drive into parking lots that had 5,500 spaces, with more to come. Shoppers could also do their banking, get gas, eat a meal, buy groceries, or even trade stocks. Moreover, they need not worry about the weather, because "our cross-walks are covered, our malls canopied so rain won't spoil your fun." The *Record*'s editorial view conveyed a sense of curiosity and excitement: "Tomorrow brings us a way of life new to this part of the world. It is a distribution technique whose end result is—has to be—a better standard of living. It is a stimulating and welcome experiment not only in marketing but in living. . .We can't wait to open this package."

Tens of thousands of shoppers flocked to the Garden State Plaza and the grand opening of Bamberger's and seventeen other stores. Nineteen more shops were scheduled to open over the next few months. At the 10:00a.m.opening ceremony an eight-year-old polio victim cut the ceremonial ribbon. Early birds grabbed the free plants Bamberger's gave children, and the supply was soon depleted. The Paramus and Plaza police kept the traffic moving and also assisted a few distraught shoppers who at the end of the day could not locate their vehicles in the vast parking lot. Some minor highway delays developed in the early evening on the cloverleaf ramps leading on and off Routes 4 and 17. But it took only about twenty minutes to empty the parking lot after the 9:30p.m.closing time. Gross sales receipts at Bamberger's exceeded expectations, and the new era of consumerism was off to a flying start in Bergen County.

The management of Bergen Mall followed the example of their counterparts at Garden State Plaza in devising a marketing strategy that took dead aim at the downtown merchants of Passaic, Paterson, Newark, Hackensack, and other competing commercial districts. During the two days that preceded Bergen Mall's grand opening its executives ran large display advertisements in the *Record* that announced their main message through a catchy if unimaginative slogan: "You'll Find It All at Bergen Mall." They featured stylized illustrations of Stern's, spacious parking lots, and elegant adjoining stores. The text described Bergen Mall as a "town in itself," where "in one magnificent shopping center, you'll find. . .'one stop' shopping. A fabulous new department store . . .Stern's. . . joined by a veritable main street of shops. . .every imaginable kind of store to answer your every shopping need." At the bottom a map showed motorists that Bergen Mall was "so easy to reach" by automobile and "a dream in park in." An insert on parking reinforced the sales pitch by highlighting Bergen Mall's "spacious 52 acre" parking lot with 8,600 individual spaces, closely and conveniently adjacent to all the stores." It boldly proclaimed: "Bergen Mall is Main Street. . . .with every shop facing the Mall. . .a complete and wonderfully convenient personal shopping center."

Thousands of eager shoppers turned out early on November 14, 1957, for the grand opening of Stern's and six other stores at Bergen Mall. They were attracted in part by the live on-site television broadcast of the *Today* show, starring Dave Garroway, who gave NBC viewers coast-to-coast a tour of the new shopping center. Crowds followed Garroway and his supporting cast and crew members wherever they went, and also pressed against the glass windows of the studio in the mall where the telecast originated. At that morning's opening ceremonies the mayors of Paramus and Maywood presented a giant key to executives of the Allied Stores Corporation, including its chairman, B. Earl Puckett. He spoke about future plans for expansion and growing annual sales in a surrounding market that he estimated would swell to about two million people. He also boasted that Bergen Mall would soon have its own Christmas tree, which would be larger than the one in Rockefeller Center.

An editorial in the *Record* on the eve of the Bergen Mall grand opening acknowledged "the dawn of a new era," with two regional shopping centers confronting each other like "dreadnoughts." The newspaper was cautiously optimistic that both malls and even local downtown districts could survive the commercial competition, concluding:: "No grass should grow in any street." The recent slippage in retail sales was not caused by the advent of the Garden State Plaza, but rather resulted from "a combination of too much inflation, sudden spot unemployment, some unreasoned forecasts of impending doom, and Sputnik." The *Record* observed that merchandising at both malls—"at its sleek, poised, modern best"—provided "quite a contrast with downtown blocks." But it added: "If it is a threat it is also a challenge, and most of Bergen County's progressive retailers have looked at it that way. These two vast centers ought to bring hitherto uncalculated purchasing power into the Bergen County area. They ought to keep the trade here that has been going away from home. They signal the end of the time when the consumer had to go expensively elsewhere for the things he needed. This is the beginning of being able to get it, whatever it is, where we live. This is a new level in the standard of living. There ought to be enough blessings to go around."

It soon became obvious that Bamberger's at Garden State Plaza and Stern's at Bergen Mall and the smaller mall shops were thriving. But on Main Street it was another story. A study of Hackensack's total retail sales lists $128 million in 1958, declining to $123 million in 1959, followed by increases to $127 million in 1960, $129 million in 1961, $137 million in 1962, and $147 million in 1963. But these figures are misleading, because they reflect total receipts from Main Street and new shopping establishments near Route Four, including the new Bergen County branch of Bloomingdale's and an outlet of Two Guys From Harrison. As early as 1958 the lesser merchants of Hackensack and adjacent towns reported significant losses of sales to the new malls. Academics were quick to report the grim news. The Director of Research for New York University's School of Retailing announced: "Main Street, as we know it, is moribund—an anachronism. It is an institution of the horse and buggy era." Shopping malls were quickly becoming the new town community centers.

Packard's huge business in at the north end of Hackensack was strong enough to withstand the challenge of the malls and survived for decades, but Arnold Constable did not fare as well. In early November 1959, Howard Kane, the manager of its Hackensack branch, acknowledged a downturn in business when he appeared before the City Council to oppose an application for a variance from a zoning ordinance requesting permission to build a service station on a lot near the store. Kane recalled that when Arnold Constable opened its Hackensack branch twelve years earlier, "we had every confidence that Hackensack would grow and prosper as a shopping center." But, he added, "the entire City is suffering a setback because of the large shopping centers which have sprung up outside the city. We have every confidence that if Hackensack is guided in the right direction, it will come back and continue to be a shopping hub and center as it has been for the last ten years. We have every intention of staying in Hackensack." He then argued that a gas station near his store would not enhance the neighborhood and would occupy space that should be utilized for more parking spaces. Arnold Constable's Hackensack branch struggled along for another dozen years, before going out of business in February 1972. Shortly thereafter its elegant first floor retail space gave way to offices of Bergen County's tax board, superintendent of elections, and other agencies. Its windows were bricked over to provide more wall space. A reporter for the *Record* mournfully described the second story as a "graveyard of broken retail dreams: storage space for old fitting-room mirrors, clothing racks, cabinets, showcases and other fixtures that still have not been sold off."

The smaller shops at the lower end of Main Street took the brunt of the damage inflicted by the Paramus malls. The increase in vacancy and turnover rates told the tale. In 1958 the city business community listed 637 retail establishments, but by 1963 that number had dropped to 551. Also, whereas even during the Depression and World War II vacancies on Main Street were virtually unheard of, in 1961 and 1962 there were, respectively, thirty-five and thirty-nine empty storefronts. Moreover, between 1955 and 1965, with the exception of shoe stores, 50 percent of the shops liquidated their inventory. The toughest years were between 1958 and 1961, with several businesses showing sales declines that ranged from 25 to 50 percent. Hardest hit were apparel shops. A modest revival of business fortunes began in 1961, especially after merchants invested in renovations and introduced more modern merchandising practices.

Hackensack's leading merchants were not about to roll over and accept defeat at the hands of the new malls. Although in December 1957 and January 1958 a few of them seemed to be in a state of denial as they minimized the longer-term impact of the malls on their shops, overall the town's Chamber of Commerce took the threat seriously. Early in January 1958 one owner told the *Record:* "People are creatures of habit.. . .and those who have shopped in the City [Hackensack] for a number of years will be back as the novelty of the regional centers wears off." That newspaper also quoted my dad's optimistic prediction for prospects for 1958. He reasoned: "World War II babies are now teenagers and their increased purchasing power should boost sales," adding that they "accounted for more sales at the store [Roses Dress Shop] during the past Christmas than any other age group." What he did not reveal at this time was that he had already protected himself by acquiring a percentage lease for a new bridal shop in Bergen Mall.

Before and after the 1957 Christmas holiday season Hackensack's Chamber of Commerce launched a publicity campaign promoting business on Main Street. One advertisement featured a map of the downtown district with designated parking areas, including a notice that all parking meters would be hooded during the holiday season. Another proclaimed "Our Outlook Is Great for '58" and thanked "Mr. and Mrs. Bergen County for the way that you made 1957 the biggest single year that the over 400 Chamber of Commerce members have enjoyed." The City Council also sponsored a large display ad in the *Record* announcing that Hackensack "has everything to offer to business firms, industrialists, and residents."

At the beginning of 1958 Samuel Hekemian, a leading realtor, expressed a more sobering view of the current state of business in town and future prospects. He estimated: "In 1957, 10 percent of the business establishments on Main Street did more business than they did in 1956, 40 percent did about the same, and 50 per cent did less business." But he also argued that "there is no need to be discouraged" so long as the town's merchants adopted modern methods of merchandizing, with proper care paid to quality and price of goods sold and courteous treatment of customers. Business consultants echoed his argument that there was plenty of business to go around, provided store owners were careful and wise about their methods of retailing. Time would tell which Main Street stores would survive and even thrive and which would go out of business.

Beginning in 1957 and continuing for the next few years, Main Street merchants took a proactive approach to the coming of the malls. Their projects included providing more free or metered downtown parking, demolishing or renovating shops, repaving and beautifying Main Street, and sponsoring new sales promotions and events to woo customers back to Hackensack. They also tried to revitalize the downtown district by applying for urban renewal funds to rehabilitate commercial zones. Another strategy was to join with churches and citizens concerned with traffic congestion in a campaign to maintain Bergen County's blue laws that banned shopping on Sundays, since the town's independent proprietors feared ruination if the malls gained the right to open seven days a week. Although Hackensack's lobbyists won that battle to keep stores shut on the Sabbath, the rest of their schemes failed to restore the city's prior privileged position as the commercial hub of Bergen County.

Traffic flow and especially parking concerns were paramount in the minds of Main Street merchants. On June 2, 1958 the City Council angered Main Street merchants by proposing a new regulation that extended metered parking enforcement in off street municipal parking lots from six days a week from 9:00am to 9:00pm, to twenty-for hours, every day of the year, except for 8:00am to 1:00pm on Sundays and five holidays. City Manager Harold V. Reilly defended the new policy as a means of paying off the debt incurred in the lots' construction and maintenance costs. He believed that the $88,000 expense of the city's municipally owned Parking Utility "should be met from revenues received from the people who use the utility, rather than be an extra burden to the taxpayers in general." He reminded the public that the new extended hours of enforcement would not apply to parking meters on public streets, where there would continue to be no charge from 9:00pm to 9:00am and on Sundays. Thus he denied that the new rules would have any negative impact on the merchants, whose stores were closed on Sundays and after 9:00pm (with only a few exceptions).

The *Record* published a letter from a disgruntled Hackensack housewife that confirmed the worst fears of the town's merchants. She recalled getting one parking ticket when she did not have a nickel for the meter and another one when one of the rear wheels of her car extended over the white boundary line of her space by only four and a half inches.. Enraged, she and her friends decided that henceforth they would go to the malls for all of their remaining Easter purchases. She estimated that the nearly six hundred dollars she and her friends spent at the malls "could have gone to the merchants of Hackensack." She ended her letter with an assessment that was bound to displease the towns' merchants:

> I can assure you I will never drive into the City [Hackensack] again. Why should I? Would you, when these shopping centers offer you more than Main Street and you don't have to worry about parking and some ridiculous excuse for getting a ticket?.... Competition is keen, and dollars are few, and a mother like me with four children. . . can relax at these centers as well, because of the interesting amusements for children and the lack of streets where children can get hurt. The merchants of Hackensack had better start doing something, or I'm afraid Main Street will become a ghost town."

She identified herself as "a Hackensack resident, an out-of-town shopper."

Several businessmen appealed to the City Council to consider eliminating all parking meters, with the goal of promoting more shopping in town. That approach, they argued, would prevent stores from going out of business and also preserve property values in the downtown district. One councilman replied by blasting the Chamber of Commerce for not appreciating that the city had created the parking lots for the benefit of businessmen. Despite the objections of the Chamber of Commerce, the City Council approved the new ordinance by a vote of 4-1. But it also agreed to appoint a committee that was instructed to seek a better solution to the parking problem.

During the early 1960s the Chamber of Commerce sponsored a number of studies and launched new promotional campaigns with mixed results. The one positive development came not in retail but in the service sector, especially in the construction of office buildings. Thus even as more stores closed on Main Street, Hackensack's continuing status as the county seat generated new demand for office space for law firms, bail bondsmen, title companies, and other judicial service firms. The new construction prevented Hackensack's economy from going into freefall. The town thus avoided the severe blight that ravaged downtown Newark, Paterson, and Passaic.

While Hackensack's merchants struggled to revive their fortunes on Main Street, the City Council started an urban renewal program that featured slum clearance and new low-income housing in several poor neighborhoods on both sides of the business district. In September 1958 the city officials applied for a federal grant under the U.S. Housing Act of 1949 to clean up several blocks along Moore and River Streets in the town center. In March 1960 they also began similar projects in the section bounded by the Susquehanna railroad on the south, Passaic Street on the north, Third Street on the West and Railroad Avenue on the east, and another area in the south end of town between the New Jersey, New York railroad on the west and the Hackensack River on the East. All of these projects would provide new housing to replaced dilapidated buildings that were scaring away shoppers and depressing property values in the city's center.

Even as my dad put in long hours at Chamber of Commerce meetings to help promote his business and others on Main Street, he knew that shopping malls were destined to be a fixture in the suburban scene. He thus applied the strategy of "if you can't beat 'em, join 'em." Leasing agents at Bergen Mall were seeking a balance of large and smaller stores, aiming to make Bergen Mall "a planned shopping city rather than just a shopping center." They interviewed and screened applicants for leases, checking the merchants' retailing experience and credentials, while also answering queries from the prospective tenants about lease terms, the kind and quality of merchandise to be featured, anticipated daily counts of customers, projected sales, and facilities at the mall. My father earned their trust and obtained a lease to open a new specialty store named Roses Terrace Shop, which would sell bridal gowns, bridesmaids and prom dresses, and accessories. In retrospect it seems like a very shrewd move, but of course you did not have to be a retailing genius to predict that the bridal market in Bergen County was going to expand enormously in the late fifties and sixties, thanks to the baby boom. In fact, when Roses Terrace Shop opened in early 1958 large crowds of prospective brides, their mothers, and their bridesmaids got up at the crack of dawn to gather outside its doors.

Many Hackensack merchants bitterly condemned my father's decision to launch a new store in Bergen Mall, viewing him as a traitor to the town's Chamber of Commerce and its campaign to maintain prosperity on Main Street. But he did remain loyal to his town. Rather than shut down his dress shop, he transformed it into a second Roses bridal store. During the 1960s a third opened its doors at the new Willowbrook Mall in Wayne, followed by a fourth (this time named "Celebration") at the more upscale Paramus Park shopping center on Route 17. My father also deepened his commitment to Hackensack by renting space next door to Roses for a new women's wear shop named "Indescribable" (my mother always claimed credit for that title). He launched three more "Indescribables" in Bergen Mall, Willowbrook Mall, and Paramus Park. Most merchants appreciated my father's continuing commitment to the Hackensack business community. He provided even more compelling proof of his affection for the city a few years later when he began a law practice in town and served as city prosecutor and municipal court judge.

It didn't take too long for the residents of Hackensack to experience the economic and political repercussions of the new shopping centers. The malls' negative impact on the downtown business district depressed the local real estate market, which in turn lowered municipal tax revenues. As stores closed landlords lowered their rents to attract new businesses, resulting in a sharp decrease in Hackensack's total tax rateables. In order to balance the budget the City Council either had to drastically cut expenses or raise the residential property tax rate. Compounding the problem was a state law that required equal assessment and the end of inequities in which property valuations ranged from 10 to 54 percent of market value. The combination of the city's first reassessment of all real estate since 1938 with the budget crisis generated a taxpayer revolt. Disgruntled residents accused members of the City Council of imposing inequitable policies and engaging in corrupt practices. The result was a half decade of political instability marked by a series of recall elections that made Hackensack look like a third world banana republic.

In 1959 irate homeowners organized several homeowner and taxpayer associations to protest the new real estate assessments and higher property tax bills, which in a few cases amounted to a 100 percent increase. They charged that Mayor Edgar P. Deuell and the City Council had favored the landlords of commercial properties at the expense of homeowners. The town's Tax Assessor, William H. Lind, denied those allegations and explained that for many years business and residential property owners had shared the tax load almost equally. He attributed the sharp increases in property taxes to the depressed state of Main Street plus the need for more equitable treatment for all groups. He also noted that though it was too late to protest the 1959 taxes, relief was on the way for 1960, thanks to the opening of a new Bloomingdale's department store at the northeast boundary of Hackensack and the completion of a few new apartment buildings.

Hackensack's homeowners, unimpressed with Lind's explanations, soon organized a grassroots political campaign to recall and replace the current administration. Henry C. Savino of the Hackensack Home Owners Association and John A. Nativo of Hackensack Taxpayers and Citizens League spearheaded a drive to gather signatures for a petition requesting a special election to recall Deuell and the other four members of the City Council. Deuell responded by accusing both men and their organizations of acting as a front to advance the power of a local political machine headed by Anthony and Dominick Fondo. Both Savino and Nativo denied those allegations, but Savino resigned as president of the Home Owners Association to run as a candidate for the City Council. Another candidate, Walter E. Nowakowski, contended that the challengers were "not against Main Street business." On the contrary, he explained that the recall leaders wanted to see Main Street grow, but not at the expense of local homeowners: "We want to help Main Street business by putting more money in the pockets of our citizens so they can spend it with our local merchants. What better way do we have of putting money in citizens' pockets than by reducing their taxes to the fair level?"

Although the Bergen County Board of Taxation and the New Jersey Treasury Department reported that Lind had acted legally in assessing property for taxation, on October 6, 1959, disgruntled Hackensack's voters removed Deuell and the entire City Council from office. They were replaced by Nowakowski, Savino, Eugene E. Demarest, Arthur C. Maurello, and Fred A. McCullough. The newly elected Council chose Nowakowski, the recipient of the most votes, as mayor and Demarest (the runner-up) as deputy mayor. The victorious party's campaign manager, David R. Smith, was then appointed to the pivotal post as Tax Assessor.

But it was not long before dissatisfaction with a new tax assessment program and factionalism within the new regime led to a revolt against Nowakowski. On May 24, 1960, Demarest, Maurello, and Savino voted to oust him as mayor and replace him with Demarest. After his election Demarest fired an apparent shot at the Fondo brothers, declaring: "The Council was faced with the choice of going down the path of political bossism. . .or down the path of government that is guided by the will of the people and who will not be bossed by self-seeking and self-appointed bosses." Nowakowski then filed a suit to regain his position. He was reinstated as mayor in January of 1961, when the Superior Court of New Jersey ruled that his ouster had been illegal.

Hackensack's City Council game of musical chairs continued with the May 1961 regular election. Although Nowakowski retained his seat on the Council, he placed fourth in the voting, trailing Peter Frapaul (the new mayor), Kazmier Wysocki (deputy mayor), and Charles E. Freeman. Frank A. Buono Jr. captured the final place. In his acceptance remarks Frapaul stated that the people of Hackensack desired "an end to the type of political maneuvering that has given a circus-like atmosphere to the conduct of our local government." Wysocki acknowledged that three different factions were represented on the new Council, which had inherited a messy problem involving hundreds of claims of homeowners disputing property tax assessments.

Two years later the protracted tax struggle and the political ambitions of former councilmen Savino and McCullough produced still another recall campaign. But this time the challengers targeted only two councilmen: Wysocki (who had become mayor after the death of Frapaul) and Freeman. In a sobering "State of the City" message in January 1963 Wysocki acknowledged that Hackensack faced several serious problems. These included "losing its position as the leading business center of Bergen County" and the deterioration of large sections of its residential community. He added that though no one wanted an increase in taxes, it was essential that the city retain the high quality of its school system, parks and recreational facilities and extensive public services. That responsibility was becoming more problematic because of declining tax revenues from the depressed business sector. This time the political and tax revolt failed. In the recall election on September 10 Wysocki and Freeman easily defeated their opponents.

With stores both on Main Street and at Bergen Mall, my dad put me and my brother to work, mostly during the summer months. He never paid us, but he fed and clothed us, kept a roof over our heads, and took care of our college educations. Changing the displays in the front window was Dan's least favorite assignment because of the time when some classmates passed by just as he was dressing the female mannequins with the latest fashions. They hooted at Dan as he arranged the clothing over the dummy's breasts and butt, heckling him about the "action he was getting." My work at Roses Terrace Shop was less exotic—helping out with the inventory, filling out forms and collecting money at the cash register when the salesgirls were busy with customers, vacuuming the carpets, cleaning out the store room in the basement, or assisting with the semi-annual sidewalk sales held in both Hackensack and Bergen Mall to get rid of unsold merchandise at discounted prices.

Sometimes my father took me to the Seventh Avenue garment district in Manhattan to pick up a wedding gown or bridesmaid's dress to replace one that had been damaged or lost in shipping. We'd go to the "Bridal Building" that housed the offices of the owners (all Jewish it seemed me), chief executives, and designers of the leading manufacturers of formal women's wear in the nation. In those days their factories were also in the district, staffed by seamstresses who were members of the International Ladies Garment Workers Union. One time I met David, owner of David's Bridals, one of the leading firms in the industry. He and my father had known each other for more than a decade, and he greeted us warmly. "Nate," he said, "Is this your son?" What a good-looking boy!" "How's your family?" My father replied: "Fine, Fine, David, How's business?" And David answered: "Oh, it's terrible, such a struggle, I don't know how long we can last with these costs and the rent here." Then more kvetching, followed by: "so much aggravation, what can I say, I should retire already, but I am too young, and my son wants to be a doctor, so there is no one to carry on." As we got into the elevator, with me holding the wrapped gown, I asked my father about David's complaints. He laughed and said: "That means he's doing great, and soon he'll raise his prices."

After I graduated from high school my dad thought it would be good for me to work at a real job and earn a few bucks, so he used his influence at Bergen Mall to get me a part time position selling lamps at Stern's four weeknights and all day Saturday (twenty-four hours a week, at around $1.35 per hour). I knew nothing about lamps, but I quickly mastered the tasks of retrieving packages of the most popular pole and table lamps from the adjacent storeroom, filling out special order forms, collecting money and using the charge card machine (pre-credit card). What I learned that summer of 1963 was that I did not want to spend the rest of my life working in a department store or running my dad's growing chain of bridal and women's wear shops. I would return to work at Roses the summer after my freshman year in college, and then again part-time for two years during the late 70s, but then my father finally sold all of his stores.

Before we got our licenses, the guys and I spent more time on Main Street than we did at the new shopping malls. Mostly that was because we could walk there. Main Street was only one block away from State Street and just a half a mile from Hackensack High School. Research assignments drew us downtown to the Johnson Public Library, and we went to see the latest films on weekends at the Fox and Oritani movie theaters. But we also enjoyed traveling to Bergen Mall or Garden State Plaza, either by badgering our parents to drive us there, or by taking public busses. One of Bergen Mall's most popular summer promotions was its free Friday evening band concerts, which attracted suburbanites who brought beach chairs to listen to the music.

After we all got our licenses we had more independence and were more able and eager to forsake Main Street and the decaying downtown of Hackensack for the brighter lights and enticements of the shopping centers. On one memorable summer weekend evening I drove Henry to Bergen Mall in my father's small, manual transmission Fiat. After the stores closed I started its engine, but when I shifted into first gear the car did not move. I tried the other gears, but the only one that engaged with the clutch was reverse. So my only option was to drive three miles back to my home backwards. Fortunately there were very few cars on Maywood Avenue, but when we were about half way to my house a policeman stopped us and asked us for an explanation. Amazingly, he let us continue and provided us with some protection along the route.

By 1963 it was clear that adolescents in our town and throughout Bergen County favored the malls, especially as they added food courts, movie theaters, and shops that catered to teenagers. High school girls like Kevin's sister Erin and Ruth Heiferman found the new malls exciting, and they enjoyed sampling cosmetics, trying on clothes, and searching for the latest music albums. They did not have enough money to purchase much, but they loved the process of looking. Just as we guys filled our leisure time with countless hours of playground sport our female classmates occupied themselves with recreational shopping. Erin considers herself to be one of the nation's pioneering "mall rats."

The malls also provided plenty of part-time jobs for teenagers. My father hired Erin for his Bergen Mall store to assist new brides and their bridesmaids when they selected their gowns or returned for their fittings. She was not very enthusiastic about her work and passed her time daydreaming and generally ignoring the customers. He fired her, but softened the blow by telling her that she was "too smart" for the job.

6. On the Eve of Destruction

In the 1950s we did not spend very much time worrying about whether we were going to be hooked up to an iron lung or paralyzed for life from polio or instantly incinerated by a nuclear attack. We were dimly aware of the Korean War, the growing hysteria over communist subversion in America, and the threat of the Soviet Union. It's not that we thought we were immortal. We knew that a deadly disease or an atomic bomb could kill us before we had a chance to grow up. But we lived happily in a state of denial. We did not allow the warnings to spoil our good times playing sports, hiking and camping on scout trips, or just hanging out, at Breslow's or each other's homes. We were suburban white boys who were blessed with loving parents who provided us with a sense of security. We sensed some of the anxieties of the adult world, but we were too sheltered or too privileged to believe we were actually on the eve of destruction.

Even as tensions between the United States and the communist regimes of the Soviet Union and China escalated during the early years of the Cold War, Americans became preoccupied with a serious public health menace that was much closer to home. Polio was a crippling and potentially deadly disease that could leave an adult or child permanently disabled or deformed, and in severe cases dependent on an iron lung respirator for assistance in breathing. Citizens were aware of polio's devastating effects in large part because of the example of President Franklin D. Roosevelt. He was stricken in 1921 when he was thirty-nine, and he required heavy iron leg braces to stand when he gave public addresses. Although adult cases were not uncommon, the large majority who suffered from polio were under sixteen. Parents feared that a child might come down with polio's symptoms—a severe headache, exhaustion, nausea, a high fever, muscle aches (especially a stiff neck), followed by the onset of paralysis. Community leaders became increasing alarmed about what appeared to be a polio epidemic when the number of cases suddenly spiked from an average 20,000 a year in the late 1940s to 58,000 in 1952. The summer season appeared to be the peak time of risk for contracting polio, and swimming pools appeared to be the venue where the virus was most readily spread. Medical researchers were then testing several vaccines that might provide immunity to polio, especially for children. Our parents were among the millions of Americans who anxiously awaited the results of these clinical trials.

Among our guys only Henry had a family experience with polio. When he was four years old, his cousin Richie Arrabito contracted polio and underwent treatment at Bergen Pines Hospital. One day Henry was horsing around with Richie's brother John and John pushed Henry down a flight of stairs. Henry sustained a minor neck sprain, but when it stiffened up over the next few days his parents became very worried, because a stiff neck was a possible indicator for polio. Thinking that it was the best placement for him, they took their son to Bergen Pines, mainly because his cousin Richie was being treated there.

The Bergen Pines polio ward had previously been used for tuberculosis patients. Desolate, dingy, and downright terrifying, it resembled a medieval torture chamber. Henry pleaded with his mother Pauline not to leave him there, clinging to her so tightly he ripped her blouse. He was given a bed near Richie, but Henry watched in horror as Richie underwent painful heat therapy that was aimed at stimulating the muscles in his legs and other afflicted parts of his body. Worst of all, Henry caught a glimpse of the large spinal tap needle, which a doctor used to draw fluid from him to determine if he in fact had polio. Clutching Pauline for comfort, he screamed throughout the procedure.

Still, Henry tried to amuse Richie. One stunt was pretending he had his head stuck in the boards at the end of his bed. This trick succeeded in distracting Richie a few times, but one evening his head actually became wedged in the headboard. The nurses ignored his pleas for help, thinking he was kidding again. Henry wriggled his head out and survived. When it became clear that his symptoms resulted from the fall down the stairs rather than infantile paralysis, Henry was discharged. Richie's condition improved and he recovered sufficiently to live a normal life with only slight long-term effects of the disease on his mobility.

Six years later the good medical news came on April 12, 1955 when federal health officials announced that a vaccine developed by Dr. Jonas Salk was successful in a field trial of 1.8 million children. The recommended treatment consisted of a series of injections of inactivated (dead) poliovirus. A few years later a rival oral live-attenuated vaccine developed by Albert Sabin supplanted the Salk vaccine. But it was the Salk version that launched the first mass inoculations of schoolchildren in U.S. history, promoted nationwide by the National Foundation for Infantile Paralysis (now the March of Dimes). By 1957 the annual number of polio cases in the U.S. had dropped to 5,600. In 1961 there were only 161.

In the spring of 1955, however, there was considerable doubt about the new vaccine. The national medical community, federal government, and the pharmaceutical companies all endorsed it, but many citizens, including some parents in Hackensack, remained skeptical because the first large batches of doses would not be ready until June. Parents worried if there was sufficient time remaining in the school year for the second shot, required for the inoculation to become effective. (Scheduling a third "booster" injection would not pose a problem, since that round could safely be held during the following year.)

On April 20, just eight days after the federal government gave its stamp of approval to the Salk polio vaccine, second-graders in Hackensack's Holy Trinity Roman Catholic elementary school were among the first schoolchildren in the United States to be injected with the drug. Cameramen filmed the historic event for local television news shows that evening, recording the seven-year-olds as they lined up, winced through their injections, and received their reward of a huge lollipop.

Holy Trinity parochial school participated in a special program that made it eligible for an early batch, but we students in the public school system had to wait two months for our initial doses. In Hackensack 1,650 pupils were eligible for the vaccine. Of this group, 1,500 children were certified by their parents to participate. Technically, the vaccination program was under the jurisdiction of the town's Board of Health, but the Board of Education provided the facilities and administered the project. In late May Dr. Edward Essertier, a Board of Education member, convinced his colleagues that it was too risky to administer one shot in June, with no guarantee that the second shot would be given sometime in July. But on June 9 Dr. Essertier and the other Board members changed their minds and endorsed the program, having been assured that a fresh batch of vaccine, manufactured by the Eli Lilly Corporation, was in the custody of the town's Public Health officer. Superintendent Hobart De Puyt then announced that all children in the first four grades would be inoculated, beginning the following Monday, with plans for the second shot still undecided. In that first round 518 students were actually inoculated—about one-third of those who were eligible. Many remained somewhat confused and undecided about the safety of the Salk vaccine.

Over the next two years the Hackensack schools completed the polio vaccination program. We were all inoculated, although a few of us took a sugar cube that contained the Sabin oral form of the vaccine. I did not receive my first injection at Hillers School, because I was sick on the date of inoculation. Since I missed out on the regular program, a few months later my father took me to another elementary school, where a school nurse administered the Salk shot. I remember being far more anxious about the needle than I was about contracting polio and being paralyzed for life.

During my boyhood I had several illnesses, including the mumps, a painful case of boils, and a bone separation condition (Osgood-Schlatter's disease). My most serious medical crisis was an appendicitis attack in late November 1955. It happened the day after my parents took my brother and me to see a midweek performance of the Broadway musical *Damn Yankees*. I loved the show, but the next morning I awoke with sharp pains in my abdomen. My dad called our doctor, who came to our house (imagine that happening today). He arranged for a surgeon to perform an emergency appendectomy at Hackensack Hospital a few hours later. When my father told me that I needed an operation I trusted his judgment and the doctor's skill. But I worried that my mother would try to delay or block the surgery, because she was a very anxious person who did not have much faith in modern medicine. She had already left the house that morning when I'd awakened with my stomach pain. When my dad called her with the news she became hysterical, but then he put me on the phone and I calmed her down and assured her that I would be all right. It took me a few weeks to recover from the surgery, because my appendix had burst during the procedure, which caused some complications and risk of infection.

The Cold War made a greater impression on our young minds than did polio. Images of a mushroom-shaped cloud looming over my head disturbed my sleep. I felt secure in my home and with my best friends even though I knew they could not protect me from a nuclear holocaust. By the time I began first grade I knew something about the Korean War, and when it ended in 1953 I was much relieved when my mother told me the good news that "they were not killing daddies anymore."

In mid-October 1952, when we were in second grade, we had an early introduction to the drama of national presidential politics. Hackensack was the site of an appearance by Republican candidate and World War II hero General Dwight D. Eisenhower, who was campaigning against the Democratic nominee, Governor Adlai Stevenson of Illinois. A few weeks before the election, our teachers marched us a few blocks over to Essex Street to see Eisenhower's motorcade en route to a 1:00 p.m. rally on the lawn outside the Bergen County Courthouse in downtown Hackensack. As Eisenhower's car passed by many of us waved tiny American flags distributed by our school.

Hackensack was a Republican town in those days, and our teachers clearly favored Eisenhower, as did most New Jerseyans. (A reporter for the *New York Times* wrote that while traveling from New York City to cover the campaign stop he saw a sign that read: "Don't worry Ike—New Jersey is safe.") At the courthouse a crowd of about 10,000 heard the "bare-headed, coatless candidate" attack President Harry Truman's spending policies as "sheer folly." Ike also called for better national leadership "to improve America's position both at home and abroad." The Republican state chairman who introduced Eisenhower told the gathering: "You're not as well off as you were even five years ago." That would certainly have been news to my parents, loyal Democrats who believed that the Truman administration had elevated our family's economic status since 1947—our last full year in the Bronx. For business reasons my father was a registered Republican during the 1950s, but his heart was with liberal causes, and he and my mom supported Stevenson. The same could not be said about his sisters, who had married rich Bergen County businessmen and were much more conservative. My parents were disappointed after Eisenhower trounced Stevenson in 1952 and again in 1956. But during those years, I liked Ike. So did Barry Vasios, whose parents supported Eisenhower. Barry taped a piece of white notepad paper with the "I Like Ike" slogan to the front fender of his bicycle. I was comfortable with Eisenhower as president, and his passion for golf may have even played a minor role in motivating me and the guys to try the game.

After Eisenhower's inauguration the Cold War heated up a bit as both the United States and the Soviet Union tested advanced hydrogen bombs. The government mandated civil defense exercises to help the

American people protect themselves in the event of a nuclear war. At Hillers our principal and teachers supervised the drills, in which pupils gathered in the basement or hallways to practice "duck and cover" procedures. We were instructed that in the event of a nuclear attack, we should not rush to a window to look at the flash of light or the mushroom cloud. Rather, we should immediately cease all activity and lie facedown on the ground in the fetal position, covering our heads with our hands. We also learned the rules for air raid drills and the advantages of families building bomb shelters in their basements or backyards. I don't think it ever occurred to me that there is not very much you can do to survive a nuclear explosion, and even if you did survive, who would really want to live in a hole in the ground for a few weeks and then try to live in a post-nuclear world?

These civil defense drills did not disrupt our education, but the frequent bomb scares, especially at State Street Junior High School, were more annoying. On those occasions it was not the Soviet Union calling, but rather an angry kid or adult playing a prank. When a bomb threat was phoned in we would file out of the building and stand on the sidewalk for at least a half hour or more. The police would then conduct a fruitless search for the bomb. For many of us, it was a welcome relief from class, except if it was very cold, which it often was, or if the interruption in routine had a negative impact on our academic work or extracurricular activities.

During the early and mid-1950s television kept us up to date on the latest news of the Cold War. One evening I was watching the *Ozzie and Harriet Show* when a bulletin interrupted the program to announce that Julius and Ethel Rosenberg had been executed for passing atomic secrets to the Soviet Union after World War II. Even at such a tender age I had some knowledge of this notorious affair, since my parents, like most liberals, doubted they were guilty. Senator Joseph McCarthy's campaign against so-called Communists in the U.S. government did not make much of an impression on me or my friends then, but decades later I met Hollywood screenwriters whose careers had been severely damaged by his witch-hunting tactics.

On October 4, 1957, one month after we started seventh grade and just a few weeks after the Little Rock school desegregation episode, the Soviets successfully launched the first Earth-orbiting artificial satellite, which they named *Sputnik* ("fellow traveler" in Russian). At first President Eisenhower and his advisers downplayed the significance of both *Sputnik* and the successful firing of an intercontinental ballistic missile as threats to America's national security. But other officials, scientists, and especially the mass media viewed the Soviet achievements as alarming evidence that America had fallen behind its powerful rival. Edward Teller, one of the scientists who developed America's first nuclear weapons, thought that *Sputnik* heralded a kind of technological Pearl Harbor. As American intellectuals agonized about why we seemed to care more about fancy cars and kitchen appliances than we did about education—especially in scientific and technological fields—the Navy accelerated its program to rocket an American satellite into space.

Sputnik was a big deal to me and my friends, twelve years old that year, as after dark on Boy Scout camping trips we searched the skies for brief sightings of that small aluminum sphere (22.8 inches in diameter and 184 pounds). On one late October weekend a scout leader soberly lectured us about the implications of this latest technological challenge from the Communists. He did not want the United States to fall too far behind the Soviets. We got the message--as American patriotic boys, we were rooting for the good guys to respond right away with proof that America was capable of being the world leader in both outer space and the mass production of consumer goods and fast food. While visiting the Soviet Union Vice President Richard Nixon used a model American kitchen to show Nikita Khrushchev how American capitalism surpassed Soviet communism in providing the masses with the most modern appliances and consumer goods. Although Khrushchev dismissed Nixon's claims, my friends and I were confident that we could bury the Russians with hamburgers and French fries. But now we wondered if they could bury us with missiles.

In November the U.S. replied to *Sputnik* with a launch of a U.S. Navy rocket. Seconds after ignition, it burst into flames and toppled over. It broke into fiery pieces, leaving its tiny four-pound satellite intact, beeping away amid the debris. (In England the *London Daily Express* proclaimed: "U.S. Calls It Kaputnik.") In late January 1958 the United States recouped some of its prestige with its first successful launch of an orbiting satellite. It turned out that in the longer run the panic over *Sputnik* benefited me and my classmates, because it prompted the Eisenhower and Kennedy administrations and Congress to substantially increase federal funding for higher education. That money turned out to be beneficial for me a decade later, as it paid for my four-year graduate fellowship at Columbia.

In the fall of 1960 we all followed the hotly contested presidential race between Republican Vice President Richard Nixon and Democratic Senator John F. Kennedy from Massachusetts. Although as a kid I had liked "Ike," by the time of the 1960 election I had switched to the Democratic side, thanks mostly to the appeal of John F. Kennedy. I did not care that he was Catholic, and I didn't like or trust "Tricky Dick" Nixon. My friends also favored Kennedy, as he appeared to be more charismatic, youthful, and dynamic. We celebrated his victory in November and his inauguration on January 20, 1961. Three months later we watched him take responsibility for the failed U.S. invasion of Cuba at the Bay of Pigs, which had been planned by the Eisenhower administration to overthrow the communist government led by Fidel Castro. Kennedy and his military commanders did not provide adequate air or naval support for the brigade of 1,500 American-trained Cuban exiles who wanted to depose Castro. It was an embarrassing fiasco for our new young president. It would set the stage for a far more threatening confrontation over Cuba.

In October 1962, as my classmates and I completed college applications and took the final rounds of the SAT exams, the Cold War threatened to explode into a hot nuclear holocaust. That month began with a boost to America's morale provided by a native of Hackensack. Walter ("Wally") Shirra, Jr. completed six orbits of Earth during a Mercury mission that lasted nine hours and thirteen minutes. On October 15 his birthplace and the neighboring town of Oradell (where he grew up) honored him with a motorcade that began at the Bergen County Courthouse and proceeded north on Main Street, with tens of thousands cheering the new hero along the way. At a ceremony in a football stadium in Oradell, James A. Webb of the National Aeronautics and Space Administration presented Shirra with a medal and read a statement from John F. Kennedy, in which the president acknowledged that the United States was still trailing the Soviet Union in the space race. He praised Shirra and the entire Mercury team for their efforts "to get our space program moving from a position of second best to one of world leadership."

Just a few days later we followed news reports that the Soviet Union was building nuclear missile bases in Cuba. President Kennedy weighed his options of doing nothing, using diplomacy to persuade the Russians to remove the missiles, attacking the missile sites by air, invading Cuba, or blockading the island. Kennedy ultimately decided on a refinement of the blockade alternative—a naval quarantine applied to all offensive military equipment headed for Cuba. We all gathered in the high school auditorium to watch televised news updates as we wondered if the Soviets would back down. We went through our normal schedule of classes and after-school sports practices in denial, unwilling to believe we might be vaporized at any moment. We were relieved when Soviet Premier Nikita Khrushchev ultimately agreed to dismantle and remove the missiles, after Kennedy secretly pledged to reciprocate by withdrawing American missiles from southern Italy and Turkey. Since Kennedy's concession was not made public until later, the standoff ended with an apparent American victory, thereby boosting our faith in Kennedy's resolve in standing up to the Communists. The New Frontier was gathering momentum with a growing space program and a strong rebuttal to a Soviet challenge.

With the Cuban missile crisis over, we could turn our attention back to school work, sports, and college applications. Dimly aware of the escalating conflict in Southeast Asia, we remained on the eve of destruction.

7. Our Sporting Lives

The Duke of Wellington allegedly proclaimed: "The Battle of Waterloo was won on the playing fields of Eton." However, he probably never actually uttered that statement, and even more doubtful is its thesis that intense athletic competition at English prep schools enabled British military commanders to conquer Napoleon. Today it is debatable whether youth sports programs and varsity athletics provide participants with an edge later in their lives on battlefields or in corporate boardrooms. At best, they prepare boys and girls for the challenges of adult life in a highly competitive culture. My friends and I believe that playing ball on public fields and competing on Little League and junior and senior high school teams taught us the value of discipline, training, and teamwork, as well as how to cope with both success and failure. On the other hand, there are plenty of people (including my son Adam) who achieve great success despite having little or no interest in sports during their youth.

Sports played an enormous role in our lives as boys and adolescents. It all began with baseball. We learned the fundamentals of the game by playing catch with our fathers in our backyards and local parks. At the age of eight we tried out for "pony league" novice teams; at nine or ten we became pint-sized ball players in full Little League uniform, playing on enclosed fields with an electronic scoreboard in the main arena, dreaming of future stardom in the Major Leagues.

Hackensack joined the Little League national organization about a decade after it was founded in 1939 in Williamsport, PA by Carl Stotz. Baseball of Hackensack, which administered our Little League program, grew rapidly after World War II, in part because of the city's increased population, but also because of the spectacular performance of our hometown team in the 1952 Little League World Series. That year our squad of eleven-to twelve-year old-boys from Hackensack won a regional tournament in Englewood and qualified for the Little League World Series in late August in Williamsport. Although a nine from Monongahela, Pennsylvania trounced our boys 10-1 in the national semifinals, they bounced back to capture third place with a 2-0 shutout of a San Diego team.

A *Bergen Evening Record* editorial titled "The Little League's A Big Thing" highlighted the "phenomenal success of Little League baseball," crediting it with reviving interest in the sport among boys, and helping to justify "baseball's claim of being our national game." The *Record* then showered praise on the squad and their coaches. The City of Hackensack honored the fourteen players, batboy, and two coaches with a siren-screaming, fire-horn blaring, twenty-five-car motorcade, with the stars seated three abreast in the back seat of open convertibles. The festivities ended in the City Hall parking lot, with speeches and display of the team's third-place trophy. The City Council passed a resolution offering special congratulations to the coaches of the All-Star team and of all the Little League teams that competed during the regular season. The tournament's officials and the press singled out Rudy Davis for his outstanding performance. A black left-handed pitcher who won two games for the team (including the two-hit shutout of San Diego), Davis also smacked seven hits in nine at-bats. At a time when most of Hackensack's elementary schools were still racially segregated, the Little League all-star team included several black kids, with Davis among the stars.

Two years later the memory of those glory days was still fresh in Hackensack when I first tried out for the town's youth draft, catching fly balls and fielding grounders in a school gymnasium. The men who had volunteered to be Little League coaches evaluated my skills. After two seasons in the league's "farm system" of informal games I graduated at ten to the roster of the "Chamber Champs" of our town's National League. One of my teammates was George Sellarole (nicknamed "G.B."), a talented athlete from an Italian family prominent in the construction business and politics in Hackensack's south end. We would renew our friendship in high school, when he became a football, wrestling, and baseball star and one of the most popular boys in our class. My friends and I were excited about participating, and we loved the trappings that encouraged our fantasies of being big leaguers. We thought it was pretty cool to wear our team caps to Hillers or State Street schools to show off our athletic prowess to our classmates—especially the girls.

Each season of our Little League careers began with an "Opening Day" celebration scheduled on the final Sunday afternoon of April. Sponsored by the City Council and Baseball of Hackensack, the annual ritual of springtime gave the mayor, Council members, and other community dignitaries free press coverage and a prime opportunity to link their political careers to America's national pastime. The event was particularly charged with partisan politics during those years when a municipal election was scheduled for seats on the City Council. The festivities began with a parade of organized by teams that were sponsored by local businesses or community organizations—car dealerships, pharmacies, fuel companies, the Chamber of Commerce, among others. Proudly wearing our full uniforms, we boys gathered on River Street and marched into Riverside (later renamed Foschini) Park. We paid little if any attention to the political speeches as we washed down hot dogs and hamburgers with sodas. Boys from four teams then got down to the real business of the afternoon, playing the first two games of the year.

When I was eleven I played shortstop and outfield and was a good enough fielder that I generally didn't worry that the ball might be hit to me in a pressure situation—I could handle it. My batting improved with experience, and I was chosen as a substitute on the team that represented our league in the national tournament. I flied out to left field as a pinch hitter in our first and only game, which we lost by a lop-sided score. But over the winter a medical problem threatened my baseball prospects for the next season. I developed a severe case of Osgood-Schlatter disease, which sounds worse than it is. It is caused by a bone separation in the lower leg just below the knee, which requires rest until the growth process provides the proper healing. By spring, after much pleading from me my doctor told my parents and coach that I could play a few innings of each game that season. One of my greatest sports thrills came when I hit a pinch-hit line drive home run over the left field fence—the first round tripper of my career. (I would hit only one more.) How proud I was when I described my "Ruthian clout" to my dad. Once again I was selected to my league's tournament team. This time we won our first game, but then lost in the next round. Looking back, I am glad that I was never in a situation where an error might have cost my team a victory. I am sure that such a mistake would have haunted me for the rest of my life. My career in organized baseball ended in 1960, after a few years playing on the full-scale diamond in Babe Ruth League and one season as a centerfielder on the State Street Junior High ninth-grade team. The left fielder on that nine was Joe Mazza, a relative of Henry's and one of the toughest boys in our class. We got along pretty well, even though I think he was a little annoyed that the coach picked me to play centerfield.

Hackensack Little League, Chamber Champs, sponsored by the Chamber of Commerce, 1958. George in back row, second from left, was centerfielder, shortstop, and pitcher.

Barry Vasios began his Little League career a year before the rest of us, because he was born prior to the eligibility date of July 1. Although we had the advantage of being nearly a year older when we joined, Barry matured early and was gifted enough to excel when he was eleven. At twelve, as a catcher for the Optimist Bees of the National League, he knocked a ball over the outfield fence for a home run. I took another homer away from him when I reached over the center field wall to catch another of his long fly balls. In his final year of Little League he made the all-star team that competed in the early rounds of the national tournament. Barry did not mind the extra pressure of a program that was modeled after Major League Baseball; in fact, he thrived on the opportunity to play ball like a pro. His success as a Little Leaguer helped boost his confidence for later athletic achievements in baseball, basketball, and football in junior high and high school.

Richie, Henry, and Barry Cohen played on teams in the Oritani league—the newest of the three divisions of Hackensack's Little League. Richie was the best player of the three and close to Barry Vasios in talent. He earned a place on the starting nine of the Buzz Saws as a nine-year-old, but despite his ability, in his very first game as a left fielder he was so nervous he almost threw up. Later he switched to the more demanding and central position of catcher. In his last two years as a member of Nat's Pipers the coaches picked him for the all-star team that represented the Oritani League in the national tournament.

Henry and Barry Cohen were not blessed with a great deal of innate athletic talent, but both practiced hard to become respectable in our sandlot, street, backyard and Little League games. Henry patrolled second base or the outfield for the Oilers, and Barry Cohen played first base and right field for the Vitamins. Henry's big moment as a Little Leaguer was not a game-winning hit or spectacular catch; rather, it was colliding with an outfield fence in pursuit of a ball that cleared the wall for a home run. Henry's heroic albeit futile effort turned him into the momentary star of the game, as a crowd of concerned coaches and parents gathered around him while he regained consciousness. That episode would prove to be one out of many such sporting mishaps he would suffer in his athletic career.

Kevin was a good all-around athlete with solid baseball skills who had the misfortune of playing on perhaps the worst team in all three of the town's Little Leagues: the Ratner Rockets of the National League. His coach was a complete incompetent with little if any knowledge of baseball. That did not prevent him from applying several bizarre baseball innovations, including an alphabetical batting order. Before long Kevin's dad, Bill, began helping out with the coaching. As a young man he had been a ringer for a New York Athletic Club nine, and later he had played softball in a Bendix Aviation company league, so he knew the game. Because Kevin was one of only two players on the Rockets who could catch a batted ball, he had to play many positions, including catcher, despite being short. He was talented enough to make the all-star team and play in the Little League tournament during our last year. In our first round game (a victory) he replaced me in left field for the final few innings, and even cleanly fielded a single on one bounce, despite being so nervous that he could barely move his legs. He credits good luck (if not Divine Providence) that the ball was hit right to him.

Despite being small, Kevin often was the catcher for the Ratner Oldsmobile Rockets.

Some of our girl classmates joined in the fun by signing up for Junior Miss Baseball—which was then new in town. It was founded in Hackensack in the spring of 1958 as the first league of its kind in Bergen County. The concept began with a questionnaire circulated the previous fall by the town's Youth Guidance Council. The girls voted overwhelmingly for baseball--"a league of their own." Dr. Jack Goldin was President and Dr. William

Nawrocki of American Legion Post #55 was vice-president. The managers of the Junior Miss teams were all women, but some husbands assisted them, including George Vasios (Barry's uncle and father of his cousin Kristine), and Tom Meehan, the manager of my Chamber Champs squad and a coach of his daughter's team. Six teams, each composed of fifteen girls, competed in the league's inaugural season.

Junior Miss baseball reflected the traditional views about athletics for girls and young women that prevailed until the women's sports revolution of the 1970s. Character development through participation and amusement counted more than refinement of skills or championship competition. Modified rules stressed feminine behavior and prohibited physical and rough conduct that was deemed too masculine and thus inappropriate for females. Dr. Goldin told the *Record*: "The purpose of Junior Miss Baseball is not to develop athletes. We have started the program to give the girls of Hackensack a worthwhile athletic outlet and make them more wholesome women." He then contradicted himself by adding: "To be sure, no women are in the big leagues. But who is to say that some girl from Hackensack might not be the first." The girls played in full uniforms with caps and sneakers (not spikes) on the same fields as the boys. All fifteen girls had to play in a game for a win to count in the standings. The ball was the size of a regular baseball, but had a softball cover. Sliding and stealing bases were banned. According to Goldin, they were prohibited "to keep this type of baseball lady-like."

Despite these modifications, many girls in our classes welcomed the opportunity to participate in a sport that they knew we loved to play. Kristine Vasios was a natural athlete and a Junior Miss League standout, as was my next-door neighbor, Carol Ferrara. Ruth Heiferman was not in their class as a ballplayer, but she could catch and throw the ball and was a decent hitter. She played first base for a nine coached by her dad. He later quit because he was upset by the foul language used by some of the girls. Sylvia Lewis recalls the summer she spent playing right field for Toby's Autos, a team sponsored by a local car dealer. She claims that her team won the city's Junior Miss championship that year—thanks entirely to her teammates, she says.

In 1984, when my son Adam was three years old, we began the time-honored father-son ritual of playing catch in our backyard in Glen Ridge, New Jersey. Adam did not exhibit much excitement for the exercise, but he seemed happy to spend the time with me. I loved every minute of it and secretly hoped that he would turn into a good ballplayer, thus enabling me to relive glorious moments from my past. Five years later, when I enrolled him in the town's Tee-ball program, it was already clear that he would be one of those boys who would reach base more often via a walk than a hit. He liked playing on a winning team when he was ten, but the next two years became a nightmare for both of us, as his squads lost practically all of their games. Adam had average baseball skills at best, but he much preferred playing Nintendo, watching television, going on Boy Scout camping trips, and just hanging out with his friends.

My psychic investment in Adam's playing the game came to a head in the spring of 1993, when he was in sixth grade, the final year of youth baseball on the small diamond. He did not want to sign up one more time, but I pressured him, and he reluctantly agreed. But he was miserable throughout the season, especially when his team lost its first nine or ten games. A bout with severe springtime allergies provided him (and me) with the excuse to quit the team. Forcing him to play that final season turned out to be a major mistake in my life as a parent. But I think (at least I hope) that he has forgiven me. In 2003, the year he graduated from college, I dedicated my book on baseball during the Civil War to him. In the preface I wrote: "He did not inherit the Kirsch family baseball gene, but he did give me much greater gifts beyond the world of sports." It took him a few years, but he eventually read it on a train ride from Boston to Newark.

During my Little League days I was an ardent Yankee fan, as were Kevin and Barry Vasios. At Hillers I was passionate for the "pinstripes," devouring team histories and biographies that chronicled Yankee greatness. Among the old-timers my favorite baseball hero was Lou Gehrig. I have an eight-millimeter home movie of my brother Dan and me wearing Yankee jackets while playing stickball in our backyard. Henry and Richie remained loyal to the ill-fated Brooklyn Dodgers, perpetually doomed to "wait until next year" for their first World Series championship—which they finally won in 1955. Barry Cohen faithfully followed the New York Giants, who had shocked the baseball world by defeating the heavily favored Cleveland Indians in the 1954 World Series.

I watched every Yankee game I could on television. The Yanks won five World Series in a row between 1949 and 1953, so I was not devastated when they lost the pennant to the Cleveland Indians in 1954 or when the hated Dodgers finally beat them in the World Series in 1955. I was thrilled when the Yankees returned to their championship form in the 1956 World Series with Don Larsen's perfect pitching in game five and the Yankees' 9-0 victory over the Brooklyn Bums in game seven at Ebbets Field. My father took me to that contest, courtesy of complimentary tickets provided by my uncle, Pincus Rizack, who obtained them through his position as Deputy Chief Engineer of the Borough of Manhattan. (He worked with New York City Parks Commissioner and city planner Robert Moses, which was a big deal at the time.) My memories of that afternoon include a corned beef sandwich at a Brooklyn Jewish delicatessen, a brilliant clear blue sky October afternoon, and Dodger fans praying for rain after Yogi Berra hit two home runs over the right field wall, Elston Howard added a solo shot, and Moose Skowron smacked a grand slam into the lower left field stands to turn the game into a Yankee rout. My dad insisted that we leave after the eighth inning to beat the traffic, so I did not have the pleasure of witnessing the Yankees' celebration after the final out. I still have our program from that game, which included a scorecard that my father kept through eight innings.

My dad was a Giants fan as a kid growing up in the Bronx and Manhattan in the 1920s and '30s. He learned the game on the streets of the city, with little or no help from his alcoholic absentee father. So Dad made sure that his family history would not be repeated with his sons, playing catch with us in our backyard, and taking us to the Polo Grounds before his beloved Giants followed the Dodgers to the West Coast. They packed up and deserted New York for San Francisco in 1958. Although he did not root for the Yankees each July he signed Dan and me up for a charter bus trip to a night game at Yankee Stadium in the Bronx sponsored by the Hackensack YMHA. I can still smell the cigar smoke and hear the roar of the crowd when Mickey Mantle came to the plate. A few fans even greeted Mantle's at-bats with boos, apparently because they were disappointed that he did not hit a home run every time he stepped to the plate.

After the Yankee victory in the 1956 World Series my devotion to them began to wane, but to this day I am not sure why. By the time I entered junior high in 1957 I had begun to switch my allegiance to the Yankees' hated rival, the Boston Red Sox. I am certain that I am not the only Red Sox fan in the world who started out rooting for the Yankees. There must be hundreds, even thousands like me, bored with the Yankees winning virtually every year, searching for underdog teams to follow. Perhaps seeing the Broadway show *Damn Yankees* had touched something in my psyche, moving me to identify with Joe Hardy's hapless Washington Senators, who could only fantasize about defeating the mighty Bronx Bombers. I could understand why a ball player like Hardy would sell his soul to the Devil to acquire fame, fortune, and a pennant for a bunch of chronic losers and their fans. Not yet twelve, I was seeking new story lines and new heroes in our national pastime. I found a true one in an aging Ted Williams. Over the next few years—the last of his career—I read everything I could find written about him, which introduced me to the long and storied history of the Red Sox. For a few summers an uncle gave us tickets to a Sunday doubleheader of my choice, and one year I watched Williams belt a long drive deep into the lower right field stands in Yankee Stadium. When the "Splendid Splinter" retired at the end of the 1960 season (after hitting a home run in his final at bat), I did not have to wait very long for a new hero. The following April Carl Yastrzemski debuted in left field. Though the Red Sox teams of the early and mid-1960s trailed far behind the haughty Yankees, the latest pinstripe dynasty was finally coming to an end.

In State Street, sports ranked just below schoolwork and family and religious obligations among our priorities, now that we had dropped out of scouting. In eighth grade I played baseball on the regulation-size diamond in the town's Babe Ruth league, and I also joined the State Street track and field team as a miler, following my brother's path.

Although I more than held my own in pick-up touch football games at the Civic Center field, I did not try out for the junior or senior high school varsity football teams. I was too small, but more important, my mother disapproved of the sport and would never give me permission to participate. The message I internalized was that football was not an appropriate sport for Jews because it was too physical and violent. When I became a sport historian, I learned that a few Jews had excelled in football—especially in the "thinking position" of quarterback, with Benny Friedman and Sid Luckman as stars. I enjoyed HHS varsity football vicariously by rooting for friends and playing trumpet in the marching band. I continued to play touch football with my brother and friends.

Basketball was another story and a lot more promising for me. It was popular among Jewish immigrants during its formative years as a "city game," my father had played the game as a kid, and my mother had no objections. My dad put up a hoop on our garage, but Richie Prager's more spacious driveway became our preferred venue during countless sessions year-round. It became a running and embarrassing joke among my friends that whenever the phone rang at Richie's house they knew that it was my mom calling telling me that it was time to come home.

Dan and George in front of the Heath Place garage. The ladder was necessary to retrieve balls that got stuck behind the backboard. Note the 1955 Chrysler in the garage. February 1956.

All that playground practice paid off, for I made the eighth-grade team at State Street Junior High School as a guard. That winter I improved my game (especially my long-range set shot) on a YMHA squad that also included Richie, Barry Cohen, and Steve Wexler. In those contests the competition was not as strong as in the public school league, but I benefited from the extra playing time and enjoyed the experience of being one of the starting five. The following year I made the ninth-grade team at State Street. Oh, how proud I was to wear that maroon and gold uniform. I was less thrilled about the bus rides to away games and the trips to practice sessions at the Broadway School in the southern end of town (in those years State Street School lacked a modern gymnasium). I was one of only three white boys on a squad of twelve. Richie had also tried out for the team, but being at an awkward stage of growth he had gotten a little heavier and slower (hence his nickname, "Turtle"). Realizing that he was destined to warm the bench, he volunteered to help Coach Kay by charting field goals attempted by our players.

Our coach, James ("Jim") Kay, was a chain-smoking gym teacher, a strict disciplinarian, and a stickler for fundamentals. He was an intense perfectionist who hated to lose, and we dreaded hearing his tirades on the few occasions when we were defeated. Our stars—guard Kenny Dixon and center Eddie Hill (six foot five inches tall) were both black. Fifty years later Dixon remembered Coach Kay as a "good human being" who was "concerned about all of his ball players" and who showed no favoritism. Kenny recalled that one time when he acted like "a complete asshole" Kay "didn't like what he was seeing," and threatened "to get another black guy to kick my ass."

At State Street during the winter of 1959-60 the starting five included four blacks and Barry Vasios, who was a guard. (In private, Coach Kay once jokingly called him his "Great White Hope.") The locker room and shower sessions with my black teammates featured some eye-opening and embarrassing moments—especially when they talked about dating white girls, or when I peaked at their privates to see if it was true that black males were better endowed than we were. (It seemed that they were.) But before long I felt comfortable with them, and they accepted me for who I was—a smart, short Jewish kid with adequate ball-handling skills and a decent outside shot, but who was no threat to make the first team. We remained friends through high school, although we were never close enough for me to fully understand and appreciate how they viewed us and how they coped with the white world. In the locker room and showers they sang their favorite "doo-wop" tunes of the late 1950s, and they were probably amused when Barry and I adopted our own theme song—Bobby Darin's "Beyond the Sea."

That year I played in only a few games and scored just ten points over the entire season, which came to an exciting conclusion in the closing minutes of the Bergen County Junior High Invitational tournament championship game on Saturday, February 27, 1960. Our State Street team, with a season record of 17-3, was seeded sixth in a field of twenty-one schools. Our opponent, the Tigers of Tenafly Junior High School (all white boys from a more affluent suburb), were undefeated and top ranked. We trailed by a score of 24-19 at halftime. After the intermission we took a brief two-point lead until Tenafly's star, Bill Parmer, tied the game at 29-all after three periods. Our prospects looked bleaker after Dixon fouled out, but we took a four-point lead after Hill opened the final quarter with a field goal and two free throws. When another of our starters fouled out, Coach Kay looked down the bench at me and the other subs and asked: "Who is not nervous?" I remained silent. He passed on me and picked a younger boy, Theodore "Bubby" Whiting, who played quite well. To this day I wonder how I would have felt if I had been the one to secure the victory. Or perhaps I might have made critical mistakes that cost our team the game, which might have haunted me for the rest of my life. The outcome was thrilling, especially considering Barry's late heroics. He scored five points in the game (five of six free throws), including the decisive foul shots in the final seconds that maintained our lead and sealed our victory by a score of 39-36. Hill was voted the Most Valuable Player of the tournament. The superintendent of schools congratulated Coach Kay and the players at the next meeting of the Hackensack Board of Education.

I contributed nothing to the outcome, yet I felt I had earned my championship trophy—labeled "Bergen County Freshman Tourney Champs"—through my participation in all the practice sessions. It turned out to be the only sports championship honors I ever received and the high point of my basketball career, even though I made the sophomore squad the next year in high school. For Barry, the tournament final became his greatest game in a career that later featured several standout performances on defense for the State Street freshman and Hackensack High School varsity football squads. For Jim Kay, State Street's victory marked his second consecutive county freshman title. A few years later he became coach of the Hackensack High School varsity basketball team, a post he held with great success until he died of a heart attack while he was still a young man.

As we entered high school in the fall of 1960 participation in sports and other extracurricular activities, not straight A's, offered entrée to the in-crowd, and, we hoped, to the hearts of girls in class. HHS athletic squads were called the Comets, which had become our school's nickname (replacing the "Colts") after Halley's Comet passed by the Earth in 1910. Earning the coveted varsity "H" letter sweater was a dream that came true for a few of us during our sophomore year.

Kevin was the first to gain entrance into the elite inner circle of student-athletes with his startling success as a varsity wrestler. His small size as a boy had been a disadvantage in sports and had rendered him vulnerable to bullying by Barry Vasios and others in Boy Scouts. But a growth spurt in ninth grade changed all that. As a sophomore he had just about reached his adult height of five feet ten inches. He was now taller, and his low weight and slight frame, coupled with his increasing strength, natural agility, and intensely competitive nature, all combined to make him an ideal candidate for wrestling. Although he was a novice (in that era Hackensack had no junior wrestling program), Coach Paul Fulton spotted his potential in gym class and recruited him. Kevin learned the fundamentals quickly and progressed rapidly. In practice he dispatched his main rivals in the 105-pound weight class, Henry Cenicola and Randy Polinsky. Randy then went down in weight to 97 pounds, and Henry became a substitute. Henry sustained his usual number of injuries, but he persevered as a second-stringer. In his senior year Coach Fulton awarded him a Varsity Letter.

Kevin performed brilliantly as a sophomore, losing only one match during the regular season, although he did not advance very far in the New Jersey state tournament. On at least one occasion he totally intimidated his opponent—one boy begged his coach not to put him up against Kevin, who although skinny still towered over him. (Kevin pinned him in thirty-two seconds.) He even attracted the attention of one college coach (from Columbia). But though Kevin took great pride and pleasure in his outstanding athletic achievement, he was also beginning to realize that his wrestling career had severe physiological consequences. In order to wrestle at 105 pounds Kevin had to sharply curtail his food consumption. He and his teammates had to pass a weigh-in, held a few hours before each match. If they were above their weight limit they put on a rubber suit and took a hot shower to sweat off the extra poundage. If they passed, the coaches rewarded them with a chocolate bar for energy for their contest. (In that era they did not understand that consuming chocolate before a wrestling match was actually counterproductive, in that it often caused a drop in blood sugar at the most critical point in the contest.) Kevin never failed to make weight, but over the course of the winter he became increasingly gaunt, to the point that his mother worried about the effects of food deprivation on his long-term health. Kevin's strict diet totally dominated his existence; he recalls that during wrestling season he never dreamed about girls or anything else. He only dreamed about food.

During the summer after sophomore year Kevin and his teammates journeyed each day by bus to a wrestling camp in Roselle Park, where he learned a lot more about the theory and practice of the sport. Food was not a problem since there were no required weight limitations. The boys could eat normally, since the morning and afternoon sessions were so demanding that they sweated off enough calories to maintain their weight anyway. Kevin gained a few pounds that summer, much to the relief of his mother. But he became quite ill at the beginning of our junior year and lost weight as a result. At the urging of his wrestling coach he joined the junior varsity soccer team that fall in order to maintain his conditioning and build up his endurance. That winter he wrestled at 114 pounds and found that the competition at that class was much more intense. He still won most of his matches, but he was not as dominant as he had been the previous year. Once again, he did not get very far in the post-season state championship.

As a senior Kevin could not play soccer or wrestle, because of a broken arm he sustained during the summer of 1962 at Boys State at Rutgers University in New Brunswick. Although Boys State was primarily an academic honors program for outstanding students from New Jersey's high schools, it also included sports. Kevin excelled in the wrestling tournament, and advanced to the final rounds. In his last match he was leading his opponent when the boy fell on Kevin's left arm, breaking it in four places. He could not continue in the match and was taken to a local hospital. Despite Kevin's loud moans for pain killers, the doctors refused to give him any drugs until his parents signed consent papers. They finally relented and gave him some medication just fifteen minutes before his mother and father arrived. Surgeons then set his arm and placed it in a cast for twelve weeks.

In retrospect Kevin's two-year wrestling career took a heavy toll on his mind and body, but it also boosted his standing among our crowd and our classmates during our sophomore year. His celebrity status as an athlete caught the eye of his first girlfriend, "Diane." She lived in the Fairmount section of town, and thus had not attended State Street, so she was new to us. Diane was Jewish, cute, pretty, sexy, funny, and artsy. She was also one of the few students in our school who was hip to the art and music scene of Greenwich Village. She had a huge crush on Kevin and she was not shy about letting him know about it, or about showing her affection in public or especially in private. Kevin soon became infatuated with her, and they were voted "sweethearts" of the sophomore class.

Unfortunately, Diane's house was about three miles from Rowland Avenue, so Kevin made many late-night bike trips home. On one occasion his bike chain broke, and he had to run the rest of the way home to meet his father's curfew. When he struggled through the door he found his dad waiting. Sweating and tired, Kevin apologized profusely, though no doubt he was happy about his deepening romance with Diane. But alas, the flame of their infatuation flickered out sometime during their junior year, when they realized they had little in common. Diane was consumed by the worlds of art and fashion; Kevin at heart was much more conservative and even reclusive. He was also much more driven to excel in academics. She and Kevin had a few more dates later in high school and one in college. They stayed in touch for decades.

I warmed the bench for the sophomore basketball team (scoring a grand total of three free throws for the whole season), but I performed much better in two sports that I had just begun to play—soccer and golf. In a gym class in the fall of 1960, a coach noticed that I had some modest ability in soccer and encouraged me to try out for the junior varsity. Kevin and Richie also later joined the squad. The three of us had little prior experience other than kicking a soccer ball around in Richie's backyard. Playing high school soccer then was no big deal, because other than a few Latinos none of our classmates had any skills or training in the sport. (Less than a decade later youth soccer would become a suburban phenomenon.) The coaches taught a crude strategy of hustle, aggression, and brute force, since only a handful on the team had any ability to control, pass, or head the ball. I improved enough to get into a few varsity games as a junior. I practiced diligently during the summer of 1962, and in my senior year became the starting right wing. (Kevin would have been my chief rival for that position, but his broken arm put him on the disabled list.)

That fall our team won most of our games, thanks mainly to the expert coaching of Robert ("Bob") Seddon, a graduate of Springfield College. A few years later he left Hackensack High School to become the baseball and soccer coach at the University of Pennsylvania, where he enjoyed great success over the next three decades. With his tutelage and inspiration I became adept at centering the ball and scored a few goals and assists. Our squad lost our league's championship to our archrival, Teaneck High School, but we upset them in the first round of the New Jersey state tournament. They were clearly the better team, but our goalkeeper made many spectacular saves and we scored a lucky late goal to win, 2-1. Afterward my teammates taunted the Teaneck team as our buses pulled away from the field. I remained silent, because although I was happy that we won I was not comfortable with rubbing salt into the wounds of the defeated. I knew that it was only a matter of time before we shared their fate.

That defeat came a few days later, when we lost in the second round to East Orange by a score of 2-1. For me the sting of disappointment over our elimination was tempered by a personal highlight, for I scored our only goal. I was playing right wing, and as I swooped down in front of the goal our left wing launched a long crossing ball toward me. After its first bounce, I half-volleyed it with my right foot into the lower left corner of the goal, just as the goalkeeper leaned toward the opposite side. It was a very pretty play and got me a loud ovation from our fans and praise from my teammates and coaches. But it was not enough for us to advance in the state tournament.

We finished the season with a quite respectable record of twelve wins, four losses, and three ties. Although the 1962 Comets soccer squad did not win any league, county, or state titles, I was more proud of my accomplishments on that team than I was of my participation on the State Street squad that won the Bergen County freshman basketball championship a few years earlier. The difference was that this time I was a major contributor to the team's success. I was also very pleased when the sportswriters who covered scholastic sports for the *Bergen Evening Record* awarded me "honorable mention" recognition on their newspaper's all-Bergen County soccer team for fall 1962. I hoped that my high school soccer experience would give me an edge in applying to selective colleges.

Playing soccer as a starting wing in my senior year earned me a coveted varsity "H" letter sweater, but more importantly, it extended my circle of friends to include boys from a variety of ethnic backgrounds— English, Italian, German, Polish, and Slavic. Tony Toriello and Richie Cavalieri both made the *Record*'s All-County First Team, and Fred London also earned "honorable mention" notice. Other standout players were Randy Polinski, Joe Gurda, John Nefzger, and Tony Matkovich. Bobby Hall—a close friend—was one of our goalkeepers..

George on 1962 HHS varsity soccer team. 1963 yearbook photo, courtesy of Hackensack Board of Education.

My golfing life had begun in 1959 at the age of fourteen. On long summer days the guys and I would sometimes play thirty-six holes on easy Bergen County daily fee courses, stopping only for a quick sandwich and a soda at noontime. Television networks were just beginning to feature tournaments as well as taped "All-Star" matches, and we got caught up with the golf boom. President Eisenhower and Hollywood celebrities like Bing Crosby and Bob Hope were promoting the sport, and the relatively low cost of a starter's set of clubs and the accessibility of public courses in suburban Bergen County facilitated the growth of the game. But it was the exploits of the professional golfers, and especially Ben Hogan, Sam Snead, and most of all, the new hero, Arnold (Arnie) Palmer, that really excited America's sports fans. In 1960 Palmer attained the heights of golfing immortality with two spectacular triumphs in major championships—the Masters and the U.S. Open. I became a big fan of Palmer's after watching his come-from-behind heroics on television.

In the spring of my sophomore year Michael Weinstein, a neighbor and the senior captain of the high school golf team, persuaded me to try out for the fourth and final place on the varsity. He was a good golfer whose family belonged to a Jewish country club, and he was a huge fan of Sam Snead, copying his swing and even wearing "Slamming Sammy's" signature hat. Michael gave me several lessons and invited me to play a few rounds on his club's course. Several times we sneaked onto a few holes on the back nine of the private Hackensack Golf Club in Emerson. I worried that we would be caught and dragged into municipal court on charges of Jews trespassing on WASP property, but nobody ever bothered us.

Thanks to Michael the coach chose me for the last place on the team, but in truth there was precious little golf talent in Hackensack High School during those years. I was thrilled to make the golf team because that qualified me for a varsity "H" letter as a lowly sophomore. I was hoping that honor would boost my popularity and my chances with girls—wishful thinking, as it turned out. For some inexplicable reason the girls turned out to be much more attracted to hulks who played football—not five foot seven inch, 145-pound golfers. I managed to win a few matches that season, but after moving up to the third position over my final two seasons I lost or tied every contest. My memories of my high school competitive golf career are a blur of duffed shots, poor chips, and missed putts, punctuated by very few pars. At the athletic awards dinner at the end of my junior year I received the golf trophy for 1962, despite the fact that I was winless. Perhaps my coach wanted to reward me for being a good captain and a good loser, but the real reason was that the boys who played in the first and second spots were both sophomores. I had a lot more fun playing with my friends over summer vacation, when I improved my game and lowered my average score to the mid-90s. In college and graduate school I carded a few rounds in the upper eighties, but I never advanced much beyond the level of bogey golfer. Decades later when I took up tennis I realized that choosing golf over tennis in my teenage years was the biggest mistake I ever made in athletics. The running and reaction skills that enabled me to become a good soccer player made me far better suited for tennis than golf.

Richie participated in sports year-round. He played soccer all three years, earning a varsity letter as a senior. In the winter he was a substitute on the sophomore and junior varsity basketball teams. In the spring he abandoned baseball for tennis, which turned out to be a great decision in both the short run and for the rest of his life. His mother had arranged for him to take some tennis lessons during the summers of 1957 and 1958, and she also took him to the Orange Lawn Tennis Club to attend the annual Eastern Grass Courts tournament. That competition attracted some of the best players in the world, because it was then a tune-up event for the U. S. Amateur championship at Forest Hills. Through practice Richie became proficient enough to play varsity doubles with Stan Rothman as a sophomore, and thus join Kevin and myself as members of the Varsity "H" club. He and Stan had a winning record, but as a junior and senior Richie lost most of his singles matches. But he distinguished himself with a few impressive victories and more than held his own against several of the best tennis players in Bergen County, adding two more varsity letters along the way.

Kristine Vasios, Barry's cousin, was among the best female athletes, but she was frustrated by the lack of opportunity to participate in competitive sports. She often invited Barry and his friends to play baseball and touch football games on a field behind her house on American Legion Drive. She was the only girl included because she had the requisite athletic ability and knowledge. Her skills improved to keep pace with the boys.

Kristine felt constrained not only by the lack of serious competition in girls' sports, but also by the old-fashioned rules—especially in women's basketball, which confined each player to a small zone on half of the court. Her passion for athletics became a sensitive issue for her when some of her classmates called her a "tomboy," which then carried negative connotations. Today, characterizing an athletic girl as a tomboy is much less common because of the greater acceptance of girls' sports. Being so labeled was one of the reasons Kristine felt "out of the loop." Yet she was also comfortable with her identity, had many friends, and did not feel ostracized or stigmatized to any significant degree. Born ten years too soon to realize her full potential in sports, she was denied opportunities that are now available to girls.

George earned 3 HHS varsity letters in golf, 1961-63. 1963 HHS yearbook photo, courtesy of Hackensack Board of Education.

Richard earned his HHS varsity letter in soccer in 1962. His right knee is bandaged due to injury. 1963 HHS yearbook photo, courtesy of Hackensack Board of Education.

Varsity sports for girls did not exist during this period because the Hackensack Board of Education and athletic administrators subscribed to a sports philosophy dating from the late 1800s. The model rejected the male system that stressed star performers and competition for inter-scholastic and intercollegiate champ-ionships. Instead, physical education faculty favored regular gym classes and inclusive intramural programs that emphasized participation and fun for all players. Kevin's older sister Erin hated the mandatory bloomer-style gym suits because they were unflattering (especially for thin girls like her).. While there were no high school varsity sports for girls, there were highly competitive after school contests in field hockey, basketball, speedball (a game in which points are scored by throwing, kicking, or heading a ball into a goal), softball, badminton, bowling, volleyball, archery, and lacrosse. There were also a few field hockey and basketball games played against other high schools.

While today girls can achieve social prominence in school through athletics, cheerleading, or pep squads, back in the 1960s their opportunities were limited to the cheerleaders, who appeared at football and basketball games and selected soccer matches, or the "Ponies," who performed dance and flag routines at marching band competitions and football games. Erin Clermont wanted desperately to be either a cheerleader or a pony, but her short stature and the fact that she was thin, not Marilyn Monroe-proportioned, worked against her in the tryouts for both. She had a better chance of becoming a Pony because she had a good sense of rhythm and easily mastered the dance routine assigned to the candidates. But at her audition she had to impress Terence McGrath, the band director, and a panel of judges, whom she found to be demanding and intimidating. She fell victim to a bad case of stage fright and panicked during her performance. The outcome was much happier for Kristine Vasios, who was both a good dancer and a talented athlete. She survived the first major competition of her life and enjoyed being a Pony during her junior and senior years. Ruth Heiferman overcame her fear of performing in public and her inherent shyness to claim a coveted spot as a cheerleader at State Street and at HHS. She liked being a cheerleader because she enjoyed dancing and acrobatics and being involved (at least indirectly) in the boys' games. She got along with the other cheerleaders but none of them were among her closest friends.

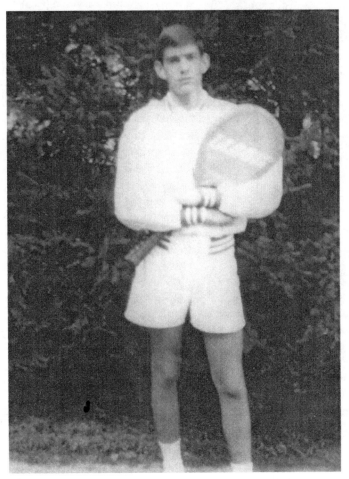

Richard earned 3 HHS varsity letters in tennis, 1961-63

A half-century ago the premier sport at Hackensack High School was football, as it is today. A boy who starred on the gridiron (or even warmed the bench) gained extra status among the student body, especially if he dated a cheerleader. Among our group of guys Barry Vasios was the only one who had the talent and the inclination to play football. He followed in the footsteps of his father by making the varsity as a sophomore, although only for the final game against traditional rival Teaneck on Thanksgiving Day. As a junior he became a first-string linebacker. Though he would never bask in the glory that a quarterback, running back, or wide receiver might achieve, as a defensive specialist he earned the respect of his teammates for his rugged play and also for scoring two touchdowns.

Playing football in Hackensack during the '60s meant performing under a head coach who carried legendary stature statewide. He was Thomas—or "Tom," or "Tommy"—Della Torre. In the 1930s he was a standout running back for Ridgefield Park High School. He then lettered in football for three years at William and Mary. A Merchant Marine officer during World War II, he left the service in 1946 as a Lieutenant Commander. He began his teaching career at Teaneck High School before World War II, but after the return of peace he accepted a position at Hackensack High School. Over the next decades he taught mathematics, coached football, helped to launch our town's Little League program, and served as athletic director of the city's Youth Guidance Council and as assistant principal and disciplinarian at the high school. Over twenty-two seasons as head football coach his teams won eight Group 4 sectional championships and ten Northern New Jersey Interscholastic League titles. For many years in the spring he also was head coach of track and field. During the final years of his career he became the HHS Athletic Director.

Della Torre was beloved by his players and many if not most of his students. Although he stood only about five feet eight, he was stocky and strong enough to strike fear into the hearts of athletes or any other student he caught misbehaving in the halls or on the streets outside of school. He was a patient and effective mathematics teacher who taught Algebra in the general curriculum. As a coach he believed in tough practices and strict discipline. He was also devoted to the single-wing offense well into the '60s, long after it had become obsolete. He combined a passion for football and an intense desire to win with a genuine concern for the well-being of his athletes and all the students—especially those who got into trouble without realizing the consequences of their actions.

When he died in November 1999 several of his star players (a few of whom also became successful coaches in Bergen County) remembered him with great respect that bordered on reverence. Some viewed him as a second father—especially those black players who were raised by single mothers or grandmothers. They called Della Torre "the great white father." On the eve of important games he would make the circuit of Hackensack's bars, looking for athletes who might be violating team rules by drinking or staying out late past curfew. He provided several of his boys the opportunity to become athletic stars, and he had enough clout with college recruiters to obtain scholarships for them. But he was also quick to punish those who did not obey his rules. He was notorious for warning male varsity athletes that we should never mix sports with girls. One of his best players, Tony Karcich, later head coach of the highly successful St. Joseph's school football program in Bergen County, recalled: "You never wanted to let him see you with a girl because he said they were poison to athletes. He would spot you and warn you to stay away until after high school." Della Torre's policy of discouraging relationships between athletes and girls even applied to honor students, including Barry, who was dating Ruth Heiferman.

Whereas Della Torre detested any romantic relationships that involved varsity athletes, he viewed interracial dating as strictly taboo. As a sophomore and junior Kenny Dixon was a talented black point guard on the basketball team and a stellar running back on the football squad. Della Torre favored Kenny by choosing him to be only the second sophomore (after the legendary Billy Harris) to be a first team running back. Kenny seemed well on his way to an athletic scholarship, until as a senior he began wooing an attractive white classmate. Kenny knew that Della Torre disapproved of his dating "Noreen," but it was up to the high school principal, Howard Bollerman Sr., to decide if any disciplinary action was warranted. Kenny believes that it was Bollerman and not Della Torre who ordered Kenny to terminate his relationship with Noreen, telling him that if he refused to do so he would not be permitted to play varsity sports. But Kenny was smitten with Noreen and chose to accept disqualification rather than capitulate to the principal's ultimatum. A half century later Dixon told me: "In my mind even being as young as I was, what did [my dating Noreen] have to do with me playing? We were not walking down the hallways holding hands and doing stupid stuff in the school, and we were not doing stupid stuff out of the school." He asked: "Where did he get the authority to play God and take away my opportunity to play sports for Hackensack High School?" A school official called Noreen's mother to persuade her to take action to get her daughter to break up with Kenny. Noreen's mother then told Kenny that his relationship with Noreen was "not right" and that he should stop seeing her. Kenny politely replied that he would stop dating Noreen only if he heard that message from Noreen herself in school.

Noreen rebelled against her mother's interference in her love life, and responded by asking Kenny to come over to her house. He initially refused, but then decided ("like a dummy" he said in retrospect) to take her up on her invitation, even though he knew that her mother couldn't stand him and that he didn't belong there. When her mom was away Kenny arrived at her house and sat down on the living room sofa to watch television with Noreen. A few minutes later her brother went to the kitchen, looked out of the window, and called out "mommy's back." Kenny recalls:

> I started sweating bullets and he says 'get into my closet.' I
> felt like I was in there for hours. Then he comes and says:
> 'It's OK, kid, she left again.' I said: 'where's my coat?' I
> mean, it was innocent, we were just sitting there watching
> TV. But I had no business being there. And that was it, I
> never went back there again.

Kenny continued to date Noreen, but it came with a price. Whenever they were together they were subject to racist abuse from bystanders. Interracial couples were still a new phenomenon in the North during the early 1960s. Kenny told me:

> I got more flack from outside than from a guy like you or a guy like Barry. I remember one time me and Noreen were walking down Main Street. Guys were standing out there and saying 'look at that nigger with that white girl.' So I just stood on the side of the street and I smiled at them, and that got them more than them calling me the N-word.

As news of Kenny and Noreen's interracial romance spread throughout the high school community, several classmates and parents openly expressed their disapproval. After a few weeks the pressure began to take its toll on Noreen. She began to lose some of her friends and feared that she was becoming a social outcast. She told Kenny that she could not see him any longer. He respected her decision and stayed away from her. But soon thereafter she reconsidered and asked one of Kenny's friends to arrange a meeting with him. When she explained that their dating had cost her several friends, Kenny replied: "Let me show you what friends are." He pointed to a few of his buddies (they happened to be in the school library) and told her: "I haven't lost a friend since you and I have been dating; those are friends." They resumed dating and remained a couple until our high school graduation, after which they went their separate ways. Kenny has not seen her since.

Kenny now realizes that his ongoing relationship with Noreen cost him his chance at an athletic collegiate scholarship. He still thinks about his confrontation with Bollerman: "I don't know if I was trying to show the powers that be that you can't tell me what to do." He acknowledges he made "a huge mistake," which he attributes in part to not having a parent to give him proper guidance. Kenny had a sympathetic, loving grandmother, but not a strong father figure who would have pushed him toward the right action. A male figure would say: "no, you go back up there and you demand to get back on that team." Kenny does not blame Della Torre for whatever role he may have had in Bollerman's disciplinary action. Kenny also concedes that Della Torre and Bollerman were consistent in their policy toward interracial dating, regardless of whether the varsity athlete was black or white. A white classmate who was not nearly as talented as Kenny was also banned from varsity sports because of his relationship with a black girl.

Years later Kenny repaired his relationship with Della Torre, whom he remembers with real affection as a coach who gave him the opportunity to become a high school star. He recalls: "Della Torre was doing what he thought was right; and he wasn't doing it to be malicious." But despite the ugly episode that ended Kenny's varsity career, all was not lost. His high school diploma and the lessons he learned on the hardwood and gridiron enabled him to have a successful career in business, even without a college degree.

Della Torre was also a larger-than-life character for non-athletes. During study halls in the auditorium crowds of students often disobeyed the rules and talked loudly, ignoring the teachers and student monitors. But when the rear doors opened and Della Torre came into view, there was total silence in the room within seconds. On Facebook a few girls remembered Della Torre busting them for smoking in the bathroom and for playing hooky to have breakfast at Charcoal Corners a few blocks from the high school. But he did have a softer side. Another former student recorded on Facebook: "He was an awesome man. He came across as such a tough guy, but he was a teddy bear at heart."

Della Torre could also be very helpful when a student needed special assistance in a crisis. One afternoon as Sylvia Lewis was walking home from school a man in a car stopped her and exposed himself. Sylvia was frightened and upset, and the next morning she went straight to Della Torre's office to file a report. She did so because she instinctively trusted him more that the Hackensack police. He immediately took down the details and notified the authorities, who soon arrested the perpetrator.

In our sophomore year the HHS football team had an uncharacteristically mediocre record of four wins, four losses, and one tie. Two of the defeats were outside of the Northern New Jersey Interscholastic League (NNJIL). The most memorable game was the final one—the traditional Thanksgiving Day clash with the archrival Teaneck Highwaymen.—for which Barry Vasios suited up with the varsity. In the third period, Bill Briggs, an end, recovered a fumbled Teaneck lateral and ran 56 yards for what turned out to be the deciding touchdown in a 12-6 victory.

The Comets would return to championship form the next year, when they posted a record of seven wins and no losses in the NNJIL. The two defeats were to non-league opponents, Garfield and Seton Hall Prep. That campaign featured a record-breaking rout of Englewood by a score of 44-0, and a season finale humiliation of Teaneck, 46-0. Barry recorded enough playing time as a linebacker to earn a varsity "H." The most thrilling moments for him were scoring his two touchdowns. One came during a 46-6 trouncing of Cliffside Park, when he intercepted a lateral and sprinted 46 yards for a touchdown; the other occurred during a 34-0 lopsided victory over Rutherford, when he intercepted a pass and ran 70 yards to score.

During Barry's senior year the Comets repeated as NNJIL champions, though this time sharing the honors with Paramus High School, which had just joined the league. The first two and the final games of that season were memorable, but for very different reasons. In the first contest, with Garfield leading 21-19 in the final quarter, one of their defenders recovered a fumble by a Hackensack halfback in mid air, and then galloped 74 yards in the wrong direction for what he thought would be a game-clinching touchdown. Instead, it became a two-point safety that knotted the score at 21 points each. With only a few seconds remaining and the Garfield

Barry Vasios earned HHS varsity letters in football in 1961-62. Although he played linebacker on defense, for this 1963 yearbook photo he posed as a running back. In my copy he wrote over his picture: "Swivel Hips Vasios, robbed of 1st team All-County." Courtesy of Hackensack Board of Education.

team on Hackensack's one-yard line, their quarterback faked a handoff up the middle and tried a bootleg run around Barry's end. Barry tackled him and the game ended in a tie. The following week, Jerry Falotico blocked a punt for the only score in a 6-0 victory over Paramus (their only loss of the year). The Comets escaped with closely fought victories over Fair Lawn (14-6), Ridgewood (6-0), and Cliffside Park (19-6), losing only a thriller to Englewood, (12-6). In the annual Turkey Day showdown with a Teaneck eleven that along with Paramus was still in contention for a share of the league championship, the Comets once again triumphed in dramatic fashion. With the Highwaymen ahead in the final quarter, 2-0, Tony Karcich intercepted a Teaneck pass on the two-yard line. Craig Jackson scored on a three-yard run late in the game to seal the victory and a tie with Paramus for that year's NNJIL football title. The Comets' final record was seven wins, one loss and one tie.

Each spring Barry also played third base on the baseball team—the junior varsity as a sophomore and the varsity for his final two years. The Comet nine did not have the glamour or the success of the football program, but nevertheless Barry persevered in the sport that he had enjoyed since Little League days. His two varsity letters in baseball raised his total to four.

While it is a stretch to attribute the outcome of the Battle of Waterloo to English schoolboy games at Eton, on a much smaller stage our sporting lives did help later in our respective careers as adults. The lessons we learned and our experiences as athletes proved valuable throughout our lives. Much more importantly, our sports participation bound us together then and later. Athletics helped us to escape from the problems and pressures we encountered in school and family. The competition put an edge on our relationships, but it also brought out our best efforts. Moreover, as sports fans, the excitement and story lines provided by the most popular spectator sports gave us unlimited topics for endless (and often mindless) bull sessions. We were not content to watch these games on television alone and isolated in our living rooms; we much preferred to go into the city to see a featured Madison Square Garden Holiday Festival or National Invitational Tournament basketball game. As we grew older, at our all too infrequent mini-reunions we tended to reminisce about our past heroics on the basketball and tennis courts, baseball diamonds, football gridirons, and golf courses, as well as the most memorable college and professional contests. Our sports addiction gave us more than just games to play among ourselves or topics for debate. Athletics bound us closer as friends.

Barry Vasios earned HHS varsity letters in baseball in 1961-62. According to his inscription in my copy of our yearbook he fancied himself a slick fielder like New York Yankees third baseman Clete Boyer. 1963 HHS yearbook photo, courtesy of Hackensack Board of Education.

8. The Blue and Gold: Class of '63

Around noon on April 15, 1963, instead of buying lunch at the Hackensack High School cafeteria, I drove home to await the postman who would deliver the news that would (I thought) seal my fate for the rest of my life. I watched him dawdle at the front door of the house across the street, making small talk with an elderly woman. Then, finally, he deposited two fat and three skinny envelopes into our mailbox.

In September 1960 my brother Dan entered Harvard College. He had scored a perfect 800 on the math section of the Scholastic Aptitude Test and had also won a National Merit Scholarship. Although he was not class valedictorian, he was an excellent student who was so confident in his prospects that he applied for admission to only two colleges—Harvard and Princeton. It was fortunate that Harvard accepted him, because Princeton did not. Sibling rivalry and Harvard's prestige motivated me to try to match his achievement. I became consumed with the idea, in fact. During one family visit to Cambridge I bought a Harvard jacket to prove it.

As Dan began his first semester in college, our father enrolled in New York University's law school. He had resumed his pursuit of a dream deferred after his graduation from City College because of the Depression and World War II, and then the demands of supporting a family. Forty-two years old and the owner of a expanding bridal and formal women's wear business, he was not satisfied with being a moderately successful merchant. He wanted a more prestigious position in life. He had somehow persuaded an NYU law dean that he could manage a part-time schedule, along with a few summer courses. In those days it was unusual for a middle-aged person to earn a law degree, but our father was remarkable and thrived on new challenges—like managing his growing retail business while earning a law degree at NYU.

With my brother in Cambridge I began my three years of high school as the only child remaining in our household. But that did not mean that I became the main focus of my parents' attention. Quite the contrary. My mom left the house early to commute to Julia Richmond High School in Manhattan and didn't return until at least 5:00p.m. Most weeknights my dad was at one of his stores or in class at NYU. So although I still slept at home and ate most of my dinners there, for most of the time I was on my own, juggling school, homework, sports, marching and concert band, and hanging out with my friends.

The guys wanted to gain admission to "good" (i.e. prestigious) colleges, so our first priority was academics. But we were also paying more attention to the opposite sex, with mixed results. Kevin, Barry Vasios, and Richard found girlfriends, and I had a few dates, but I was way too shy to approach female classmates whom I did not already know from Hebrew school or State Street Junior High. School dances were decidedly "uncool," so on weekends we went to a few parties where we played the hip music on our stereos. Chubby Checker taught us "the twist," and we slow danced to the sounds of Bobby Darin, Elvis, the Platters, Sam Cooke, the Drifters, and Ray Charles.

Sophomore year passed in a flash, and after Dan returned from Harvard in June he found a summer job in Manhattan. We all looked forward to a new adventure at the end of August. My parents had always dreamed about a family vacation in Europe, and they could now afford to take us along on a trip to England, France, and Switzerland. My dad had booked a discounted travel package. It included a regularly scheduled flight to London and a return trip with a charter company called President Airlines. But when we returned to Paris for our flight home we learned that President Airlines had suspended its service after one of its planes crashed in Ireland, killing all 109 people aboard. My dad borrowed enough money from one of his sisters to pay the airfare for my parents and me to return to New York on Air France. (Dan had already planned to spend a few more days in Europe before beginning his sophomore year at Harvard.) We were much relieved when our plane touched down safely in Queens. My friends welcomed me back. I had endured an anxious conclusion to a wonderful trip, just after my sixteenth birthday. I realized how fortunate we were that our family was not booked on the ill-fated President Airlines flight.

Back in school for my junior year, I felt more pressure to maintain high grades and prepare for the standardized tests that would be critical for my application to Harvard. In high school I was a more diligent student than my brother, but I could not match his performance on the SAT exams. My scores were respectable, but not high enough to guarantee admission to Harvard, Yale, or Princeton. I also had to consider the competition of the guys—especially Kevin, who set the bar very high with his brilliance and incredible work ethic. Not surprisingly, Kevin aced the SAT tests. Nearly a half century later he recalls that he still views his mastery of them as the "zenith" of his life, adding, "if life were a multiple-choice objective aptitude test, I would be emperor of the world—I was made for those tests." I dimly recall feeling a bit smug when my score on the Advanced Mathematics Achievement Test was slightly higher than his, but that only happened once. As far as the Ivy League went, I would also be up against Barry Vasios, Richard Prager, Steve Wexler, and a few others. I realized that this was not necessarily a zero sum game; we could all be accepted by our first-choice colleges (although that was highly unlikely) or we could all be rejected. I also believed then that our friendships were strong enough to survive any outcome. (I was right about that.)

Although Hackensack High School did not offer girls the same opportunities as boys in competitive sports, it did provide them with an equal chance to excel in academics—at least if they were enrolled in the College Prep curriculum. That academic track was closed to virtually all of the black and many of the Italian and Polish girls, most of whom took classes in the Commercial curriculum to prepare for secretarial or clerical jobs. (Most of the black and many of the Italian and Polish boys pursued a General track that included advanced instruction in such subjects as wood and metal shop and mechanical drawing.) Among the white girls, Ruth Heiferman, Sylvia Lewis, Susan Toscano, and Mary Anne Cunningham were high achievers in College Prep courses, but they were not as driven as we were to gain admission to the most selective colleges in the country. Ruth's romance with Barry Vasios that began in tenth grade may have boosted her academic performance through a very friendly rivalry (despite her disclaimer that she was never a competitive person), but she also credits the collective influence of us guys. Decades later she paid us all a great compliment when she told me: "You guys were way more important to me than I was to you. You provided a wonderful support system." She explained: "I think my attitude toward men in general was shaped by being around you guys, who were respectful, appreciative, and admiring; I had a very nice experience from the time I was in elementary school and up."

My parents did not push me very hard to aim for admission to an Ivy League or other prestigious college. They didn't have to, because I was self-motivated and had my brother as a role model. The other guys weighed differing factors in selecting their preferred list for college applications. Kevin's mother was highly attuned to matters of social class, in large part because she grew up in an orphanage and wanted a better life for her kids. She and Bill Clermont knew that a degree from an elite college was a passport to more opportunities and wider experiences. Barry Vasios became interested in Yale primarily because of its stellar reputation. He was also friends with Tommy Blanck, who had just enrolled there. Richie was primarily interested in premed programs, since he wanted to follow the example of his physician father. Henry and Barry Cohen were not as proactive in the process of college applications, although they were both leaning toward Rutgers, mostly because it was inexpensive and had an excellent academic reputation.

Although the teachers and curriculum at Hackensack High School provided us with a solid foundation for college, our secondary school preparation was clearly a cut below that offered at the nation's elite public and private schools. I benefited more from the courses in mathematics, English, and social studies than those in foreign language and science, while my friends' experiences differed according to their talents and interests. We continued to dislike the experimental Illinois "new math" curriculum, which in tenth grade covered geometry. Richard and Barry Cohen struggled with its formulas and theorems, while Kevin, Barry Vasios, Henry, Steve Wexler, and I had much success with the Illinois system. Fortunately, during our junior and senior years Art Collard applied more traditional methodology to expertly guide us through Advanced Algebra, Plane Geometry, and other topics in College Prep Math. My parents already liked Collard because when my brother Dan graduated from HHS he had written them a note in which he praised Dan's performance and cooperation in class. Collard helped us prepare for the math sections of the SAT and his instruction enabled me to excel in the introductory calculus course I took in college. Kevin enjoyed math more than his other subjects but later regretted that HHS did not offer calculus, since the introductory physics course he took during his first semester in college required a basic knowledge of calculus. Although he enrolled in calculus that term, it took a while for him to figure out how to apply it to physics.

Having a mother who was an English teacher gave me a big edge in that subject. As a sophomore I thoroughly enjoyed reading *Julius Caesar* and other classics with Maria Costa. She was spirited and enthusiastic and I sensed that she relished the challenge of teaching our section of honor students. In eleventh grade Don Otis introduced us to the masterpieces of American literature. He was a novice teacher when my brother Dan was one of his students, and he and his classmates liked Otis a lot. One time they had some fun with him after he alerted them that during the next session a supervisor would observe his teaching. The students then conspired that when the administrator came to class they would all remain silent for ten seconds after Otis asked his first question. The next day they made Otis sweat as they counted to ten before they all raised their hands, laughing as they responded with their literary insights. A few years later my friends and I appreciated his informal and friendly teaching style as we read works by American novelists and poets. His class was of great help to me in college and graduate school.

We all benefited from the high quality of our social studies teachers. Harold Bloom was a gifted story teller—especially about his experiences in the Army during World War II. His classes in World History and U.S. History were well organized and thorough. He taught Barry Cohen the value of outlines and note-taking, which served him well at college and later in his career as an educator. Bloom was promoted to chairman of the Social Studies department in 1963, assistant principal in 1966, and principal of HHS in 1970. Leonard Rosenberg introduced us to a working-class and common people's perspective on U.S. history before the revisionist view of "history from the bottom up" became fashionable (and controversial) in high school and college curriculums nationwide. While teaching full time at HHS he earned a doctorate in Political Science at the New School for Social Research in Manhattan. Somehow he found time to coach the varsity tennis team, with Richard as one of his premier players. Rich did not take any history courses with him, but remembers Rosenberg as a gentleman who was encouraging and reasonably proficient in the sport. Four years after we graduated Rosenberg finally finished his thesis—a 530 page study of the political thought of William Paterson, a Founding Father from New Jersey. Fittingly, Rosenberg then joined the faculty of William Paterson University, where he had a long career as a professor and chair of the Political Science department.

In foreign languages the French instructors applied the traditional methods of teaching grammar, vocabulary, and literature, but the Spanish faculty introduced an experimental approach that used audio learning rather than standard textbooks and writing and reading assignments. A few of us complained that the new curriculum did not adequately prepare us for the College Board Achievement Test in Spanish. Kevin liked his Spanish teachers, who were friendly and fun in class, but he had more difficulty with that subject than with any other, mainly because of the experimental audio learning approach. His understanding and performance improved dramatically when the curriculum started to incorporate written materials, because he could see the words spelled out. Henry excelled in his three years of Spanish and won the medal in that subject at an honors assembly in June. I never studied Latin with Edward Kulaga, but my friends viewed him as an eccentric but effective teacher. He recognized Kevin's talent and took him into New York City for a Latin contest in which Kevin performed quite well.

Barry Vasios, Kevin, and I all did well enough in the natural sciences, but Richard and Henry were more talented and more drawn to those subjects. Mary Whelan's biology course was demanding but she was very kind and genuinely concerned about our progress. Richard has little recollection of even taking high school physics, but he had no difficulty with biology and chemistry as he prepared to apply to medical school. Henry was an excellent student in all the sciences, but was particularly enthralled with chemistry. During our senior year our chemistry teacher, John Petix, recognized his natural aptitude in that subject and took a special interest in his progress. That course provided the foundation for Henry's professional success in science and business.

We also participated in extracurricular activities other than sports. Henry, Barry Cohen, Steve, and I joined the marching and concert bands. I played the trumpet, Henry and Barry were clarinetists, and Steve was a percussionist. In our sophomore year we benefited enormously from the talent and discipline of the music director, Owen Fleming. We played arrangements of classical pieces that were demanding but very satisfying to learn, including the *1812 Overture*, which we performed at band competitions, and the *Merry Wives of Windsor* and the final movement of Tchaikovsky's *Symphony in F Minor*, which we played in May at the spring Symphonic Band Concert.

I would only benefit from Fleming's expertise for one year. He precipitously departed for California in the summer of 1961 amidst rumors (but no proof) of scandal. Unfortunately, his replacement, Terrance McGrath, was simply not in his league. I soon learned how quickly a music program could decline when the director lacked the essential skills and leadership qualities. Although I was tempted to quit (as did a few of my friends) I decided to stick it out for my final two years. I probably thought that being in the band might make me seem more "well rounded" in the eyes of college admission officers, and that dropping out might hurt my chances at the most selective schools. In our senior year McGrath threw Barry Cohen out of the band after he chose to go to a dental appointment rather than band practice. Steve Wexler left the band to earn spending money in an after-school job. Henry lasted through the fall term of our junior year.

My seventeenth birthday was a big deal for me, because at that age New Jersey residents became eligible for a learner's permit for a driver's license. I passed a course in Drivers Education that summer, and my dad let me practice with the family's aging 1955 Chrysler. On August 28 I obtained the permit at the Motor Vehicles Center in Wayne and scheduled my road test for September 28. It rained that morning, and I worried about passing the parallel parking requirement, which had given me some difficulty in practice sessions with my father. My anxiety increased when I had trouble starting the car because of a faulty ignition. My dad accompanied me. I wore my Harvard jacket for good luck, hoping that it would impress the instructor. He gave me a break by permitting me a second try at parallel parking. I passed and now "had my wheels." I felt that I had advanced further into adulthood, as I was now much less dependent on my parents and older brother for transportation. We were all responsible kids, and none of the guys was a reckless driver. But it was an age before mandatory seat belts, and I shudder now when I consider the risks we took in the cars that Ralph Nader would soon condemn as "Unsafe At Any Speed."

In December I mailed applications to five colleges: Harvard, Princeton, Brown, Dartmouth, and Cornell. I was hopeful that my soccer performance would help me gain an edge at Harvard and especially at Brown, where my coach had some influence. In February I became obsessed with negative thoughts and worried about what I would do if all five institutions turned me down. I went to the guidance office and found a catalogue for Lake Forest College in suburban Chicago, which had a good reputation. I thought that if I received five rejection letters I would try to talk my way into Lake Forest over the summer.

Our senior class trip at the end of March provided a welcome distraction for me and the guys as we sweated out the final few weeks before we got the results of our college applications. At six in the morning of Friday, March 29, 1963, three busloads of sleepy Hackensack High School seniors began a 4-hour journey to Washington—the far-off land of Jackie and John F. Kennedy's New Frontier. On our bus a slumbering figure awoke shortly after departure—the "Worm" (Henry) had turned. He amused us with a nearly nonstop comic commentary as we headed down the New Jersey Turnpike. A Friday of shrines and museums in D.C. gave way to a wild motel night of music and room-hopping, followed by guerrilla raids with water balloons. Saturday witnessed a full day of touring the Capitol, the White House, some steps, the Wax Museum, the Lincoln Memorial, more steps, many more steps, and the motel again. For nourishment there were meals at Hot Shoppes. Saturday evening began on a wild note, but the

12:30a.m.curfew brought out the faculty chaperones—Elmer Kruper, Donald Otis, and Carol Falleni—better known as Elmer Ness and the Enforcers. On Sunday we stopped at Annapolis before heading home. On our bus Henry led us through the highlights of our trip, including changing the guard, a la Arlington. Over the final few miles he guided us through a hilarious comparison of the historic sites of our nation's capital and Hackensack.

So now it was April 15, 1963—COLLEGE DECISION DAY. The two fat envelopes the postman brought conveyed congratulatory letters and registration forms from Cornell and Dartmouth; the three skinny envelopes contained a rejection from Princeton and waiting list notifications from Harvard and Brown. I walked upstairs and collapsed on my bed. A wave of disappointment engulfed me as I contemplated my next moves.

I got up and drove back to high school with my mixed report and learned that Yale had admitted both Kevin and Barry Vasios, but only Kevin had gotten into Princeton. He had filed applications to eight institutions: six of the Ivies (all but Harvard and Columbia); the University of Virginia (because of its honors program); and Amherst. He dismissed Harvard because he thought of it as a decidedly "uncool" place for nerds. He was accepted by all of his choices except Amherst, which put him on its waiting list. He narrowed his choice to Princeton, Yale, and Brown. The Brown admission office ardently tried to recruit him by inviting him to a small exclusive dinner for accepted students in Manhattan, hosted by Thomas Watson of IBM. Over the next two weeks he visited the Princeton campus on a beautiful, sunny day, and toured Yale during a miserable rain and wind storm. He was captivated by Princeton's picturesque collegiate beauty and uninspired by New Haven and the Yale campus, except for its attractive courtyards. He chose Princeton primarily because of good weather on the day of his visit. His decision made his mother happy. She thought Princeton was more prestigious than Yale.

Barry Vasios applied to Princeton, Yale, Rutgers, the University of Virginia, and Washington and Lee. He was admitted to all of them except Princeton, which was disappointing because it was his first choice. Still, he was thrilled by his acceptance at Yale, though it offered him very little financial aid. He described his standing in a note to his friend and current Yalie Tommy Blanck as "Boola boola, no moola." But his mother came to the rescue and obtained a student loan for Barry from her boss at the Hackensack Mutual Savings and Loan—the bank where she had risen from teller to Treasurer over her three-decade career.

Richie, Barry Cohen, and Henry did not apply to the most selective schools in the nation. Although Richie had won a major community service award at State Street and had excelled in most subjects, his difficulties in his mathematics courses prevented him from graduating with a high class rank. That pretty much ruled him out as a candidate for the Ivies and other highly competitive universities. He wanted a college with a solid premed program and a school where he could continue his tennis career. A Bergen County tennis champion, Bill Taylor, recommended that he apply to Ohio Wesleyan University, because it had a strong premed program and a respectable tennis team. Richie had followed Taylor's advice and had been accepted there early in the fall, so the pressure had been off him for a while. Richie did make the waiting list at Colgate, but chose to go to Ohio Wesleyan.

Barry Cohen also struggled mightily with math courses, but he loved social studies and did very well in Harold Bloom's World History class and in the required two years of U.S. history. His brother Bobby was then finishing his senior year at Rutgers College in New Brunswick. Barry wanted to live away from home, so Rutgers became his first choice, because it offered him the best education at the lowest cost to his parents. He also applied to and was accepted by Penn State, Temple, Fairleigh Dickinson, and Bridgeport Universities.

The modest means of Henry's parents made it highly unlikely that he would attend an expensive private college, but that option had vanished in early 1962. One evening, after he and Kevin had gone to see the film version of Arthur's Miller's *A View From the Bridge,* he came home to find that his father had suffered a heart attack. Enrico had been working two jobs, including an evening shift at the post office, in order to build up a college fund for his son. That would no longer be possible. Two years of unemployment ensued, which required that Henry take care of his own college expenses. So his college application process and decision came down to a simple matter of family finances. At least for his first year, Henry would have to be a day student, which limited him to schools in New York City or northern New Jersey. Since he was interested in a career in pharmacy, he filed applications to the schools that specialized in that field at Columbia, St. Johns, Brooklyn College, and the Newark campus of Rutgers.

Henry and Steve Wexler also applied for five-year Naval Reserve Officer Training Corps Scholarships. That program paid all expenses for an undergraduate degree, but it required five years of service as a naval officer after graduation. Both were accepted. Henry decided he did not want to devote that much time to the U.S. military. Ultimately he chose to attend Rutgers University's campus in Newark, primarily because it had a first-class undergraduate pharmacy program. On the other hand, Steve accepted the scholarship, but even though he was admitted to both Cornell and the University of Wisconsin, he could only use his Naval ROTC funding at Wisconsin, because all of the places under that program at Cornell had already been claimed by other applicants.

Over the last two weeks of April I tried to gain admission to Harvard off of the waiting list by asking my brother (who was a member of the fencing team) to contact its soccer coach on my behalf. But Harvard's coach did not view me as a very promising prospect. As for Brown, its soccer coach was sympathetic but told me that if I really wanted to enroll there the best he could do for me would be to arrange an interview with the admissions committee, where I could try to talk my way in. In the meantime my parents took me to Ithaca to visit Cornell. It was early spring and the campus was spectacular. Plus Cornell was coeducational and Dartmouth had no women, which became the deciding factor. So I would go to Cornell, which, I was soon to learn, was populated with hundreds of freshmen who didn't get into Harvard, Yale, or Princeton, but were determined to gain acceptance four years later into the law, medical, or graduate schools of those or comparable elite institutions.

My friends and I coasted through the final months of HHS, reaping academic awards in June and waiting for the new challenges of college in the fall. Kevin graduated first in our class (out of 396 students) and won the Women's Club Civic Award, the Mathematics Association of America Medal, the Hackensack Good Government League Award in Mathematics and Science, and the American Legion Scholarship and Citizenship Award. I ranked fourth overall, second only to Kevin among the boys. .Barry Vasios graduated seventh and captured the Knights of Columbus Junior Citizenship Award, Steve Wexler was eighth and won the General Supermarkets Citizenship Award, and Henry was thirteenth. All of us earned membership in the National Honor Society.

Among the girls Ruth was sixth in our class and a popular cheerleader. Despite all of her accomplishments, she was modest, self-effacing, and shy. Because of these qualities for many years I mistakenly thought she had low self-esteem, but she later explained to me that she knew she was just as smart if not smarter than all of us, except Kevin. She was just not as competitive or ambitious as we were. She did not think of herself as being either superior or inferior to her classmates, nor did she think she had accomplished anything very special. Rather, she was grateful that she had been born with some talent, and she had tried to make the best of her ability. All of her hard work paid off, for she received a scholarship to attend Douglass College, a highly selective school at the New Brunswick campus of Rutgers University. Ruth was admitted to Mount Holyoke (though turned down by Pembroke) but chose Douglass because she and her father agreed that the marginal academic benefit of attending the more prestigious Mount Holyoke was not worth the substantial additional cost. Her decision was not solely based on the financial factor. She also detested snobs and viewed Mount Holyoke as an elitist institution. Thus she felt more comfortable attending Douglass College because it was more egalitarian.

Sylvia Lewis graduated third in our class and also won the Hackensack Alumni Scholarship, the Helen Clarke Mathematics Award, and the American Legion Scholarship and Citizenship Award. Her older brother was a graduate of Cornell, and she was accepted off of Cornell's waiting list about one week after I was admitted. The Hackensack Alumni Scholarship provided her additional support to the substantial financial aid package Cornell offered her. My friends and I were very pleased to see Sylvia honored, especially since she had experienced far more family hardship than any of us. Another brother had died in childhood of disease, and her father had suffered a fatal heart attack when she was in elementary school.. Remarkably, she managed to sustain an energetic and upbeat spirit—a true zest for life—despite this misfortune.

National Merit Scholarship Finalists: Ruth Heiferman, George, and Kevin, receiving congratulations from HHS principal Howard Bollerman Sr.

Although the Hackensack public school system did not award any prizes specifically designated for minority students, three black classmates received partial college scholarships at the annual Mary McLeod Bethune Scholarship Fund dinner, held at the First Congregational Church in early June. The featured speaker was Dorothy Height, president of the National Council of Negro Women. The recipients and the institutions where they planned to enroll were Willie Belle Davis (Paterson State), Josephine Pegeese (Montclair State), and David Macdonald (Hampton Institute, Virginia). Macdonald also excelled in athletics, garnering Coach's Awards in Cross Country and track that evening at the annual Varsity-H program at the High School. Another speaker, Rabbi Martin Freedman, a civil rights activist from Paterson, told the honorees and guests that "new vistas are opening for the Negro college student because knowledge is power and...civil rights jobs in the South are now being opened to Negroes." He reminded the gathering that "a unique challenge faces the entire American community, to stand on the values of old phrases of freedom and equality which are now being revitalized." In addition to Davis, Pegeese, and Macdonald, a few other black graduates from the class of 1963 went on to attend college that fall. Two of them, Eddie Hill (St. John's) and Gilbert Finney (Texas Southern), had been premier players on the State Street Junior High School basketball squad that won the Bergen County Freshman Tournament back in 1960.

Voted "Most Studious," Sylvia and George. We would remain studious as classmates at Cornell. 1963 HHS yearbook photo, courtesy of Hackensack Board of Education.

On graduation day, Thursday June 20, 1963, I played my trumpet for the final time. The HHS marching band inaugurated the proceedings at the Athletic Field with the "Processional March," as a looming severe thunderstorm watch threatened to wash out the rest of the program. It turned out to be the shortest Hackensack High School Commencement to date in its 67-year history. After the invocation by the Rev. J. Benton Rhoades, Dolores De Donato completed her speech on "The Life that Awaits the Graduates." John Anderson, my classmate since State Street, then began his address on "The Role of Individualism as Reflected in the Graduates." The civil rights movement was in full swing, and the faculty's choice of John as a commencement speaker signified a long overdue recognition of the contribution of black students to our school. But shortly after John began his remarks a downpour disrupted the proceedings. The principal, Howard Bollerman Sr., halted John's talk and ended the ceremony. The audience of 3,000 parents, relatives, and friends dashed for their cars, and the graduates ran to the school gymnasium to collect our diplomas. As it turned out, the storm quickly passed through town. The commencement exercises could have resumed outdoors. But instead we skipped the rest of the program except for the benediction delivered in the gymnasium by Rabbi Kleinman of the Hackensack Hebrew Institute. In keeping with the spirit of the times, he asked that the graduates "look upon the knowledge they have gained, not merely as a tool for personal gain, but also as a means to serve their fellow man." We then dispersed to our celebrations. John Anderson never completed his speech, and sadly, a few years later he died in a traffic accident.

MOST LIKELY TO SUCCEED
Ruth Heiferman—Kevin Clermont

H H S

FAVORITES

WITTIEST
Henry Cenicola—Ann Yervanian

1963 HHS yearbook photo, courtesy of Hackensack Board of Education.

On the day of our graduation the guys shared good memories and positive feelings about our time at Hackensack High School. We were blessed with good friends, and we had enough success in sports to feel good enough about athletic performance. We got along well with the girls, and a few of us even felt the pangs of puppy love. Although some of our peers viewed us as "nerds" or "grinds," we were respected and well treated by most of them. In Kevin's view we were never as popular as some of the more affluent kids from the Fairmount section or Emerson, who had the money to purchase great clothes or cars, or the more charismatic Italians from the south end of town. On the other hand, Rich was oblivious to the social class structure of HHS, perhaps because he was quite content with his life of studying, playing sports, and dating an attractive girl from Rochelle Park who was one year younger than us. Our friendships with the black athletic stars gave us some status among their friends and shielded us from the bullying that a few of them inflicted on several of our classmates. In Kevin's words, "We brilliantly navigated the blackboard jungle aspect of high school." The same could also be said about our experiences previously at State Street, which more closely resembled the *Blackboard* model.

Whenever I think about our senior year romances and especially our sexual initiations (or lack thereof), the highlight will always be Henry's fling with a spirited and sexy Italian-American junior. I have no idea whether he was the first of us to lose his virginity. Because of my shyness (or respect for their privacy), I never asked Kevin about Diane or Barry Vasios about Ruth or Richie about his girlfriend. We had a theme song for Henry that spring— the Chiffons' "He's So Fine."

I passed the summer of 1963 working at my part-time job selling lamps in Stern's at Bergen Mall and spending some of my free time with my first real girlfriend, Peggy Yervanian, the younger sister of Ann Yervanian. (Ann was a talented classmate and one of the stars of our senior class production of "Bye Bye Birdie.") My weekly take-home pay after deductions was under thirty dollars—not enough to make a dent in my Cornell tuition but sufficient to cover dates with Peggy at the movies and at the Jersey shore, plus a few rounds of golf. My flirtation with Peggy was young and innocent and did not last very long into my freshman year in college, but it was sweet nonetheless.

At the end of August Barry Vasios, Richie, and I invited three girls (including Barry's sweetheart Ruth but not Peggy) to join us for a week--at separate boarding houses--at Point Pleasant at the Jersey Shore. On my eighteenth birthday, August 28, 1963, we drove to Asbury Park, where they treated me to dinner and a surprise birthday cake. We ended the evening by seeing *Lawrence of Arabia* at one of those huge movie palaces that screened premier films. On that same day a historic event transpired in Washington. Martin Luther King Jr. delivered his "I Have A Dream" speech at the Lincoln Memorial, which would become the most famous address in the history of the civil rights movement. At the time I was much less concerned about the long term historical significance of that date, because turning eighteen meant that I had acquired the right to vote and consume alcohol in New York (but not in New Jersey). I also became eligible for military service and was required to register for the Selective Service system, a.k.a. the Draft.

Barry Vasios, Kevin, and I were the last to leave for college. In those days, Yale, Princeton, and Cornell had freshmen orientation in mid-September. On our final night together before we went our separate ways we drove around Hackensack, speculating on what the future might hold. We were wistful in recalling some of the good times we had enjoyed together since we first met at Hillers School. Fired up and confident that we were prepared for the new challenges that lay ahead, we were eager to get started. We had new worlds to conquer.

9. Halls of Ivy, Rutgers, and Ohio Wesleyan

As Kevin, Barry, and I passed the waning days of summer in Hackensack before heading to Princeton, New Haven, and Ithaca, Barry Cohen, Henry, and Richard began their college lives in New Brunswick, Newark, and Delaware, Ohio. By mid-September we had all scattered to our destinations. Except for Henry, we were now free from daily contact with our parents. None of us had spent more than a few weeks away from our families. We now had to learn how to fend for ourselves, living away from the security and comfort of our homes.

Barry Cohen's parents drove him to the Rutgers New Brunswick campus and helped him move into his room in Mettler Hall, a dormitory that was then only one year old. In the 1960s, Rutgers College was well respected as an academically intense institution that attracted highly motivated students and offered a first-class education at a state-supported discount price. Among Barry's classmates were several who had been admitted to Ivy League schools, but who chose Rutgers because it was such a good bargain.

In fact, Rutgers might very well have become an Ivy League college, if its nineteenth-century administrators had been more skilled managers and fundraisers. Founded in 1766 by the Dutch Reformed Church and originally chartered as Queen's College (to honor King George III's Queen consort, Charlotte of Mecklenburg-Strelitz), it is the eighth oldest college in the United States and one of only two colonial colleges that later became public universities (the other is William and Mary). Financial difficulties forced it to close its doors for two extended periods during the late 1700s and early 1800s. Queen's College reopened in 1825 and was renamed Rutgers College in honor of Revolutionary War hero Colonel Henry Rutgers, who expressed his appreciation by giving the college a $200 ornamental bell and a $5,000 bond. In 1864 Rutgers became New Jersey's land-grant college under the terms of the Morrill Act of 1862. In 1945 and 1956 the New Jersey legislature consolidated several of its schools and programs and designated the new entity as "Rutgers--the State University of New Jersey."

Barry started out as a Liberal Arts student, taking introductory-level courses in the humanities, social sciences, and physical sciences. Problems with his first roommate during his first few weeks motivated him to find another one, who later flunked out. He kept in touch with friends from Hackensack High School who were attending Rutgers, and made a few new ones, including his future roommate Bob Bloom. In his education classes he got to know Jim Valvano, a basketball star for the Scarlet Knights who later achieved fame and fortune as coach of the North Carolina State University basketball team, which won the national championship tournament in 1983. Like Princeton, Rutgers College was still all-male, although Douglass College (an elite state-supported women's school) was close by. But the Douglass coeds took most of their classes on their own grounds, with infrequent visits to the Rutgers campus. Barry went to a few social mixers, but since he was quite shy he did not have much success with the Douglass ladies, especially since many of them still clung to boyfriends from their hometowns or were more interested in upperclassmen.

Whereas the rest of our parents dropped us off on our first day at college and wished us good luck as a rite of passage, Henry simply took the local 102 bus to the Newark campus of Rutgers. It was not that his parents loved him less or did not think that starting college was a big deal. Rather, his use of public transportation reflected his different family and financial circumstances. Neither his mother nor his father owned a car. Henry's parents were immensely proud of his achievements, but they were not able to provide the same degree of guidance and financial support that the rest of the guys got from our mothers and fathers.

Henry was a beneficiary of the decision of the Rutgers Board of Trustees to strengthen public higher education in an urban environment by expanding the university into Newark after World War II. In 1946 the Trustees approved a merger with the University of Newark. The newly reorganized Newark Colleges of Rutgers University included a College of Arts and Sciences, a School of Business Administration, a Law School, and the College of Pharmacy, in which Henry enrolled. Each held equal status with the other colleges of Rutgers, but the classrooms, laboratories, and other facilities used by students on the Newark Rutgers campus were generally in rehabilitated residential and office buildings and factories, and were inferior to those available to their counterparts in New Brunswick. During Henry's undergraduate career the state of New Jersey built a large modern campus for Newark Rutgers between Washington and High Streets, adjoining the New Jersey Institute of Technology and forming the University Heights district of the city. But most of the new classrooms and laboratories were finished after Henry's graduation. His use of the new facilities was mostly limited to his many hours of study in the Law School library.

Ninety percent of Henry's classmates at Newark Rutgers were commuters. The vast majority were Jewish; most of the others Italian. Newark's Jewish population had been plummeting since the end of World War II, but those who remained viewed Newark Rutgers as an inexpensive first-rate option for an undergraduate degree and a gateway to graduate, law, or medical schools.

Henry soon tired of his daily commute by bus to Newark, so he bought a used Volkswagen to get to his classes and his jobs at the Fairmount Drug store in Hackensack on weeknights and his aunt's glove factory in Hillsdale, New Jersey on weekends. When he was not at home helping his parents, in class, in the library, or at work, he stole a few hours for recreation and joined a fraternity—Tau Delta Phi. Henry's Italian Roman Catholic heritage posed no problem for its predominantly Jewish membership. But first he had to endure the hazing rituals of the brothers. They were mostly silly tasks like wearing a burlap shirt, running errands for brothers, or doing pushups on demand. On Hell Weekend there was no physical or alcohol abuse, but there was much sleep deprivation and attempts to goad pledges into fighting each other. Henry formed close friendships with Steve Ulin and Joel Baum, enjoyed the frat parties, and played on several of its intramural and intra fraternity athletic teams. During his freshman year, when he still lived at home, and throughout the next three years when he rented an apartment in Newark, Tau Delta Phi provided Henry with an active social life and a welcome refuge from the burdens of his financial, academic, and family responsibilities.

At Newark Rutgers Henry also gained a new nickname, "Hank." As we got older we only occasionally called him "Worm," but he took on a new name when he entered an intramural wrestling tournament. The college's varsity wrestling coach, Robert Mizerek, the supervisor of that event, suggested that Henry adopt a tougher name to help him advance in the competition. He recommended "Hank." While that nickname does not appear likely to strike terror into the heart of an opponent, it did wonders for Henry. Despite his less than stellar record on the HHS varsity wresting team, in the intramural Newark Rutgers tournament he won the 119 pound championship as a freshman and the 126 pound title as a sophomore. Henry ran with his new nickname, his classmates and fraternity brothers began calling him "Hank," and it became his preferred name for his remaining years in college and throughout his long career in the pharmaceutical industry. His Hackensack buddies and I always found it a little odd when others call him "Hank," but his new nickname served him well in his professional life as a scientist and businessman.

Richard's journey to college was the longest from Hackensack, as he and his parents drove 586 miles west to Ohio Wesleyan in Delaware, Ohio. Founded in 1841 by two members of the town's Williams Street Methodist Church, it was one of the first colleges named for the founder of the Methodist movement, John Wesley. In the 1960s it had a liberal arts orientation and a coeducational enrollment of less than 2,000 students. Richard chose Ohio Wesleyan because of its small size, the reputation of its premed program, and his good prospects for making the varsity tennis team.

During the fall semester Richard took mostly science courses. His recreational and social life consisted of occasional tennis practice sessions with Bill Taylor, a sophomore and a former Bergen County singles tennis champion. Richard's friendship with Taylor earned him the status of honor (or first) pledge among the freshmen selected for membership in Sigma Phi Epsilon fraternity, with Taylor as his big brother. His fall tennis practice sessions with Taylor also helped him hone his skills for the competition for the varsity, which would begin its spring season with tryouts in February.

At Newark/Rutgers Henry lived two lives. By day he was a serious student who was elected Parliamentarian of the Economics Club (top: front row, second from left). On weekends he was the fun-loving "Hank" of Tau Delta Phi fraternity and Vice-President of the Inter Fraternity Council (bottom: center wearing toga). Photos from 1967 yearbook, *Encore.* Courtesy of Rutgers University, Newark, NJ.

My parents and I drove from Hackensack to Ithaca and stayed overnight in a motel in Collegetown, just across Cascadilla Creek gorge on the southern edge of the Cornell campus. The next morning I moved into my freshman dormitory room, 109 Founders Hall, bid my folks a fond farewell until Thanksgiving, and greeted my roommate "Rodney," from Tenafly. We had met at a mathematics competition earlier that spring, and once we learned that we were both going to Cornell we requested a double room to share. Within a few hours I also met several other floor mates with whom I bonded right away: Jim Cohen and David Hamburger (both of Elkins Park, PA), and Tim Wright (son of a Cornell professor in the Agriculture College).

In April of 1963 *Time* magazine described Cornell as "the happy hybrid of U.S. higher education...an Ivy League school with a Big Ten flavor. . . Part of it is private and impeccably elite; part of it is public and happily egalitarian." Its new president, James A. Perkins, formerly vice-president of the philanthropic Carnegie Corporation, was taking over the reins of a school that noted Cornell political scientist Clinton Rossiter called "the most unmanageable, undirectable university in the country." Founded by Ezra Cornell in 1865 as New York State's land-grant institution, with the assistance of Yale's Andrew Dickson White, within a few decades it had become a world-class institution of four private and four public colleges. In founding an institution "where any person can find instruction in any study," Ezra Cornell advanced the democratization of American higher education by authorizing the admission of women and applicants from all races, classes, and creeds.

In my freshman year Cornell had 11,823 students (one-third female), and I was one of the 2,892 undergraduates enrolled in the College of Arts and Sciences. That year it cost my parents $1700 in tuition and $366 for my room, plus around $1,500 for meals and personal expenses. The privately endowed Arts College was the most selective and most prestigious, followed closely by the colleges of Engineering, Architecture, and Hotel Administration. Arts students viewed the Hotel School as a trade institution for business types who took gut courses in wine tasting and fine cuisine. We respected Engineering and Architecture students because of their intense workload, and we recognized the high quality of the state-supported Industrial and Labor Relations college but we looked down on those admitted to the less selective Home Economics and Agriculture colleges. (We had no interaction with students in the graduate level Veterinary College.)

As I began my four years at Cornell I was not worried about flunking out (which was a rare outcome in all of the Ivy League schools); but I still wanted to excel academically. I signed up for courses in Calculus, the first half of the History of Western Civilization, English Composition, American Government, and French Literature. My Hackensack High School courses in Mathematics, English, and History had prepared me well for those subjects, but I was on shakier ground in French and American Government. I had senior professors in French (David Grossvogel), History (Eugene Rice), and

Government (Andrew Hacker). Grossvogel was intimidating but fair; Rice was a remote figure, standing on a platform in a large auditorium as he lectured about ancient, medieval, and early modern history. Hacker had a critical and sarcastic air about him and a habit of talking for only about 30-40 minutes out of the scheduled 50-minute period. He was a misplaced New Yorker who later left the wilds of Ithaca for a position at Queen's College in the City University of New York. My History and Government classes met twice a week for lectures and once a week for a discussion session led by a graduate student. My first "prelim" (hour exam) was in my best subject, Calculus. I survived a five-minute panic attack just before it began and then aced it with a grade of 100. My first tests in French, History, and Government did not go as well, but my English instructor liked my papers.

As I diligently read and completed class reading and writing assignments, I chased my athletic dream of making the freshman soccer team. During Orientation I practiced by myself and with a few other prospects, and played well enough in tryouts to be selected for the squad. The star of our team, Seth Dei, was a native of Ghana. His father held a powerful (but somewhat precarious) position in his country, and Seth's family had sent him to the States for his secondary and college education. During the five-week season I started most of the games at right or left wing, scored a few goals, and recorded a few assists. My sports highlight of that fall came in our opening game on October 11, when I scored the winning goal with twelve minutes remaining in a 4-3 victory over Cortland. The next day the *Ithaca Journal* reported my heroics. I proudly sent its account of the game to my parents with a note: "Enclosed is my first collegiate press clipping. You can't imagine how happy I was when the ball went into the goal." Our squad had a very successful season, winning seven out of eight games. The only blemish was a tough 1-0 loss to Ithaca College. I wrote my parents: "It was "Hackensack-Teaneck style, with us the losers." That fall Cornell's varsity soccer team's record was an underwhelming 0-8-1. Its new coach, Jerry Lace, saw that help was on the way and was optimistic for Cornell's soccer program for 1964 and beyond.

I was still writing to my high school girlfriend Peggy, but I also eyed the co-eds sitting next to me in class. My prospects for a date with any one of them seemed remote at best since there were far more men than women at Cornell (especially in the Arts College) and the freshman women were more interested in upperclassmen. An article in the *Cornell Daily Sun*'s Orientation Week issue quoted a counselor's advice: "Better get these girls now, boys, next week will be too late." Although I quickly made a few female friends among my classmates, I did not date any of them until my junior year. One of them eventually became my steady girlfriend during the spring term of my senior year.

Peggy came up for Fall Weekend in early November. We had a good time at a Saturday night Four Preps concert that also featured the standup comedy of a young Woody Allen. The *Sun*'s critic was lukewarm about the

Four Preps' performance, but was decidedly more appreciative of Allen's self-deprecating Jewish humor. Allen quipped that he had sold the rights to his romantic life to Parker Brothers, so they could make a game of it. The weekend was fun but soon afterwards Peggy and I stopped dating. She was a senior at HHS and immersed in its social life; I was trying to adjust to my new world at Cornell. I don't recall any dramatic quarrel or incident that terminated our relationship. We simply agreed to part ways.

Kevin and his parents drove one hour south from their home on Rowland Avenue to Princeton during a heavy rainstorm. The miserable weather contrasted sharply with the sunshine that flooded the campus during their previous visit, when the elements and the picturesque setting had persuaded Kevin to choose Princeton over Yale. After the Clermonts struggled across muddy lawns to unload his clothing and supplies, they discovered that Kevin had been assigned to a single room on the top floor of a dormitory with three other students. The showers and toilets were located in the basement.

Bill Clermont, unhappy about Kevin's room assignment, loudly complained about it to Princeton's housing officers, insisting that Kevin be reassigned to a better room. He was convinced that Kevin was given such poor housing because he was a lowly public school student (from Hackensack, no less), and that the prep school boys would never have been subjected to that kind of treatment. The fact that at least one of the other three was from a private school did not deter Bill. As a result Kevin's name was put on a waiting list for a room change, which came through about a month later.

Kevin's new quarters was a two room suite with only one roommate, a Hungarian refugee. The son of a minister, he was unable to adjust to college life and was extremely antisocial. He seldom left the room and passed the time drawing pictures of naked women that he copied from *Playboy* magazine. He never went to class, and he refused to talk to anyone—especially Kevin. (Once he went fifty-five consecutive hours without uttering a word.) He soon grew resentful that Kevin was doing normal things like attending classes and studying, so he would turn off Kevin's alarm clock in the middle of the night, apparently hoping that Kevin would sleep through his first class. Kevin then became wary about spending time in his room, so he stayed in the library as long as possible each night. To compound the problem, the new room was on the fifth floor of the oldest dormitory on the Princeton campus, a medieval structure named Witherspoon Hall. Once again, the bathrooms were in the basement, and here you had to step over steam pipes to access them. (Some students urinated off the roof or out a window in the middle of the night to avoid walking down and especially back up the stairs.) Kevin later learned that his new room assignment had become available only because the previous occupant had moved out, presumably because he could not tolerate his suitemate.

That fall Kevin was also struggling with an introductory physics course. He had signed up for it without realizing that it required a basic calculus class, which he was taking simultaneously. Our mathematics courses at Hackensack High School had adequately prepared us for college calculus and Kevin excelled in that subject. But it took nearly the entire semester before his Princeton calculus class provided the concepts and formulas he needed to understand and solve the physics problems. Crazy as it seems now, given Kevin's initial problems with physics, his tense relations with his disturbed roommate, and conflicts with his English instructor in a composition class on Shakespeare, he feared he might flunk out of Princeton. He was so miserable that beginning in November his mother picked him up each Friday afternoon and drove him back to college on Sunday evening, so that he could spend the weekend at home. And get his laundry done.

Kevin's career at Princeton coincided with a critical period of change in the institution's long and distinguished history. Founded in 1746 as the College of New Jersey by a dissident sect of "New Light" Scottish Presbyterians, the Princeton name was adopted informally after the Civil War and then officially in 1896. Although not the southernmost of the Ivy League schools (Penn holds that distinction), Princeton was commonly known as the most northern of the southern colleges in the United States. Among the elite northeastern private universities, it was the one most preferred by aristocratic young gentlemen of the South. During the Civil War a significant portion of the student body sympathized with the Confederacy, and some dropped out to fight (and die) for the Lost Cause.

When Kevin arrived on campus Princeton remained a bastion of white southern male upper class Christian privilege. It had no women, a tiny number of black undergraduates, and a social class system based upon a hierarchy of eating clubs that humiliated those with little or no family status or wealth. During the early 1900s an increasing presence of Jewish students at Princeton generated resentment among the WASP majority. As a result its admissions office limited Jewish enrolment to about 3 percent—roughly the Jewish segment of the nation's population. It was also virtually impossible for Jews to gain admission into the eating clubs. Prospects for Jewish applicants brightened after World War II, and by 1960 they constituted 15 percent of the student body.

Strict rules governed student conduct. Undergraduates were not permitted to operate or maintain a car within an eight-mile circle centered on the university. They could not marry, unless they obtained the permission of the Dean. Freshmen were also required to attend Princeton's non-denominational (but Christian) chapel services half of the Sundays in each term. Jewish students could meet the mandatory chapel requirement by going to their own services rather than the Sunday liturgy held on campus.

The most significant and costly question that President Robert Goheen pondered during the mid-1960s was whether Princeton should admit women. In 1965 a *Daily Princetonian* editorial lamented "the profound unhealthiness of the Princeton undergraduate's social life with women," which it described as a week of studying, followed by "superficial, orgiastic weekends." The result was "abstention, frustration, and unhappiness." Given the scarcity of women on campus and Kevin's proclivity for spending most of his waking hours either in class or in the library, his dating life was minimal. During his freshman year it consisted of one evening with his former high school girlfriend Diane, and a few more with a Douglass College friend of Ruth Heiferman's. The lack of undergraduate women on campus, the inconvenience and expense of boarding dates for five or ten dollars in off-campus rooming houses over the weekends, and the virtual absence of female tenured professors all combined to create a sexist environment at Princeton. A prime manifestation of the Princetonian view of women was the tradition of "spooning" whenever a student brought a date into a dining hall. Undergraduates would rate the physical attributes of the guest by banging their silverware on the tables, with the loudest reception reserved for the most attractive women. The *Daily Princetonian* lobbied for coeducation as "the solution for Princeton's social illness," but Goheen remained opposed to the idea, stating publicly that "Princeton has no problems that coeducation would cure." Goheen did permit an early trial with a small group of coeds on the Princeton campus that began in the fall of 1963. Five young women from a Cold War-inspired Cooperative Undergraduate Program for Critical Languages lived on campus and took courses in foreign languages and world cultures.

As for racial integration, the number of African American students admitted to Princeton each year during the 1950s could literally be counted on the fingers of one hand. Most of the few black undergraduates were foreign students from Africa. But with the pressure applied by the civil rights movement in the South and anti-discrimination legislation approved by the New Jersey legislature and signed by the governor, Princeton was forced to reexamine its policies on racial matters. In October 1963 a visit to Princeton by an avowed segregationist, Governor Ross Barnet of Mississippi, sparked widespread protests from Princeton students and town residents. In response Goheen pledged to work toward achieving "equal and open opportunities" for all. He and the new director of admissions, E. Alden Dunham, started a new recruitment program to bring more black students to Old Nassau. That nationwide campaign increased the total number of black undergraduates from seven in 1962 to 41 in 1966 and 318 in 1970. But the university's new initiative to admit more black students was not welcomed by all. Students from the south still hung Confederate flags on dormitory walls—though classmates thought that they did so more to display southern pride than to oppose integration at Princeton.

Barry Vasios's mother and uncle drove him to New Haven—his father missed the grand occasion due to illness. Barry moved into a three-room suite in Wright Hall (two bedrooms and a living room) with two roommates, both of whom were graduates of private prep schools. After his mother and uncle helped him unpack Barry immediately reported for his work/study job, which required that he serve food and clear tables at the Berkeley College dining hall. He needed the $500 he earned at that employment, because Yale had not awarded him either a scholarship or a loan to pay for tuition, fees, and room and board.

At the time Barry entered Yale the administration was reviewing a Freshman Year Report prepared by an advisory committee (appointed by President A. Whitney Griswold) that evaluated admissions and financial aid policies. The committee members pointed out that several promising students who were offered only a job or a loan chose not to enroll at Yale because their families could not afford the expense. They specifically criticized the prevailing system of mandatory bursary work, concluding that it "brings hardship to some students, especially those who are promising but at the outset less well prepared, in that it prevents them from making the most of their educational experience at Yale." They recommended that freshmen (like Barry) who needed financial aid should be offered a scholarship, a loan, or both, with no other demands. Taking on a job for extra money would then be purely voluntary. Yale adopted the new system the next year. The Freshman Year Report also recommended that Yale place more emphasis on intellectual distinction in admissions decisions.

As Barry began his freshman year he was self-conscious about his public school background, modest socioeconomic status, and self identification as a Greek-American. He found that at Yale, even more so than in multi-ethnic Hackensack, newcomers were often categorized by their last name. That often led to ethnic stereotyping which in Barry's case frequently resulted in questions that he found to be disrespectful or insulting. The nature of his job naturally heightened his sensitivity toward social class divisions at Yale, especially during dinners on special weekends, when he wore his white uniform jacket and waited on his more affluent, well-dressed classmates and their dates. His crew cut from his Hackensack High School days was also a social class marker, since most of the other Yalies had longer hair styles and looked like John F. Kennedy. Barry took his job seriously, however, and volunteered for overtime to earn extra cash. He used the additional pay to buy his class ring. He was rewarded with a glowing recommendation from the manager of the Berkeley College dining hall, which, when combined with Yale's newly implemented more liberal financial aid policy, helped him gain a scholarship, loan, and a better job as a sophomore.

Though social class distinctions were certainly evident at Yale in the mid-1960s, new admissions policies and a system of residential colleges promoted a more egalitarian ethos—even though Yale still remained all male and enrolled very few black students.. Barry's class was the first at Yale in which graduates of public schools outnumbered those from prep schools—

though only by a slight margin. The shift toward more financial aid for students from working-class families came too late to benefit Barry when he was a freshman, but it helped him considerably over the next three years.

Yale's residential colleges also fostered a more democratic atmosphere. During the mid-1920s both Harvard and Yale adopted the model of Oxford and Cambridge in England, housing undergraduates in residential quadrangles, thanks to the generosity of Edward S. Harkness, a graduate of Yale's class of 1897. Initially, incoming students were permitted to indicate a personal preference for a residential college, which tended to foster social class, athletic, and other distinctions among them. In 1954 Yale began to randomly assign freshmen to a college. The goal was to encourage the mixing of students from public and private high schools and of different ethnic, religious, and socioeconomic backgrounds. All freshmen dined in a common hall, but each lived in a dormitory that was affiliated with a particular college. Barry was assigned to Pierson College, where he resided during his sophomore, junior, and senior years.

Barry's academic career at Yale got off to a good start with an advanced placement course in English poetry that began with Chaucer, a survey of world history, a physics class designed for liberal arts majors that did not require calculus or a lab; elementary sociology, and Spanish (his weakest subject). He was anxious at first that he did not know anything and that he might flunk out. But by the spring term he realized that his Hackensack High School preparation and his work ethic gave him certain advantages over the prep school students, many of whom were enrolled in courses at Yale that they had previously taken and thus could slack off. Over time he got the impression that Yalies from public schools were somewhat smarter and more focused on academics than their preppie counterparts, many of whom cared more about partying.

Barry studied long hours, but he also took time off on the weekends to enjoy the social life available to Yale freshmen, especially on the fall football weekends. He was still dating Ruth, so he invited her up to New Haven for the game, dinner, and a dance afterward. Ruth loved going to Yale to visit Barry. She liked the residential college system and appreciated that she was always treated well by Barry's friends. She viewed him as an outgoing, social person who enjoyed being at Yale, and who overcame whatever feelings of ethnic or social class alienation he may have initially harbored as an outsider.

At midday on Friday, November 22, 1963 shots rang out in Dallas, Texas that sent shock waves throughout college campuses. I learned of the assassination of John F. Kennedy early that afternoon. I was in my dorm room at Cornell, preparing to walk up Libe Slope to attend the weekly discussion section of my Government course. The class still met, but we quickly abandoned our reading assignment for a collective grief session punctuated with speculation about what the death of the young president might mean for the U.S. and the world. After class I walked around in a daze for a few minutes, trying to decide if I should continue with my plan to go to a barber shop in Collegetown that afternoon for my first haircut in nearly three months. I had arrived in Ithaca with my standard fifties classic crew cut, but after a few weeks of college I felt that longer hair was more suitable for the new me. So I let my hair grow out, but it needed to be trimmed before I returned home for Thanksgiving the following week. Given what had just transpired in Dallas, going for a haircut seemed like such a trivial, inappropriate, and even downright disrespectful thing to do. I thought about going back down Libe slope to return to my room to deal with Kennedy's death with my friends. Instead, I went to the barber shop for my haircut.

On that day Kevin was sitting in the office of Princeton's French Department in East Pyne Hall, on some administrative mission. He recalls: "I heard someone say that the President had been shot. I was so wrapped up in my university transition that I thought the reference was to the president of Princeton University. For the life of me I could not imagine why someone would shoot the university president." Before long he discovered the truth and headed home.

Henry's immediate reaction to the news mirrored Kevin's. He was on his way to a freshman composition class, wondering whether he should pledge a fraternity, when a classmate told him that the president had been shot. At first Henry thought that Rutgers' president, Mason Gross, had been the target. In the writing class the instructor led the students in a discussion of what might happen if the president was incapacitated but still alive. Henry was so devastated by the assassination that on Saturday he and a few of his Newark Rutgers friends drove four hours to Washington and waited all night on a long line with an estimated 250,000 other mourners to view Kennedy's coffin in the Rotunda of the Capitol building. On Sunday morning Henry and his friends paused for about thirty seconds before the remains of the slain president. They drove back home that evening.

Richard and Barry Cohen both had exams scheduled that day. At Ohio Wesleyan Rich heard the news just prior to a chemistry test that was proctored by a substitute for the course's instructor. The examination was not postponed because no administrator had the authority to do so, although several students were distraught and weeping. Richard took the test. When Ohio Wesleyan (and virtually all colleges in the U.S.) cancelled classes on the following Monday, the day of Kennedy's funeral, Rich decided to go home earlier than he had planned.

Barry Cohen learned the news as he filed out of an exam at Rutgers. Shocked and upset, he left a group of students who were milling around in a state of confusion and went to his brother's apartment. (Bob Cohen was a graduate student that year.) He woke him up, turned on a radio, and heard that the president had died. They decided to go to Hackensack for the weekend to cope with the tragedy with their parents..

Barry Vasios had just left the Berkeley College dining hall after his lunch time food service shift when he heard a radio blaring the news through an open dormitory window. He went into a kind of shock. He felt a chill, put on a jacket, and went to the Yale chapel. The Harvard-Yale football game scheduled for the following day was canceled. Barry was upset later that evening when he heard loud noise coming from a drunken group of Yalies who were partying as if nothing had happened. He viewed the Kennedy assassination as a national tragedy and thought that all of his classmates should show proper respect.

Like my Hackensack buddies, I felt the urge to go home, but I also did not wish to miss my classes on Tuesday and Wednesday mornings. I decided to abandon my perfect record of class attendance and began my Thanksgiving break four days earlier than I had planned. On Saturday evening I packed a suitcase, walked downtown to the Ithaca bus station, and waited for a bus that would take me to the Port Authority Bus Terminal in New York City. The bus broke down en route, and I did not arrive home until around eight on Sunday morning. I had not alerted my parents about my early arrival, so they were surprised but glad to see me. I was relieved to crash in my old bed. Over the next few days I watched the television reports of Jack Ruby's shooting of Lee Harvey Oswald, Kennedy's funeral, and the first days of the administration of Lyndon B. Johnson. I reconnected with my Hackensack friends. We shared stories of our first months of college. The day after Thanksgiving we played touch football at the Civic Center field, just like old times.

After Kennedy's assassination we all returned to our respective campuses, bracing for winter and our first crack at final exams. We looked forward to the spring semester, when we would narrow down our choices for our majors. All of us except Richard were satisfied with our choice of college. When Richard returned to Ohio Wesleyan after Thanksgiving break he began to feel increasingly isolated in the Midwest and had second thoughts about attending such a small college. In February he had a long talk with his parents about transferring. He took a fair amount of grief from his fraternity brothers when he told them that he was considering leaving Ohio Wesleyan— especially since they had picked him as honor pledge. So for the time being Rich put up with the hazing of what the brothers called "Help Week." He did everything he was supposed to do, since he would not know the outcome of his applications to transfer until the end of the academic year. In the meantime he ingratiated himself with his fraternity brothers and did whatever chores they required of him, since that was the way he viewed his entire life—a series of academic, social, and personal tasks to complete.

Richard's spirits rose greatly in the spring, as the weather improved and he performed quite well in the classroom and on the tennis court. He takes pride in his undefeated record of two wins and no losses in NCAA varsity tennis competition.(He is certain that one victory was in singles; he believes that the other one was in doubles). His coach did not include him as the number five or six singles player in their match against mighty Ohio State University that spring, so Rich did not contribute to the upset victory by the "Battling Bishops" of tiny Ohio Wesleyan over the Buckeyes of Ohio State. By the end of the year Richard earned his freshman numerals, but he did not compete in enough matches to win a varsity letter.

During the spring Richard traveled to Colgate in upstate New York and the University of Pennsylvania in Philadelphia for campus visits. He applied to those schools plus Columbia. A conversation with the Colgate tennis coach convinced him that he was good enough to make the varsity team there. In June he went to Philadelphia for an interview at Penn, which accepted him a few weeks later. Once Rich learned of his admission to Pennsylvania he stopped visiting other colleges, but as the summer began he had some final doubts about his decision to leave Ohio Wesleyan. He loved his life there in the spring. The weather turned nicer, he was playing tennis every day, and he was feeling more comfortable with his fraternity life. He was generally more confident and happy, which made it harder for him to leave Ohio Wesleyan.

That summer Richard returned to Hackensack Hospital for his second stint of service there. During the summer of 1963 he had worked as a janitor and washed walls, among other menial tasks. In 1964 Richard was one of six operating room technicians hired by Hackensack Hospital for that summer. He claims that he landed this job on his own, and that his physician father pulled no strings for him.. He trained as a scrub operating room technician, learning how to handle and pass surgical instruments to the surgeons during hernia, gall bladder, and a few chest operations.

When I returned to Cornell in early December to complete the fall semester I felt the full force of my first Ithaca winter. There were three inches of snow on the ground and the hills were treacherous. Two weeks later the temperature plunged to 4 degrees. With the excitement and fun of frosh soccer over, and with the icy blasts of wind and snow sweeping across the campus, I braced myself for the second round of hour exams. For the first time in my life I struggled with alternating bouts of depression and anxiety. Heart palpitations about a week before Christmas break sent me up the hill to the university health clinic. A nurse assured me that stress caused my symptoms, telling me that they were common among freshmen and not life-threatening. I took some comfort in her diagnosis, but the problem would not go away anytime soon. Cornell's academic calendar in that era did not help. After a two-week holiday break we had to endure three more weeks of classes before the grueling ten-day final examination period. For the first and only time of my life I started marking off the days on my calendar; hoping that the torture would soon end. All of my hours in the library paid off, because I did pretty well, earning respectable grades and just missing making the Dean's list.

With my first term behind me and feeling more confident about academics, for the spring term of 1964 I registered for the second halves of the courses I took in the first term, substituting Comparative Government for American Government. In February I flirted briefly with the fraternity rush, but instead for our sophomore year David Hamburger, Jim Cohen, and I found an off-campus apartment on Stewart Avenue, right on the edge of Fall Creek gorge. As the semester began my roommate, Rodney, started sleeping twelve hours a day, missing most of his classes. After a poor performance in his courses that spring he took a leave of absence from Cornell and did not return during our college years. My social life that semester was pretty minimal, highlighted only by watching February cable television broadcasts in Founders Hall lounge of the Beatles performance on the Ed Sullivan Show and Cassius Clay's victory over Sonny Liston for the heavyweight championship of the world.

At the end of my first year at Cornell I made the Dean's List and the Freshman honor society, Phi Eta Sigma. When I returned home just after Memorial Day I could finally relax. In June my parents and I drove to Cambridge to attend Dan's graduation from Harvard and to help him pack for his move home. As Dan and I drove back to Hackensack he shared his sense of relief and surprise that he had managed to earn his bachelor's degree in Mathematics without attending most of his classes and without doing much of the assigned work. Clearly, he and I had the exact opposite approach to college. But Dan had an uncanny ability to cram for exams and still receive respectable grades. He spent most of his time at Harvard practicing his fencing skills, which ultimately gained him All-American honors in that varsity sport during his senior year. His talent in taking standardized tests also paid off when he aced the Law School Aptitude Test. He applied to New York University Law School, and his interview there went so well that he was accepted and awarded a Root-Tilden Scholarship, despite his mediocre academic record. Dan spent the summer working in New York City and courting his new girlfriend, Laura Sue Siner, a freshman at Boston University whom he had met at a fencing meet. I helped my dad in his bridal store in Bergen Mall, hung out with my friends, and played golf once a week.

Kevin's fortunes at Princeton improved dramatically after Thanksgiving. In late January his mastery of calculus enabled him to ace both the math and physics final examinations, and he also earned high grades in history (Western Civilization) and French. His only low mark in his entire Princeton academic career was in his English writing class—the equivalent of a B-minus. He made the Dean's List, as he did every subsequent semester. His dorm situation also resolved itself when his Hungarian roommate flunked out—a rarity in any Ivy League school, but a more probable outcome when a student never attended class or completed any assignments for his courses. Kevin was assigned a new roommate, Wade "Chip" Boggs, a wealthy upper-class southerner from North Carolina who played on the tennis team and later joined one of the more exclusive eating clubs. Although socially Chip was far removed from our Hackensack crowd, he and Kevin became good friends. Kevin also strengthened his friendships with future roommates Paul Schmidt and John Lavieri.

By the spring of 1964 Kevin fully recovered from the trials of his first few months and was devoting all of his energy to his course work. The result was spectacular success in the academic arena, but a social life that left much to be desired. That imbalance in his life would remain a problem for the rest of his college years at Princeton.

For Kevin the summer of 1964 brought a one-month return to misery, when Freddy London, a Hackensack High School classmate, got him a job in a medical supply company in Lodi. To qualify for employment there Kevin had to join the Teamsters union. His co-workers were mostly Hispanics. It was brutally hot in the factory, there was no air conditioning, and his work assignment was to bend thousands of pieces of copper tubing at four places so that they would fit inside sterilizing equipment. Kevin's technique was to make all four bends in each tube before proceeding to the next one. His foreman chided him, "Hey, smart college boy, can't you think of a better way to do this job?" He told Kevin he could accomplish a lot more if he made the first bends on all of the tubes, then the second bends, then the third bends, and then the final bends. That method was indeed more productive, but it turned an already tedious task into one that was incredibly more boring. Kevin lasted only three weeks in the Lodi job, but fortunately his mother was able to get him a position in the mail room at the Ford Motor Company, where she worked. It was like a country club compared to the Lodi plant, says Kevin.

Barry Vasios felt more at ease at Yale during the spring term of 1964 and gained confidence in his academic work—earning A's in all of his courses except Spanish. He also strengthened his friendships with his closest friends, including Tim Weigel and Gene Siskel. Weigel was raised in the suburbs of Chicago and was a graduate of Lake Forest High School, the captain of Yale's freshman football team, and later a star running back for the Yale Bulldogs varsity. A history major, after graduation he became a television sports anchorman and reporter in Chicago. Siskel came to Yale from a boarding school (Culver Academy in Indiana) and majored in philosophy. He later became well known nationally as a movie critic and co-host with Roger Ebert of their popular weekly television show.

Barry tried out for the Yale freshman baseball team in late winter inside the indoor Cox batting cage. After two or three weeks of practice he, Henry Jones (a black freshman from Arkansas who later became a federal judge), and several others were cut. It was a blow to his ego, because of his high school achievements, especially on the diamond. He later learned that most of the Yale freshman baseball players had already been recruited from high school, and the coaches did not need or want many substitutes. So Barry had to settle for competing for Pierson College in Yale's intramural sports leagues. He played on Pierson's baseball nine all four years, serving as captain as a senior. He also participated for a few seasons on Pierson's touch football team and its basketball "B" squad.

Yale remained a college for men only during the sixties, and as at Princeton, there were stirrings of protests and demands for the admission of women. As a freshman Barry signed a protest petition and marched in a demonstration for coeducation. In the meantime Yale men had several options to meet females. New Haven had a Catholic college, Albertus Magnus, and Southern Connecticut State College was a short ride from campus. There were also weekend mixers when Yale's residential colleges arranged for busloads of women to descend on the campus from the all-female "Seven Sisters" schools. As at Princeton, young women who dated Yale men often endured the humiliating tradition of "spooning" when they dined in the Freshman Commons. That hall was huge, and as they walked and waited on the long line for their food freshmen would rate their physical attributes by striking their silverware on the tables according to a code—one rhythm for the most attractive; another for the least alluring.

During the summer of 1964 Barry worked as a technician and repairman for the appliance division of Sears, Roebuck. He got the job through a high school friend, Bobby Hall. He installed air conditioning units, which generally posed no problems. But when Sears was out of stock for air conditioners, he installed ice makers in refrigerators. That required some skill. Although Barry and Bobby were supposed to be "factory-trained technicians," they learned it all on the job.

On one memorable occasion Barry was working alone connecting an ice maker in an ancient large house in Passaic. The task required that he close the cold water valves in the basement, drill a hole in a cold water pipe, run a water line from the pipe in the basement to the ice maker in the back of the refrigerator, and then open the cold water valves in the basement. When he was finished Barry packed up his tools and was walking back to his van when he heard the lady homeowner calling to him: "Sir…Sir. . . I hear a trickle; could you come back and take a look?" Barry started walking down the stairs to the basement and saw a box floating by. He realized that he had mistakenly opened a valve that controlled the water supply to the radiators, which quickly filled up with water. The resulting water pressure then blew out an old joint and caused a flood. Barry had to clean up the mess and apologize to the woman, but at least no one was in any danger. That was not the case at another misadventure, when Hall drilled directly into a gas line instead of a cold water pipe. That precipitated an emergency call to the local utilities company, which closed off the entire street.

Back in Hackensack the rest of the guys began to call Barry "Rudy the Repairman." We also warned our parents that they should not purchase anything from Sears that required installation by a Yale history major.

10. College Men

In September 1964 each of us began our sophomore year more confident in our academic prospects. With the exception of Richard, we were returning to a familiar college environment. Rich was at a new school in Philadelphia—a major East Coast metropolis that dramatically differed from the midwestern small town setting of Ohio Wesleyan. He had to orient himself to daily life at the University of Pennsylvania—his class schedule, roommates, dining options, recreational opportunities, and all the rest of college life. As a transfer student Rich had to rely on his own initiatives in adjusting to Philadelphia and Penn.

Barry Cohen drove down to Philadelphia with Rich and helped him move into a dorm suite that had a living room and two bedrooms. His new roommates, Steve Sandler and Michael Parr, were not exactly thrilled with the prospect of sharing their place with a newcomer. As the new guy, Rich slept in the living room. He took a whole semester to adjust to the class schedules at Penn, though he did not find it difficult to adjust to the urban environment of Philadelphia. Growing up in Hackensack, he had often visited New York with family and friends, which prepared him for city life. He spent most of his time in the library. Playing on the tennis team was out of the question, mainly because Penn's squad was loaded with talent and Rich was unwilling to devote the enormous amount of time and energy required for him to have any chance to make the varsity.

As sophomores each of us had to choose a major. Barry Cohen confirmed his intention to major in Social Studies and Education, while remaining enrolled in the School of Arts. He took courses with several outstanding history professors with national reputations as scholars. One of the most celebrated was Richard P. McCormick, author of the bicentennial history of Rutgers University and father of a future president of Rutgers. Barry admired McCormick for his carefully structured and crafted lectures, his vast knowledge and passion for American history, and especially his love of Rutgers. He recalls the day when McCormick scolded his students after they performed poorly on an examination, reminding them that were getting an Ivy League quality of education for a state university price. Barry also liked his class with Warren Susman in U.S. cultural and intellectual history. Susman was not as organized or as easy to follow as McCormick, but he was highly animated and stimulating as he paced across the room, smoking a cigar.

During his first three terms at Newark Rutgers Henry followed the curriculum required for students in the College of Pharmacy, but in the spring of his sophomore year he transferred to the College of Arts and Sciences because he had decided to major in Chemistry, with Biochemistry as his minor. At the beginning of sophomore year Henry realized that commuting to Newark from Hackensack was costing him too much time and money. So he rented a room in a building in Newark that provided cheap housing for Rutgers and New Jersey Institute of Technology students. He then looked for jobs in Newark. His life became a routine of classes and studying during the days, working jobs at nights and most weekends, and parties on Friday and Saturday evenings. Towards the end of his sophomore year Henry started working in the Rutgers bookstore, which qualified him for a special $1,200 scholarship. Since it came with the condition that all of the funds had to be spent in the bookstore, he started a small business whereby he would purchase books and supplies for his friends, and they would reimburse him for the costs and his time and trouble.

Henry's fling with his high school flame flickered out during his freshman year. In August of 1964 he met Betty at a bar just across the border that divides Bergen County in New Jersey from Rockland County in New York. It was a favorite watering hole for New Jerseyans, since the legal drinking age was only eighteen in New York.. A graduate of Westwood High School, Betty had just celebrated her eighteenth birthday when Henry approached her that evening. She already knew that he was from Hackensack, thanks to a conversation a week earlier with Randy Polinski, an HHS classmate who had been on the wrestling team with Henry and Kevin. She recalls her first impression of Henry: "I can still remember his ... big, smiling face. I can still see the light shining on his face on the dance floor. He was a happy soul, with a happy-go-lucky smiling face."

Betty is the oldest child of a large family from Westwood. Her father was a former First Lieutenant and pilot in the Army Air Corps who had bombed Nazi military sites during World War II. Her mother, a Belgian, lived directly across a field from her dad's military base camp. After Germany surrendered in May 1945 they were married. Betty was born at a U.S. Army base with American citizenship because her father was an American citizen. Nine months later the family of three moved to West New York, then relocated to Cliffside Park for a few years. They finally settled in a house in Westwood after Betty finished fourth grade. The birth of five siblings (three brothers and two sisters) increased the household to eight. After Betty's high school graduation she enrolled for two semesters of night courses at the Teaneck campus of Fairleigh Dickinson University. By the following year she enrolled full time as an Elementary Education major, with financial assistance provided by a work-study scholarship.

Henry and Betty started dating on and off over the following year, but before very long Betty knew that she had found her soul mate. One evening, as Henry was driving her to a fraternity party in his old Volkswagen, she thought to herself: "This is the man I'm going to marry. As God is my judge, I knew it, I just knew it." As she got to know Henry's family she was impressed by their sacrifices for him. On his part, as an only child Henry was intrigued by Betty's large family.

Henry ("Hank") and Betty, mid-1960s.

Henry took Betty to several fraternity parties in Newark during his sophomore year. Betty thought his frat brothers were a bit on the wild side, and she appreciated how protective Henry was and how he never put her in an uncomfortable situation. On one occasion they left a private party early because Henry did not like the scene there, which may have involved drugs. In truth, whether or not he was with Betty, he was rarely out of control. He recalls only three occasions when he woke up not knowing his whereabouts and not being where he was supposed to be.

The difference in their religious upbringing did not inhibit Henry and Betty's deepening romance, but it did present a problem for their parents. Although Betty's mother was raised as a Roman Catholic, she deferred to her husband's devotion to Protestantism. Betty's family initially joined the First Baptist Church in Cliffside Park (NJ) and later became members of the Reformed Church of Westwood when they moved to that town. Betty knew that Henry's Catholicism would be troubling for her dad, so she did not initially tell him Henry's last name. Henry's parents were also concerned about Betty's Protestant heritage. His mother, Pauline, liked Betty very much from the beginning, but as a devout Catholic she worried that if her son was not married in the Roman Catholic Church he risked living in sin for the rest of his life.

Cornell permitted sophomores to bring a car to campus, so in September 1964 I drove my Volvo (passed down from my dad) to Ithaca and my first experience with apartment living. I arrived at the place David, Jim, and I rented on Stewart Avenue about ten days before the beginning of the semester because of preseason varsity soccer practice. Coach Lace favored me at first because of my performance as a freshman, placing me on the starting team ahead of a few upperclassmen. But a knee injury in an early match soon relegated me to the bench, and after it healed in mid-season I did not see enough action to earn a coveted varsity letter sweater. Despite the infusion of talent from the previous year's stellar freshman team, the varsity won only one game, lost six, and tied two. My chances for more playing time in the future seemed doubtful.

I remained undecided between English (my mother's influence) and History (my favorite) for my choice of major. I made a big mistake enrolling in a Fundamental Physics section that was designed for science majors when I could have opted for the much easier "Physics for Poets," which was available for liberal arts students. Foolishly, I thought that my high grade in calculus would indicate a similar outcome in physics, but I did not realize that while my math skills were excellent, I always had problems with spatial relations. Midway through the fall term I was lost, and considering my poor performance on the final exam I was lucky to escape with a B-. But I enjoyed my first try at American history—a survey class with Paul Gates.

My dating experiences were disappointing, bordering on discouraging. For Fall Weekend I invited a girl from Englewood whom I had taken out a few times in high school. She was the daughter of close friends of my parents, and although we had a good time at a party and a Peter, Paul, and Mary concert (Peter Yarrow wrote "Puff the Magic Dragon" while he was a Cornell undergraduate during the 1950s), she became ill on the long bus ride back to New Jersey. That was the effective end of our relationship. I spent a particularly awkward evening with a very sexy young woman from Ithaca College who had been the girlfriend of one of my teammates on the HHS soccer squad. When I picked her up at her dorm I found out that she was one of the most popular female freshmen, apparently because she had hooked up with numerous Ithaca College men. She was "too fast" for me in those, more innocent days, and I never asked her out again. But having "wheels" meant that on most of the weekends my friends and I could shoot pool, go to the movies and sporting events, or just listen to music at home.

The fall term of my sophomore year ended in late January with an intense and grueling final exam schedule followed immediately by a trip home, just in time to be the best man for Dan's wedding to Laura Siner on Saturday, January 30, 1965. I drove back to Hackensack at night on

Wednesday, picked up my tuxedo the next day, and tried to think of a few words for a toast at the reception. Our family was in a festive mood that weekend, after several months of tension and anxiety. Three months earlier Dan had told our parents that he wanted to marry Laura, even though he risked forfeiting his New York University Law School Root-Tilden scholarship that was restricted to unmarried students. Our parents did not believe that Dan was ready for matrimony and harbored some doubt about whether Laura would be a good life partner for him. Fortunately, Dan loved Laura and her parents proceeded with the wedding plans. He lost his funding (but not the honor) for the Root-Tilden Scholarship for the rest of that semester, but the grant was renewed his second year. Dan and Laura raised three daughters—Jennifer, Gabrielle, and Elissa—and became the patriarch and matriarch of a large and loving family that now includes six grandchildren.

At the end of sophomore year I chose History as my major, with a double concentration (not minors) in English and Government. An incident in an English literature class would be a foreboding of my future as a college professor. On the day we were supposed to discuss E. M. Foster's *Howard's End,* the instructor came down with a bad cold and lost her voice. Without any advance notice, she asked me to lead the discussion. Fortunately, I was well prepared and did it successfully. And I enjoyed doing it—my first as a college teacher.

When Kevin returned to Princeton for his sophomore year he felt confident about controlling his destiny on the academic front, but admission to a selective club depended on more subjective personal matters. Social status was still the most powerful factor, more than race or religion, among the undergraduates and the greatest divide was between the graduates of private and public high schools. Since 1958 the number of Princeton students from public institutions had exceeded those from private academies, and the financial aid policy had shifted to a "need-blind" basis. Both developments pointed toward the future democratization of the college. But in 1965 the distinction between public and prep school still carried great significance for the "Bicker" system—the time-honored tradition that governed admission to Princeton's eating clubs.

Bicker Week occurred in February, when officers of the eating clubs conducted extensive interviews with sophomores in their rooms, and then offered bids to those chosen. The clubs provided meals and were the center of social life on campus, so it was imperative that a student receive at least one bid. Otherwise, he would effectively be excluded from most parties and other social events. Moreover, since the common dining halls were open only to freshmen and sophomores, anyone not selected would have to find sustenance "elsewhere," on or off campus. That problem was partially remedied in 1961, when the administration inaugurated the Woodrow Wilson Society as a dining alternative for a small number of those students who did not join an eating club. The sixteen eating clubs ranged in prestige from top-ranked Cottage and Ivy, followed closely by Cap and Gown, Colonial, and Tiger Inn (whose members were either athletes or scions of affluent and well-connected families) to the more democratic clubs (such as Campus and Quadrangle). There had long been dissatisfaction with the clubs over the excessive cost of meals compared to the common dining halls; the anti-intellectual club culture; and the bicker selection system itself. Many criticized Bicker's tendency to put too much emphasis on conformity, as well as the psychological impact it had on those who were rejected. In 1950 a group of students campaigned for reforms that would guarantee that 100 percent of all sophomores receive at least one bid. The new system worked well until 1958 when 23 sophomores were excluded, including 15 Jews. That year was labeled "Dirty Bicker," and the resulting controversy led to new calls for reform.

The outcome for Kevin turned out to be favorable. After what he recalls as a "zero" social life during his first three semesters, his prospects improved dramatically when he was invited to join Campus, then considered the most desirable of the more democratic clubs. Campus selected outstanding students, and Kevin had a near perfect academic record. (Campus Club by itself has graduated more Rhodes scholars than any other college or university except four.) That year about 96% of his class found places in the eating clubs, leaving the remaining four percent to fend for themselves and deal with the stigma of being viewed as the class outcasts or "losers."

Being a member of Campus Club brightened Kevin's life considerably over his final two years. Although he still had some difficulty making new friends, he spent a lot of time there at night and on weekends shooting pool and playing intramural touch football. His life remained a constant academic grind, but at last he had a refuge. As a break from his studies he also served as an Orange Key guide, shepherding prospective applicants and their families around the campus. He was also vice president of Princeton's chapter of the American Institute of Mining Engineers, and a member of the Cenacle Film Study Group. He visited Princeton's two movie theaters as frequently as possible.

At the end of his sophomore year, Kevin chose Geology with a concentration in geophysics as his major, and economics as his minor. It was a precocious and smart move, because the environmental and ecology movements that swept across the nation were still a half decade away. (The first "Earth Day" was April 22, 1970.) Few students at Princeton had any interest in geology, or especially geophysics, so as a result, the senior professors in those fields, all of whom had national or international reputations, actively recruited Kevin. He finished his fourth semester with the highest grades he had earned to date. He was halfway through his Princeton career, and his star was rising.

Back in New Haven for his sophomore year, Barry Vasios continued to hold a work-study job, but his scholarship and loan considerably reduced the financial burden on his parents and himself. In addition, he had landed a much less demanding position as a college aide for his remaining three undergraduate years. His duties included checking out and shelving books in the Pierson College library, delivering campus mail, and managing Pierson's intramural program. He also performed tasks for Pierson College's Master—a senior faculty member who served as both administrator and advisor for residents. Quincy Porter held that post during Barry's first two years.

In academics Barry confirmed his decision to major in history. Yale's history department required that all majors select two areas of concentration. Barry picked American and Russian history—not a surprising choice since this was the peak period of Cold War tensions between the U.S. and the Soviet Union.

Yalies who craved membership in a selective, prestigious society could still join a fraternity or an "above ground" or "underground" secret society. Yale had banned fraternities for a while but during the mid-`60s s era there were perhaps five with memberships that reflected social class differentiation. Some were for jocks; others were for preppies or "cool guys." Secret societies had been at Yale since the nineteenth century. The so-called "above ground" secret associations—like Scull and Bones and Scroll and Key—had buildings called "tombs," because they were built in a classical marble style of architecture. Barry joined one of the "underground" secret societies. It did not have an actual clubhouse but rather met in a house rented from a yacht club situated on the coast just east of New Haven. It included a broad spectrum of people who met for dinner about twice a week. Barry enjoyed their company and conversation, and his inclusion was further vindication that he belonged at Yale.

The summer of 1965 marked the midpoint of both our college careers and the 1960s, although in terms of seismic political and cultural change that decade was just getting started. The Kennedy assassination, intensification of the civil rights demonstrations in the South, Malcolm X's rejection of racial integration and demands for black separatism and nationalism, Cassius Clay's destruction of Sonny Liston and metamorphosis into the Black Muslim Muhammad Ali, and Beatlemania highlighted our freshman year. Over the summer Congress passed the landmark Civil Rights Act of 1964. Signed into law by President Johnson in early July, it ended legal discrimination in the U.S. on the basis of race, color, religion, or national origin in federal programs, voting, employment, and public accommodations. In the fall we were all relieved that Johnson easily defeated Barry Goldwater, a conservative senator from Arizona, in the presidential election. Johnson's easy victory and the election of a large majority of liberal congressmen in both houses enabled his administration to gain passage of the historic Voting Rights Act of 1965 (which finally guaranteed the right to vote for southern blacks) and also a series of laws in his new "War on Poverty" program. These federal acts initiatives founded and funded early childhood education (Head Start), antipoverty (Community Action) and urban reform (Model Cities) initiatives. Most ambitious and costly were the new national health care plans: Medicare for those over sixty-five and Medicaid for poor people who lacked private health insurance.

While all six of us had liberal leanings and were sympathetic in principle to equal opportunity and assistance for the poor and disadvantaged, none of us felt so alienated from mainstream capitalism and American political institutions to organize or join a chapter of Students for a Democratic Society (SDS) or engage in any form of radical activism. At least not yet. Like many of our middle-of-the-road peers, it would be foreign and not domestic affairs—and especially the military draft—that grabbed our attention during the summer of 1965 and for the next five years.

The Cold War was becoming decidedly hot in a remote land called Vietnam. Although by choosing Johnson Americans had seemingly rejected Barry Goldwater's belligerent foreign policy, Johnson took a major step toward escalation of American involvement in Southeast Asia in August 1964 after North Vietnamese patrol boats attacked U.S. destroyers in the Gulf of Tonkin. Johnson ordered retaliatory raids and Congress passed the Gulf of Tonkin Resolution that gave him the authority to "take all necessary measures to repel any armed attack against the forces of the United States and to prevent further aggression." The following February he began Operation Rolling Thunder, a massive bombing campaign against targets in North Vietnam and along the Ho Chi Minh Trail in Laos and Cambodia. In July 1965 he told the American people that hundreds of thousands of additional American troops were required to fight the Vietnam War. American forces in Vietnam peaked in 1968 at around 536,000. The draft of new recruits would be expanded to meet those figures, and we all were likely to be called to duty.

As President Johnson was launching his Great Society at home and stepping up anticommunism in Southeast Asia, Kevin and I spent the summer of 1965 touring Europe. Initially we planned our trip to begin with a month at the University of Paris studying French language, followed by another month of travel through France, Spain, Italy, and Germany. For transportation we would pick up a French Simca that Kevin's dad (a fan of foreign cars) had purchased in advance. He then arranged for Kevin to pick it up in Paris in late June. We would then drive it for about eight weeks, and drop it off in Hamburg for shipment back to the States.

I flew to London in mid-June with a Cornell group and spent a week sightseeing with my friends until Kevin arrived. A few days later we traveled to Paris, where we checked into our rooms at the Cité Universitaire. We did not last long in the academic program, because after a week Kevin got bored and suggested—more like announced—that we should drop out, do some more sightseeing in and around Paris, and then hit the road for a grand tour of the continent. His change of heart surprised me because Kevin was never one to quit anything, especially classes, but apparently he thought that his course was pointless, or he just did not feel like studying in the summer. I was more than willing to comply, because I was having trouble understanding my professor, and when he called on me I could barely speak. We stayed in Paris for another ten days, during which we drove to the cathedral at Reims, saw a Saturday night performance of Carmen (my favorite opera since ninth grade) at L'Opera, and joined the crowd for the Bastille Day celebration on July 14th.

On the road, taking turns driving the brand new Simca, we headed south toward Spain. We stopped at Poitiers and Lourdes, where we watched thousands of mostly elderly pilgrims praying in front of a grotto where, supposedly, a miracle occurred in 1858. Kevin and I got the feeling that those who journeyed to that holy site in hopes of cures from their illnesses did not appreciate our presence, so we cut short our stay. After crossing the Pyrenees we spent a night in Zaragosa before continuing to Madrid and its spectacular El Prado museum. Then on to the Mediterranean, where we checked into a sunny little resort just south of Barcelona for a few days of much needed beach time. I vividly recall our afternoon excursion to the Plaza de Toros to see toreros torment, wound, and kill their four-footed opponents. I viewed bullfighting as fascinating but also barbaric—more theater than sport.

Over the last days of July we crossed back into the south of France, passing through Nimes, Avignon, and Marseilles before spending a few days on the beach at Cannes. In early August we reached Rome, toured the Coliseum, Roman ruins, and the Vatican, but cut short our time there because of the oppressive heat. It remained steamy in Florence, where we were awed by the masterpieces in the Ufizzi gallery. With only three weeks left on our trip we set off for northern Italy and Switzerland, where we rested for a few days at Zurich.

Next stop was Germany. Just four years earlier East Germany had raised the Berlin Wall between the eastern and western sectors of that divided city. Western tourists were permitted to visit East Berlin, although U.S. government policy was to discourage tourism in that hot spot of the Cold War. We obtained a document issued by the State Department's Bureau of Security and Consular Affairs that warned American citizens that visited the "Soviet zone of Germany" and Berlin that the U.S. government did not maintain diplomatic or consular missions in East Germany, and thus was "not in a position to extend to American citizens traveling in the Soviet Zone the consular and protective services customarily available to American citizens traveling to foreign countries." Because of the risks involved traveling in or through the Soviet Zone was not recommended "except on the basis of pressing considerations." The directive reminded us that entering "certain countries" without a visa might result in arrest and detention for "illegal entry."

We did not have any "pressing considerations" for our foray into East Germany, and we had not yet applied for the required entry visas. We started driving, choosing the shortest route to Berlin, which began at East Germany's southern border with Switzerland. We did not know that Westerners were only allowed to travel to Berlin via one highway—and it was not the one we were on. As we drove through several border towns we found one that appeared to be a crossing point into East Germany. It had only a few soldiers at the check point, although they were armed with automatic weapons. As they stopped us, I jokingly suggested to Kevin that we run our tiny Simca through the barricade and outrace the guards to East Berlin. But of course when they turned us away we followed their orders to take the long circuitous route to the only highway open to tourists, which extended one hundred miles from West Germany's eastern border to Berlin.

When we arrived at the designated border crossing to East Germany we filled out the paperwork to obtain temporary visas and received instructions on how to proceed to Berlin. An armed guard told us to fill up our tank with gasoline and drive on the highway without stopping and without exiting before we reached the West Berlin border. We were surprised to see people on the overpasses in East Germany staring down at the traffic on the autobahn below. We took that as a sign of their unhappiness with their lives under a communist regime. (Or maybe watching cars speeding along on the Autobahn simply gave East Germans something to do. With no speed limits, perhaps it had the same appeal as attending Nascar races has today.) At the border of West Berlin guards from both sides inspected our vehicle for contraband, weapons, and stowaways.

West Berlin was an oasis of capitalism, democracy, and western popular culture that had been rebuilt during the two decades that had passed since Germany's surrender in World War II. We rented a room in an apartment of a kind, middle-aged woman. She had pictures in her living room of her late husband wearing his Nazi military uniform. He had been killed during the war. I do not think that I told her that I was Jewish; I felt some sympathy for her loss, but secretly I was happy that our side had killed enough Germans to win the war.

We went through Checkpoint Charlie on foot into the comparatively desolate wasteland of East Berlin. We had a decent meal at a modest restaurant, but the contrast with West Berlin was striking. There seemed to be certain metro subway routes that ran under sections of both parts of Berlin, but the trains did not stop at any of the East Berlin stations. We returned safely back to West Berlin.

A few days later we backtracked through East Germany to West Germany, where we stopped at Hamburg to drop off the Simca for its shipment back to New York where Bill Clermont would retrieve it. In that town we first learned of the race riots in Harlem in New York and in the Watts district in Los Angeles, which we watched on television sets in our hotel lobby.. We noticed that European critics of the United States seemed fascinated by the status of blacks and were fond of pointing out the hypocrisy of Americans who preached equal rights but practiced racial discrimination.

The final phase of our European adventure took us via train and boat to Copenhagen, followed by another train to Brussels, Belgium and my flight home via Sabena Airlines on the day before my twentieth birthday. Kevin stayed on, as his trip still had a few days remaining. It had been an excellent and edifying adventure. Sharing travel had strengthened our friendship, even though at times we got on each other's nerves and needed to spend a few hours apart.

I needed a few days of decompression before I drove back to Ithaca. In my last letter to my parents that summer I wrote: "All I want for my birthday is some Hackensack scenery and good old middle-class bourgeois America and people who speak English."

While Kevin and I toured Europe in his dad's Simca, the other four guys were sweating through the summer of 1965 earning a few bucks performing mostly menial labor tasks. Barry Cohen worked for the Hackensack Board of Education, cleaning and whitewashing bathrooms, locker rooms, halls, and classrooms. When he returned to Rutgers as a junior he continued to live in a new high rise dorm on George Avenue, not far from the center of the Rutgers campus. He remained enrolled in the School of Arts and not in the School of Education, although he was now fully committed to the curriculum of a Social Studies/Education major, preparing to be certified as a teacher of Social Studies (not just History) in secondary schools.

In the summer of 1965 Henry divided his time between classes in Newark, several jobs, and weekends at a house his fraternity rented at Bradley Beach. After switching out of the College of Pharmacy he had declared a major in chemistry. In order to add a minor in biochemistry he had to complete additional advanced electives. That required that he take nine credits in core curriculum humanities and social science courses during the summer session. He worked until midnight at a wire factory in an industrial section of Moonachie, where he rolled wires onto large spools and prepared them for shipping to hardware stores and contractors. At Bradley Beach he refreshed (or more often exhausted) himself with Jersey Shore fraternity crazy days of sun and fun.

As summer's end Henry and a few roommates moved into their Newark apartment above a furrier's shop just behind the rear entrance to Hahn's Department Store. This would become his home base for the remainder of his college career. As cashier and manager of the Washington Diner in Newark he supervised staff schedules, making sure that all positions were filled each day. He earned a decent wage and got all of his meals free. On weekends when he visited his parents he sometimes returned to his aunt's glove factory in Hillsdale for a few extra dollars. For fun he had his fraternity life, plus an occasional night out at local concerts that featured the Motown sound, which had become hugely popular among the black population and throughout mainstream white culture. When famous or even lesser Motown groups appeared in Newark, Henry and company would travel a few blocks downtown to see their shows at the RKO Proctor's Theatre. Sometimes they were the only white people in the audience.

In 1965 Richard completed his third summer at Hackensack Hospital and his second stint as an operating room technician. He and three roommates moved into a third-floor walkup on Thirty-sixth Street in Philadelphia. His top priority was preparing for the Medical College Admission Test (MCAT). Rich's major of Religious Thought was highly unusual for a premed student, rather than a major in one of the physical or biological sciences. He used his remaining free electives to fulfill required courses in biology, chemistry, and biochemistry. Since Religious Thought electives at Penn attracted very few students Rich could enroll in small classes that were taught by some of the most brilliant Religious Studies scholars in the United States. These included Robert Kraft, a specialist in the history of Judaism in the Judeo-Christian period, who became a pioneer in applying computer science technology to ancient texts, and J.P. Pritchard, who linked religious thought to archeology.

Rich approached his Religion classes with rigor, memorizing long sections of the Bible. He did extensive research for his papers. As a junior he took over a carrel in the library without permission (they were reserved for the use of graduate students or undergraduate honors students) and loaded it with books. When a librarian discovered his encroachment he was summarily kicked out. For his senior research paper he went beyond the requirements and wrote a one hundred page treatise entitled "Interpreting the Sanhedrin in the Second Jewish Commonwealth," which focused on an aspect of Jewish history at the time of Jesus.

Rich claims he opened and closed the library practically every day, and thus had very few dates and no girlfriend—"either in fantasy or in real life." The problem was not a paucity of females, for unlike Princeton and Yale, Penn was coeducational. Although there was a separate College for Women, they attended the same classes as the men. For respite he relaxed with a few close friends, especially Carl Wiesenthal and Steve Sandler. During his junior year and part of his senior year he volunteered for some community service once a week teaching reading to underprivileged children.

Back at Cornell in the fall I moved into a two-bedroom apartment in a new building on Thurston Avenue and awaited the arrival of my roommates— David Hamburger, Jack Roth, and Tom Lieder. Jim Cohen had decided that he needed some separation from David. Jack was a new friend, a midwesterner whose father owned a large department store in their home town, La Port, Indiana. Like many of us, he had been disappointed when he was not accepted by Harvard and was determined to gain admission to an elite law or medical school. He had an incredible capacity to study longer and work harder than any other person I knew in college. Tom was a native of

Shaker Heights, Ohio, a twin, and a kind and caring person. He was struggling to cope with the enormous workload assigned to engineering students. He transferred to the University of Michigan after his junior year.

The fall 1965 semester was an intense mix of coursework and soccer, with little time for relaxation. A highlight was a history honors proseminar with Professor David Brion Davis, a Pulitzer Prize winner. He became a helpful advisor and mentor. That semester I also took a creative writing class. I was under the illusion that I might have a future as a novelist, especially after my instructor praised a short story I wrote about college life. I sent it off to Kevin at Princeton, and after a few weeks he mailed me his six-page handwritten review, which was mixed at best, but tilted heavily to the negative. He admired my writing style and the story's "technical aspects," but he was much more critical of its development of themes and characters. I valued his comments as constructive criticism and resolved to sign up for one more creative writing course in the fall of my senior year.

That autumn my collegiate athletic career came to an end, not exactly in a blaze of glory but at least with the satisfaction of finally earning a varsity "C" letter sweater. My season began auspiciously when I scored a tying goal against Rochester in the first half of a seesaw battle that our team ultimately won, 5-3. The highlight of my varsity soccer career came in early October at 19:30 of the second half of a match against Colgate, when my second and final goal of that season put us ahead, 4-1. The sportswriter of the *Cornell Daily Sun* reported: "Kirsch scored on a play that made watching the game worthwhile." As he recounted the action, a Cornell player stole the ball from the Colgate defense, then passed it to a teammate "who fed to Kirsch who kicked the ball perfectly from a bad angle to score." We triumphed 5-2. But although we had a good team that year, some injuries to key players and much mediocre play resulted in a lackluster season. I played as a reserve wing in Ivy League home games against Harvard and Princeton and matches at Dartmouth and Penn. My parents drove all the way up to Ithaca the week after the Rochester game to see me play against Princeton. A few weeks later I was disappointed when they traveled to New Haven for the Yale match, but Coach Lace kept me on the bench throughout the game. Richard watched me play three quarters of a game that we lost to Penn in Philadelphia. Our team wound up with a record of 6-4-1.

At times I look back on my soccer career as a waste of time, but I remain proud that I was the only one of the six guys who earned a varsity letter sweater in college. I wore it to class and around campus over my final three terms, still stuck in a "Big Man on Campus" mentality more reminiscent of the 1950s than the mid-1960s. In an era of antiwar, black power, and women's rights protests, flower children, marijuana, and rock and roll, letter sweaters on campus were decidedly "uncool". But I remained trapped in a Hackensack High School mindset when it came to sports.

As I completed the spring term of 1966, the Vietnam draft loomed as a frightening possibility, especially since it seemed likely that exemptions or deferments for graduate students would soon be eliminated. Antiwar sentiment was growing on campus, though the full fury of student demonstrations was still a year or two away. I was also feeling academic pressure. My greatest challenge was Professor Davis's survey of modern American cultural and intellectual history. Although he had been my professor in a small seminar for prospective history honors students the preceding term, now I was one of more than one hundred students in a large lecture. I eagerly poured over such classics as Henry May's *The End of American Innocence*, Richard Hofstadter's *The Age of Reform*, Alfred Kazin's *On Native Grounds,* and Robert Penn Warren's *All the King's Men.* I completed the semester on a high note, acing Davis's class and an introductory macroeconomics course with Alfred Kahn. I wound up on the Dean's List for the second time.

George scrambling for the ball for Cornell in a varsity soccer match against Princeton, October 1965 (ended in 1-1 tie).

That spring I made a few trips to Cortland State College (about a half hour away) in search of female companionship. I had a few dates with a Cortland coed whose home was on Long Island, but we lost interest in each other after a month or so. One weekend I drove to New Haven to visit Barry Vasios. He fixed me up with an attractive blond (a "white ace" we called her) who was pleasant company but not a serious candidate for a long-term relationship. Basically I spent most of my time in class, in Olin library, or in our apartment listening to the Beatles, Rolling Stones, Byrds, Motown groups, and, with Vietnam increasingly on my mind, the protest songs of Bob

Dylan, Joan Baez, and especially Phil Ochs and his "Draft Dodger Rag" and "I Ain't Marchin' Anymore."

The summer of 1966 turned out to be the exact opposite of 1965 for me, more of the same for Barry Cohen and Richard, and new experiences for Henry, Kevin and Barry Vasios. Instead of touring Europe, I remained at home in Hackensack, living a life of leisure, essentially as freeloader. I rationalized my wasted time as a reward for my hard labor the past year in college, but I should have earned some spending money working for my father or at some minimum wage job. Barry Cohen got a promotion at his job from maintenance man to painter for Hackensack's Board of Education, while Richard continued as an operating room technician at Hackensack Hospital.

The summer of 1966 was especially hectic for Henry because he took biochemistry courses at Drew University in Madison, NJ and at Newark/Rutgers. He also found a new job in Moonachie at a Dr. Scholl's foot products factory. He worked there for two weeks, anxiously waited out a one-and-a-half week strike by the local chapter of the Teamsters Union, and then benefited with extra overtime. Thanks to the generosity of an affluent alumnus, his fraternity upgraded its summer lodging to a spacious house in Interlaken, an upscale and more private community on the Jersey Shore. Sun and surf ruled the day, followed by barbecues, drinking, and dancing at night. Henry's romance with Betty was becoming more serious. She remembers the beach gatherings at Interlaken as much calmer than the wilder fraternity parties in Newark. One time Barry Vasios visited, and Henry fixed him up with a good-looking girl he knew. Their date started off well and seemed to be heading toward greater intimacy, until she confided that she was recovering from a case of trench mouth. That cooled things off considerably.

I soon became bored with reading and a weekly round of golf, so during a July trip to the Jersey Shore I decided to write, direct, and edit a surfing movie. The project became "Ride the Wild Sand," an 8-millimeter, 30-minute short, shot in brilliant color. The feeble minimalist story line told the tale of a summer romance. Barry Vasios was the male lead, and Henry's girlfriend, Betty, played Barry's love interest. Henry did not mind our choice of Barry, since he represented an "All-American boy" hero. Betty was a bit self-conscious at first about being cast as a sexy starlet, but she got into it as all in fun. She also thought it was "sweet" of us to include her in our inner circle. An added bonus of this project was that we got to know Betty much better that summer. We all liked her and thought she provided a stabilizing force on Henry, perhaps keeping his wilder side in check and helping him focus on his life's goals. Years later she told me that that we were much different from Henry's Newark Rutgers buddies—more controlled and proper, with more interesting conversations. Meeting us opened up new avenues and worlds of possibilities for her.

In this, my first and last foray into the world of cinema, I shot several comic flashbacks and interludes, including one scene with Henry asleep and buried in sand, waking up to a clock radio that was plugged into his bellybutton. Another featured me as a lifeguard, jumping off a high stand and racing into the water to rescue some unseen drowning surfer. For filler I used shots of the guys dancing on the beach and body surfing on the gentle waves--since none of us knew how to use real surfboards. I stuck in a few seconds of Barry Vasios coming out of his Sears van in his "Rudy the Repairman" uniform and Richard eating a bunch of grapes under a small tree. (I got the idea that eating grapes was sensuous from the film *Tom Jones*.) All of the guys appear in the movie except Kevin, who was in Red Lodge, Montana, on a Princeton geology field mapping project. I spliced the segments together in the basement of my house, recorded a sound track (mostly Beatles music) to accompany the film, and had a big opening (and closing) night party at the end of August at my house, with live music supplied by Steve Wexler's younger brother's rock and roll band.

On some Sunday mornings during the summers of 1966 and 1964 a few of the guys and I played softball on the Civic Center field. My father, then nearly fifty years old, often pitched—sometimes for both sides. His participation angered my mother, who resented his absence from the house for a few hours—especially when she wanted to spend the day in Manhattan. Their Sunday morning fights were a symptom of serious marital problems that became more pronounced after they became empty-nesters. Their age difference was now becoming more of a problem. My father had a lot more energy than my mother, but the more serious issue was that their career cycles were out of synch. Dad was still expanding his retail business and had begun investing in real estate; he also had earned a law degree and opened a small practice. On the other hand, my mother's daily commute to Manhattan was wearing her out and she was approaching the end of a four decade teaching career. She believed that her needs should come first and thus resented my father's desire to play softball on summer Sunday mornings.

Our nickname for my dad was "All-State Nate." He seemed to accept that moniker as a sign of his honorary membership in our gang, despite the generational gap. Sometimes I sensed that he thought we should pay him more respect, especially after he was appointed City Prosecutor in the spring of 1966. He looked forward to the weekly games, and thoroughly enjoyed the action, sometimes even risking injury. One time I got very angry at a neighborhood kid and former classmate who knocked my father down during a close play at second base, slightly injuring him. The offender outweighed Nate by at least fifty pounds. When I scolded him for his rough play he brushed me off by saying that if my father was too old he should not be competing with us. (The young man later became lead guitarist and vocalist for a popular rock 'n roll group.)

A few other former high school classmates stopped by for a week or two to participate or just to catch up on the latest news. One time the star pitcher and shortstop of my Little League team (the "Chamber Champs") showed up. A superb athlete, he had not participated in high school sports because he had dropped out of school to join the U.S. Marines. We speculated that he did so because of a sibling rivalry with his older brother, who was a cadet at West Point and the "Golden Boy" of his family. When he appeared at the Civic Center field he had just returned from a year in combat in Vietnam. He seemed very glad to see us all but was quite subdued. He did not want to talk about his wartime experiences. We did not press him for details, but clearly he had been profoundly shaken by the ordeal.

Kevin was elected to Phi Beta Kappa as a junior—a distinguished achievement. As an upperclassman Princeton's geology and geophysics faculty treated Kevin like a graduate student, giving him his own office and laboratory, along with other special treatment. The geology department was perhaps the best one in the United States.. Kevin's professors included Harry Hess, a giant in the fields of geological geophysics and oceanography, and Erling Dorf, Glenn Jepsen, Robert Hargraves, Sheldon Judson, John Maxwell, Robert Phinney, Alfred Fischer, Franklyn Van Houten, Hollis Hedberg, and William Bonini. Fred Vine and Jason Morgan, young graduate students with offices on Kevin's hall, went on to revolutionize the field of plate tectonics.

For his junior essay Kevin wrote a report on characteristics of earthquakes. It was a serious, graduate-level scientific paper that summarized two semesters of research and required an oral defense. Kevin had already reaped some of the rewards of being an honors student in geology. He had spent the first part of the summer of 1966 in a geology research camp at the Yellowstone-Bighorn Research Association (YRBA) in the Bear Tooth Mountains outside of Red Lodge, Montana. The work was fascinating at the YBRA, but Kevin still had enough leisure time to enjoy the stupendous scenery—and go cowboy. In a letter to me he described his clothing as "blue denim from head to foot, straw cowboy hat, the whole works!" He signed it: "Hud."

In August and early September Kevin worked at Teledyne, in Alexandria, Virginia, where he did research on earthquake analysis. There he assisted a Turkish geophysicist on a secret project that concerned the limited test ban treaty of 1963, which permitted the continuation of underground testing of nuclear weapons. Kevin helped to prepare studies which investigated whether it was possible to tell the difference between an earthquake and an underground atomic test. The results indicated that it was not possible to do so, because an underground atomic test set off earthquakes that were much greater than the effects of the bomb itself. The policy implication for the United States was that it should not sign a more extensive treaty limiting underground testing because it was not possible to devise a means of verifying underground tests of nuclear weapons.

Barry Vasios spent each of the summers of 1965 and 1966 in two very different worlds, and his experiences reflected contrasting aspects of his personality. During June and July he was "Rudy the Repairman," working for Sears installing air conditioners and ice makers and trying to fix other appliances in northern New Jersey. But during August he was a companion for the grandchildren of the distinguished statesman Averill Harriman. He got that position through his classmate, Tim Weigel, who was captain of Yale's freshman football team. The student athlete who earned that honor in that era was offered the opportunity to spend the following summer working as a tutor for the children of Dorothy Schiff's brother on the family's Oyster Bay, Long Island estate. Weigel accepted that position. The following spring, the Schiff family learned that Averill Harriman's daughter and son-in-law, Kathleen and Stanley Mortimer, were also looking for a young man to serve as a companion for two of their children. The Schiffs asked Weigel if he could recommend a friend. Tim nominated Barry, who drove to Harriman, New York for an interview with the Mortimers. During that session Barry couldn't help but notice a photograph on a table that pictured Kathleen with Winston Churchill, Josef Stalin, and Franklin Roosevelt. (Kathleen had accompanied her father to Moscow during Harriman's diplomatic service there during World War II.) The Mortimers offered Barry the job of supervising the recreation of their two youngest sons in August. His tasks included taking them for a swim in a pool in Tuxedo Park or in the Harriman's private lake on top of a mountain near Woodbury Commons. Barry joined the family for dinner on most evenings, which produced an awkward moment for Barry when he was served a soup (borscht) that he had never seen before. He asked about its ingredients before he tasted it.

A highlight of Barry's life as caretaker for Harriman's grandchildren occurred on the evening of August 15, 1965, when he escorted them to the first Beatles concert at Shea Stadium. That event set current records for attendance (55,000) and gross revenues ($304,000) for a popular musical show, proving that outdoor concerts on a large scale could be successful and profitable. Whether it was an artistic success is another matter. Security guards had a difficult time containing the unruly, hysterical, and loud crowd. Barry, the Harriman kids, and most of the rest of the audience heard very little of the Beatles' performance.

Barry's continuing employment as a college aide and his good work for the Harriman family also served to gain him additional entreé into the Yale upper crust. As an upperclassman he assisted Pierson College's new Master, John Hersey, the distinguished journalist and author of *Hiroshima*, the classic account of the U.S. first nuclear attack on Japan. When Barry was a senior, Kingman Brewster, the university's president, was searching for a tutor for his youngest son and asked Hersey to recommend a student for the job. Hersey knew Averill Harriman's daughter, Kathleen Mortimer, from the time they both resided in Moscow during World War II. Hersey was very fond of Barry and also knew that Kathleen was quite pleased with Barry's work as companion for her sons, so he recommended Barry to Brewster. Thus, beginning with his friendship with Tim Weigel, Barry was able to capitalize on Yale's "old boy" network. (As an undergraduate he was also friendly with George Pataki, who later became governor of New York.)

Brewster was pleased with Barry's tutoring of his son and invited him to have dinner with his family several nights a week. That produced another embarrassing food incident when artichokes were served. Barry watched the others at the table remove the leaves from the base, but he did not realize that only the fleshy part of the leaf was edible. He tried to eat the bitter top section, with predictable results. He did some more observing until he finally figured it out. Dinner gaffes aside, his time in the Brewster mansion enabled him to forge a connection with Yale's president that would grow stronger during his law school career.

11. Class of '67

In September 1966 we began our senior years in college, and by the end of October we were all twenty-one. Which meant we didn't have much time left to decide whether to search for full time employment after graduation or apply to graduate school. If it had been peacetime our decisions would have been difficult enough, but the Vietnam War complicated our futures further. It was now highly likely that graduate students would soon lose their deferments for military service.

During the fall semester Barry Cohen fulfilled his student teaching requirement in a ninth grade world history class at Highland Park High School. It was a prime assignment for him in a middle-class town adjacent to New Brunswick. He needed an automobile to commute to that school, so over the summer Barry and his father shopped for an inexpensive used car in Passaic. A Ford dealer talked them into buying a worn out Falcon for $200. They purchased it even though it did not start on the first try, and the salesman had some difficulty getting it running. Barry had a few adventures with that vehicle, including one time when he beeped the horn, which was mounted on the steering wheel, and it fell off into his hand. Another time the muffler needed to be replaced, but Barry could not afford it. He took it to a garage and told its manager that he had only ten dollars in his pocket. The man offered to install a new muffler if Barry worked for him for one full day, cleaning the bathroom, sweeping the floor, and doing simple maintenance around his shop. Barry agreed and got through the semester with that car.

Positive evaluations of Barry's student teaching by a Highland Park teacher and a supervisor from the Rutgers education department and higher grades in major courses earned him honors recognition on the Dean's List during his final three semesters. Barry wound up with a low B average for his college career. As his graduation approached he decided to earn a master's degree before he started his teaching career. He was accepted at the University of Maryland.

In his final year at Rutgers Barry rented an apartment off campus with a few friends on Suydam Street. His social life improved, although only marginally. He went to a few mixers with Douglass women, but due to his continuing shyness he had only a few dates. Occasionally he returned home on weekends or visited Rich at Penn or Kevin at Princeton. Mostly he continued his previous routine of studying four nights a week from 6:00 p.m. to midnight and Sunday afternoons, hanging out with friends, and attending sporting events and movies. He was a rabid fan of the Rutgers' basketball team and especially valued his friendship with Jim Valvano, a starting guard for the Rutgers team. In their senior year the Scarlet Knights defeated Utah State and New Mexico in the first two rounds of the National Invitational Tournament. They lost in the semifinals to Southern Illinois, which defeated Marquette in the championship game. Walt Frazier (later a superstar with the

Knicks) of the victorious team was named the event's Most Valuable Player. Rutgers won third place by defeating Marshall. For recreation Barry played basketball a few evenings a week in an intramural league.

In reflecting back on his four years at Rutgers in New Brunswick, Barry appreciates the high quality education he received at a state university discounted price, which prepared him for a successful career as a high school teacher. He remembers the daily grind of classes, studying in the library, taking exams and writing papers, eating meals, bull sessions in dorm rooms or in his apartment, and then getting up the next day to repeat the same routine. He did not care much for the New Brunswick environment, and the social life available on campus left much to be desired. But in the end he got a good grounding for a successful professional life.

In his senior year Henry completed his required advanced chemistry and biochemistry courses and worked at Dr. Scholl's factory on weekends. He also wrote his senior thesis on "The Conductivity of Molten Electrolytes." In compiling the results of his laboratory experiments Henry built up a database that impressed his professors and earned him high marks. He used this research as part of his presentation at job interviews in the spring of 1967. At graduation Henry had the satisfaction of knowing that his four years of hard work in classrooms, laboratories, libraries, and at his numerous jobs had all paid off. Newark Rutgers became his steppingstone to a successful professional life in science and business.

During his final semester at Newark Rutgers Henry signed up for the college's Army ROTC program, expecting that his induction and basic training would occur in the summer or fall of 1967. But he never had to serve a single day in the military. A bizarre injury, the latest incident in the series of mishaps he'd experienced as a youth, was aptly timed. After a New Jersey Army ROTC meeting the recruits played a softball game together. Henry, sliding into second base, dislocated his hip. He wound up in a hospital in Newark. When he reported for his pre-induction Army physical a few weeks later, a doctor disqualified him from the ROTC program. However, Henry was still eligible for the draft. He made an appointment with Dr. Prager, who wrote a letter to the local draft board recommending that Henry be granted an exemption from military service because of his bad hip. When the draft board called upon Henry to report for induction into the Army, he presented the reports of Dr. Prager and the other physician who had examined him for ROTC. He was reclassified as 4-F and became the first of our group to know that he would never risk his life in the Vietnam War.

Richard relocated to a one-bedroom apartment (with one roommate) on Forty-Second Street and Pine in Philadelphia at the beginning of senior year, and then started the grueling process of medical school applications. Penn had a premed advisory board, which advised applicants and helped to process letters of recommendation, MCAT scores, transcripts, and other paperwork.

Rich applied to about ten medical schools. Early in the fall he had an interview with a representative from Downstate Medical School in Brooklyn. He was one of perhaps 50 to 100 candidates from Penn. Halfway through their session the interviewer stopped and asked: "Are you Jack Prager's son?" Rich felt this boded well and promptly replied: "Yes, Sir." In November Rich received an acceptance letter from Downstate. Although his record was good enough to earn admission on his own merits, he thinks he also benefited from his father's early career as a hospital administrator in Brooklyn and his dad's prior connection with Downstate's interviewer, whom he had worked with in a Long Island hospital years before.

Penn's medical school showed a strong interest in Rich, placing him on the waiting list and keeping him as an active candidate right down to August 30, 1967. Up to that last day Rich still hoped that Penn would accept him, especially since Hackensack friend and recent Yale graduate Tommy Blanck had just finished his first year there. So in the end Rich committed himself to Downstate. After the long process was over he realized that he would have gone anywhere, even Bologna in Italy, if necessary, to get into medical school. (Several of his friends took that route.) His attitude was that he only needed one acceptance. Once he got into Downstate he had the opportunity he needed, and he took full advantage.

Gaining admission to Downstate so early in the process relieved Rich of much if not all of the intense pressure he had endured for years, and now he could relax, play recreational basketball practically every day, and concentrate on completing his senior thesis.

When I returned to Ithaca early in the fall for preseason soccer practice I fully intended to compete for a spot on the first team, but after a few days I realized that I no longer was willing to make the commitment of time and energy required by intercollegiate athletics. I told Coach Lace that I was quitting to devote more time to my courses and applications to law and graduate school. He told me that he had penciled me in for the second string, so it was unlikely that I was going to see much action anyway. As it turned out, if I had remained on the squad I probably would have played a lot, due to serious injuries sustained by our star, Seth Dei, and a few other key forwards. I continued to play in pickup games and intramural leagues in soccer, touch football, and basketball, mostly with my close friend Marty Leeds. Since varsity athletes were prohibited from competing for an intramural team, I had to assume a false identity to play for Marty's soccer squad.

Now I could concentrate on my courses in American constitutional law with Walter Berns, a two credit supervised reading tutorial on the Progressive era with Richard Polenberg (his first year on the faculty), and American Foreign Relations with Walter LaFeber. He had earned his doctorate at the University of Wisconsin under William Appleman Williams, a historian who pioneered the view that U.S. presidents, secretaries of state, and diplomats aimed to create a "Rising American Empire." Williams and his disciples (including LaFeber) argued that the U.S. frequently used force to acquire land and foreign markets, at the expense of Native American Indians, Mexicans, Latin Americans, and Asians. LaFeber's writings and lectures focused on economic and strategic factors that shaped U.S. imperialism, but he was not a Marxist in that he did not condemn capitalism as the root of all evil in U.S. diplomacy. He became my primary academic role model, and we established a lasting professional relationship. His revisionist interpretation of the history of U.S. diplomacy profoundly influenced my views on American foreign policy in general and the Vietnam War, antiwar protest movements, and the draft in particular. The radical students who enrolled in his classes were often frustrated with his unwillingness to become more politically active by openly condemning what they viewed as the evils of American capitalism and imperialism. But I admired his stance as a detached scholar who critiqued American foreign policy but who (to my knowledge) never became personally involved in any antiwar protest movements. I respected his stance as an intellectual who may not have been temperamentally suited to be an activist, but who did have a profound influence on his students and the broader public, including policy makers in Washington.

Although I was still unsure of whether I would sign up for the Graduate Record Examination (the top graduate history programs did not require it), I took the Law School Aptitude Test in November. After a sleepless night I was groggy during the crucial morning sessions, and wound up with a disappointing score in the mid-500s. I submitted law school applications to Harvard, Yale, NYU, and Columbia, even though my heart was pulling me toward graduate studies in history. In December I filed applications to the graduate history programs at Columbia and Harvard.

During the spring term I completed three courses to fulfill the remaining requirements for a B.A. One was my senior honors thesis, "The Transportation Act of 1920," supervised by Professor Polenberg. It was a rather dry piece on federal railroad policy and legislation under President Woodrow Wilson during and after World War I—a far cry from my later writings on the social and cultural history of American sports. In April I received the exciting news that I had been selected for membership in Phi Beta Kappa. In May I successfully defended my thesis before a committee of Polenberg, Paul Gates, and Edward Whiting Fox (a Europeanist). Gates, an expert on the American West, treated me like a graduate student, peppering me with questions that went far beyond the scope of my essay and my knowledge. Fortunately, Polenberg came to my rescue and made sure I graduated with honors—magna cum laude in history, with distinction in all subjects. I also made the Dean's List for the third time.

My moment of truth in choice of a career path came midway through the spring term. In mid-February I was accepted into Columbia's graduate program in History, with a decision on financial aid to follow in early April. In early March a medium-size manila envelope from Harvard Law

School's admissions office appeared in my mailbox. I guessed that it contained good news, unlike the thin envelope containing the rejection letter from Harvard College that I had opened four years earlier. As I read the words "It is with great pleasure" I felt a wave of satisfaction. But by 1967 I knew enough about law school and the legal profession to realize that I was better suited to the study of history and a lifetime of college teaching. I was mindful of the irony of my decision to decline a place at Harvard Law School after an adolescence of obsessing about attending Harvard College. But I was more mature now, and realized that my prior infatuation with Harvard had a lot to do with sibling rivalry, self-esteem, and prestige.

On March 4 I wrote a long letter to Harvard Law School's dean of admissions, stating that I had decided to enroll in Columbia's Graduate School. I added two more single-spaced pages to recommend my roommate, David S. Hamburger, who had also applied. The dean responded with a very gracious reply, but later sent David a rejection letter. It turned out just as well, for David barely lasted through his first year at the University of Pennsylvania Law School. He then dropped out, headed west for California, completed a few semesters at UCLA's graduate program in film studies, and eventually became a successful movie director and producer. In late March Columbia awarded me a four-year faculty fellowship that paid for tuition, fees, and a modest living stipend. This was icing on the cake. It saved my parents nearly twenty thousand dollars. Rejection letters from Yale Law School and Harvard's graduate program in History did not detract from my sense of achievement or spoil my jubilation.

The late spring of 1967 was a magical time for me, as I alternated hours of study, research, and writing with afternoon and weekend rounds of golf on the Robert Trent Jones course at Cornell. Then more good news arrived from the office of Senator Clifford Case of New Jersey. I had applied for several summer internships at various agencies and congressional offices in Washington, with the assistance of a Cornell placement bureau. Senator Case's executive assistant informed me that I had been selected to be one of four summer interns in his office that year.

Living and working in Washington that summer carried another plus—my girlfriend "Judy," a lively, cute, and very smart Cornell French major, lived in the upscale northwestern section of that city. Judy and I had known each other since freshman year, when we were in a few classes together, but I had never asked her out on a real date. That was partly because of my shyness, but also because I viewed Cornell coeds as unapproachable academic superstars who were only interested in older men. But now that we were both seniors the odds had tilted more in my favor, and our attraction to each other became stronger. In March we began spending more time together, hanging out with friends on campus, visiting parks, dining at inexpensive restaurants, and then spending private time together back at her apartment or at mine. I looked forward to sessions of summertime romance with Judy, before she sailed off for a year-long fellowship in France.

Since I had no final exams that spring and there was a ten-day break between the end of the term and graduation, I headed back to Hackensack with a car-load of my belongings. While at home the Arab-Israeli Six-Day War broke out on June 5, as Israel launched a preemptive attack on Egypt, and ended on June 10, after Israel had routed the forces of Egypt, Syria, and Jordan, seizing control of the Sinai Peninsula, the Gaza Strip, the West Bank of the Jordan River, and the Golan Heights. As I drove back to Ithaca for graduation, I felt intense pride as a Jew in the military power of the Jewish state.

On graduation day, Monday, June 12, 1967, I introduced my parents to Judy and her family. They greeted me warmly and I looked forward to getting to know them over the summer. I bid farewell to my roommates and friends. I expected to keep in touch with David, Tim Wright, Jim Cohen, and Sylvia, but I doubted that I would remain close with Jack. Marty Leeds had been accepted to NYU's doctoral program in clinical psychology and we had agreed to rent an apartment together in Manhattan. The next day I was back on the road for Hackensack, and about a week later I headed south for my internship and what I hoped would be an exciting summer with Judy and my fellow Cornellians who had landed internships in Washington.

In his final year at Princeton, Kevin finished his senior thesis, a bound, hundred-page treatise titled: "A Computer Program for Gravitational Attraction of Arbitrary Three-Dimensional Bodies, with Application to the Crazy Mountains and Little Rocky Mountains, Montana." It was later published in 1971 in the *Transactions of the Society of Mining Engineers*, using the computer modeling program that Kevin had developed.

The Geology Department gave Kevin a lot of support, and paid for the time he charged on Princeton's IBM mainframe computer. Competition for use of that machine was intense, and the cost was very high. His senior thesis required a lot of coding in Fortran on IBM cards. His program resided on a huge stack of cards, kept in a big specially designed cardboard box. He would submit his box for a run, and return 24 hours later to get the results. Debugging a program was painful—it could take another 24 hours to learn that you had left out a semicolon in the third line, or whatever. The process took months. To maximize his use of time on this project Kevin decided to stay at school for the winter break, when turnaround time on the computer dropped to minutes, since there was much less demand for use. Kevin amused himself during computer downtime by reading Arthur Conan Doyle's "The Hound of the Baskervilles." The dorms were empty. That story was not a good choice of reading matter for a person all alone on a rather creepy Gothic campus. Kevin remembers feeling terrified as he read the tale.

One Friday afternoon, just before the computer facility shut down for the weekend, Kevin submitted another run. Unfortunately, he had mistakenly inserted a loop into his program, which didn't stop running for nineteen hours, because no technician was present. Kevin got a bill for more than $10,000 (at a time when tuition, room, and fees were $2,400 a year and his eating club cost $1,200 a year). The Geology Department picked up the tab, but it was still quite a traumatic experience for Kevin.

Despite Kevin's achievements in geology and geophysics, he had come to realize he did not want to become a scientist. In awe of his professors, he concluded that he could not match their intellects and succeed at their level. But like the rest of us, he was fully aware of the Vietnam War and the draft. Kevin had not paid much attention to the first stirrings of student unrest over the war in 1965, when Jerome Hoffman founded Princeton's chapter of Students for a Democratic Society (SDS). As an upperclassman he took little interest in the fledgling antiwar movement, other than hoping that the protesters would "get me out" of the draft.

As a short term solution to the draft threat Kevin applied for a Fulbright scholarship in international economics at the University of Nancy, France. In particular, he intended to study American investment in Western Europe. If he were awarded that grant, he would be exempt from military service for at least one more year. He also decided to file applications to Harvard Law School and Harvard Business School. Both accepted him, but after he accepted the Fulbright grant each informed him that he would have to reapply if he wished to seek admission for the following year.

At the commencement exercises on June 13, 1967, at the end of Princeton's 221st year, Kevin delivered the Salutatory Address. The time-honored Princeton tradition required that the talk be given in Latin. The graduates received a copy of the Latin speech which included footnotes (also in Latin) that prompted them to react vociferously and enthusiastically to specific words or phrases. The rest of the audience got the address without the cues.

Kevin began by welcoming and praising his alma mater, its president, trustees, deans, administrators, and professors, as well as the parents, relatives, friends, and other guests in the audience. His tribute to the impact of Princeton's professors on his own education drew a loud laugh, as he proclaimed: "Compare those ignorant youngsters in the first year of our apprenticeship with these learned men here! . . . Indeed, your training has so profoundly influenced me that no longer do I seem to be the bare-foot boy from Hackensack." ("Enimvero doctrina vestra me tam multum permovit ut non iam esse videar puer pede nudo Hackensackiensis.") His salute to his classmates highlighted noteworthy news, in particular Yale's proposed plan of cooperative education with Vassar (never consummated). "Although we watch hopelessly as those Vassar girls and those Yalies, frivolous creatures of leisure, enter into their abandoned partnership," he stated, "nonetheless the genius of our scholars and the trophies won by the athletes of the Princeton Tiger please us mightily and offer consolation." Further, "Even though in the College Bowl the knowledge of trifles acquired by the scholars of Agnes Scott overcame our powers of cogitation, from our victory in the Trivia Bowl won this year the Princeton education can accurately and truly be estimated." Kevin's reference to the impending admission of women triggered a thunderous ovation: "Through these four years we have made innumerable male friends, but very few female friends, of whom the former were more numerous, the latter fewer than perhaps was healthy. As Woody Allen, that sanctified man and patron of bon vivants, has said, 'Henceforth you may fail with a better class of women.' ("Ut dixit Woodyus Allen, vir sanctus et patronus bene viventium: 'Dehinc licet vobis vos perdere cum meliori ordine feminarium.'") He concluded: "Therefore let us rejoice while we are young— particularly with our diplomas from Old Nassau. And so friends, hail and farewell."

Kevin at Princeton graduation after delivering his entertaining Salutatory Address, in Latin. He was no longer "the barefoot boy from Hackensack [Hackensackiensis]."

Later in the graduation exercises president Robert F. Goheen announced that the Board of Trustees had authorized a study of the possibility of admitting women. Student pressure for females on campus had been building for several years, especially after the *Daily Princetonian* had applauded a new campus group, Students for Women at Princeton (SWP). Its members wanted to end the "stereotyped Princeton weekend syndrome," when young men "imported" dates from nearby colleges at considerable hassle and expense, leading to "its weary obsession with packaged, quick-thaw sex and forced pantomime of the 'good time.'" Goheen conceded: "Clearly the time has come, when a university such as ours, with so profound a sense of obligation to the world in which it exists, must look again to whether it can largely ignore the educational needs of one half the human race." He also acknowledged the presence of an unauthorized female sitting in the midst of the degree candidates. She was Christine Jones of Charleston, West Virginia, a student at Wellesley College and the date of Raymond Webster of Boston. He had borrowed the cap and gown from a sick friend and had smuggled her in amongst his classmates as a "good form of protest" in behalf of the cause of coeducation. Goheen then conferred honorary doctorates on nine men, including civil rights leader Whitney Young and two New Jersey statesmen, Governor Richard Hughes and Senator Clifford Case. Arthur J. Goldberg, U.S. Representative at the United Nations, was also scheduled to receive an honorary doctorate, but could not attend because of the continuing crisis in the Middle East, fallout from the Six Day War.

Kevin has mixed feelings about his four years at Old Nassau, with the positive effects of his academic training and achievements outweighing what he remembers as "the sickest social environment you could imagine." On the negative side, he recalls the racism and especially the sexism. Coming from a coeducational high school, it seemed unnatural not to have women in his classes. Moreover, when females did arrive as dates, horny undergraduates often viewed them as mere sex objects. He also detested the social class hierarchy that elevated preppies over public school students. He blamed Princeton's administration for helping to institutionalize social class privilege by not providing alternatives to the bicker system of selecting members at the eating clubs, which often humiliated and demoralized students. Bicker still dominated the social scene at Princeton, but student protests of the era, the recruitment of African-American students, and the coming of coeducation precipitated changes a few years later. In 1967 a lengthy student report on the eating club problem, combined with an investigation by a faculty committee, led to reforms in the next decade. These included the building of several residential colleges and the opening of more dining facilities. The result was a sharp drop in patronage of the clubs by upperclassmen, which led to the demise of a few of them and the consolidation of several others.

Although Kevin concedes today that he might have been happier at Yale, he is certain that he benefited immensely from Princeton's emphasis on undergraduate education. Ever since Woodrow Wilson's term as its president, Princeton had stressed the importance of teaching among its professors, even as it also demanded the highest standards of scholarship in research and publications. On balance, Princeton provided Kevin with the chance to reap the rewards for his hard work. The college's administration and faculty recognized his achievements, and his family and friends showered him with praise. He especially treasures a belated congratulatory note he received in early January 1970 from his Aunt Jo's friend, Tennessee Williams, who wrote: "I felt almost as proud as if I were a member of your family when I read the clipping about your fabulous scholastic achievements."

Barry Vasios devoted countless hours to the study of American and Russian history at Yale. His favorite professors were John Morton Blum, an expert on U.S. history from the 1880s to the age of Eisenhower, Firuz Kazemzadeh in Russian history, and Charles Garside, a spell binding specialist in world history who left Yale for Rice University in 1966. Like so many Yale undergraduates, Barry was in awe of legendary art history professor Vincent Scully (not to be confused with the longtime sportscaster for the Brooklyn Dodgers!)

When Barry entered Yale the admissions office had secretly projected that he would compile a C- or D+ average (he learned that when he peaked in his file). Instead, he became an honors student with a nearly straight-A record in History. An administrator had taken such a dim view of his academic prospects because Yale had too small of a sample of students from Hackensack High School to properly predict how well they were prepared for college. Barry thought that in those days Yale admitted "probably twenty-five guys from Andover, and an equivalent amount from Exeter, from Hotchkiss, from Lawrenceville," so its staff had a pretty good sense of how they would perform academically. On the other hand, Barry concluded: "if you came from a small high school they had no idea how to predict your grade point average at Yale."

Barry distinguished himself as a history major through his outstanding work in his required junior thesis and his performance on his comprehensive examinations as a senior. Unlike Princeton, Yale did not require a senior thesis for all students; like Cornell, it mandated a thesis for honors in history. The subject of his junior thesis was the political careers of black men from South Carolina and Virginia who were elected legislators during Reconstruction. For his primary sources he used mainly contemporary newspapers, including the *New York Times* and periodicals from Charleston, South Carolina, and several Virginia towns. In his senior year Barry and all of the other history majors were required to pass comprehensive examinations. His scores placed him fourth out of approximately four hundred who took the test. His performance prompted a call from the History Department's office, informing him that if he revised his junior thesis he would graduate from Yale with High Honors in History, along with the cum laude recognition he had already earned for his high grade point average in all subjects. But the term had just concluded, it was June, and Barry had already been admitted to Yale Law School. He decided that he preferred to relax for the two weeks that remained before commencement.

Barry knew that he wanted to be a lawyer by the beginning of his senior year. Partly it was the influence of his father, who had spent his adult life working as clerk of Hackensack's Violations Office and later as clerk of the Municipal Court. He often told his sons stories about his experiences with judges he had worked with and cases he had witnessed. Barry saw his dad as someone who had not had the opportunity to become a lawyer, so that inspired him to pursue the vocation himself.

At Yale's student career advisory office Barry examined a chart of data compiled from recent Yale undergraduate applicants to elite law schools that plotted their grade-point averages and LSAT scores against the outcomes. It was clear that his record virtually guaranteed his admission to Penn's law school and was probably strong enough to gain acceptance to Harvard Law School (which had an entering class of about 550). But Yale Law School was more of a reach. He applied early in the fall to those three schools. Penn accepted him within a few weeks in November; Harvard's affirmative decision arrived in December; Yale admitted him in February.

Barry, Kevin, and I could have been classmates at Harvard Law the following spring. It did not turn out that way, because Kevin spent a year in France before choosing Harvard Law School; I preferred Columbia's PhD program in History; and Barry decided to study law at Yale rather than Harvard.

Barry was thrilled to remain at Yale for his legal studies. The only drawback was that he was not satisfied with the financial assistance Yale Law School had offered him. While relaxing before his graduation, he went to the Office of Financial Aid without an appointment to request more financial assistance. He explained to the Dean of Financial Aid that his parents did not earn very much money, they had already sacrificed a great deal for him, and it was simply not fair to burden them any further. Barry did not request a scholarship; rather he asked for a substantially higher loan. To his surprise, the Dean responded with a hearty "You're right!" and asked his secretary to pull Barry's file. After a quick glance he approved a hefty increase in the loan.

Barry today professes an unconditional love for his alma mater. He enjoyed living in Pierson College, he made lots of friends, he dated enough to have a happy social life, and he had sufficient fun for periodic relief from the grind of classes, term papers, and exams. Yale provided him with a great education, especially as a history major. "I remember Yale like it happened yesterday," he told me. "Yale was like going into a different world, I was learning all the time."

In June 1967, four years after graduating from Hackensack High School, we all returned to our home town, trusting our parents to safeguard our newly minted college diplomas in family archives. Two of the guys planned to stay in Hackensack for a while, while the rest of us were just passing through for short visits with our siblings, mothers, and fathers. Barry Cohen and Henry moved back into their childhood bedrooms; Richard and Kevin traveled to

Europe, Barry Vasios returned to New Haven, and I journeyed to Washington.

Barry Cohen did not return for another sweltering season painting school hallways and classrooms as an employee of Hackensack's Board of Education. Instead he found a better job as a counselor at the YMHA's new summer camp at Darlington Park in Mahwah, at the northern end of Bergen County. The old cramped recreational facilities of Hackensack's YMHA on Essex Street no longer pleased Jewish parents. Moreover, many upwardly mobile Jews had departed Hackensack, Teaneck, and other central Bergen communities to migrate north to the greener pastures of Ridgewood, Tenafly, Woodcliff Lakes, and Allendale. Barry signed up for the job at Darlington mostly because the experience would enhance his resume and help him secure a full-time teaching position at a secondary school. Each day he'd pick up fourth and fifth graders in a station wagon, driving a circuitous route that began in Closter, wound through Harrington Park, Westwood, and Ridgewood, and then headed north to Mahwah. Barry then spent the day guiding them to swimming lessons, arts and crafts classes, and softball and basketball games. It was tiring, but less tedious than painting rooms all day.

In July Henry vacated his downtown quarters in Newark near Hahn's department store and moved back to his family's apartment on Arcadia Road in Hackensack, just a few weeks before deadly rioting broke out in Newark's black ghetto. Henry could see the trouble coming, in that conditions in black neighborhoods were deteriorating, ghetto residents viewed the Newark police as an occupying army, black leaders (especially Imaru Baraka) were talking revolution, the Italian element in the North Side was intolerant and hostile, and the Jews were fleeing, One of Henry's apartment mates was still living there when the rioting began and was trapped for three weeks in the gunfire exchanges and standoff between local black residents of Newark, city and county police, and young and inexperienced civilian soldiers from a New Jersey National Guard unit. Safe and sound back in Hackensack, Henry became the first of the guys to start his professional career, when he became a full-time employee at Shulton Corporation in the consumer goods and pharmaceutical industry.

Before Richard began his four-year grind at Downstate Medical College in Brooklyn he treated himself (with some help from his parents) to a grand tour of Europe. In mid-June he spent three days with Kevin in Paris, and then followed him to Vannes in the Brittany region of northwestern France, where Kevin was just beginning an internship. After a short stay there he met my Cornell roommate, Jack Roth, in London. Like Richard, Jack was taking a well-earned vacation before beginning medical school (Johns Hopkins) in the fall. In England they attended a premier tennis match at the Wimbledon tournament. Next they headed to the European continent for stops at Florence, Monaco, Geneva, Paris, Amsterdam, etc. When they reached Paris in early August they rendezvoused with Kevin, who was taking a short break from his job in Brittany. They told him about their night of "gambling'" at Monte Carlo, where Richard and Jack won $5.50 and $60 respectively. According to Kevin, girl action for both was "virtually nil."

Barry Vasios's plans to secure an internship in Washington that summer did not work out. Instead he went to work for Richard C. Lee, the Democratic mayor of New Haven, in that city's redevelopment office. In 1967 Lee was nearing the end of an eight-term, sixteen-year career as New Haven's mayor and had gained national notoriety as "Mr. Urban America" for city redevelopment projects financed by federal and state grants.

Barry got the Lee internship through a combination of old-boy social networking and old school Irish boss politics. He had met the mayor one evening when he was tutoring the youngest son of Kingman Brewster. Mayor Lee had stopped by for a talk with Brewster, who then introduced him to Barry. After some conversation about urban renewal issues, Lee graciously offered Barry a ride home to Pierson College in his limousine. During the short trip Lee inquired about Barry's ethnicity. He recognized "Vasios" as Greek, but wondered about his first name. Barry of course knew that Lee was an Irish politician, so he stretched the truth a little by telling him he was part Irish (his godfather was Irish). Lee seemed pleased and asked Barry about his summer plans. Barry had been greatly influenced by the inner city riots of the summers of 1964 and 1965. He wanted to do something constructive that would address the root causes of racism and poverty in the nation. When Barry told Lee that he was looking for a job in city planning or urban renewal; Lee suggested that Barry work for his administration.

Barry had a posh residence that summer in New Haven. Brewster invited him to "house-sit" his mansion while he and his family were on vacation. In late June he began his City Hall job at the New Haven Redevelopment Office, but he soon became bored with the paperwork. He asked to spend a day at the Family Relocation Office and was so inspired by what he observed he got reassigned there for the duration of his internship.

Federal law required that every urban renewal agency must ensure that all persons who had been displaced by slum clearance projects were relocated in "decent, safe, and sanitary housing." Barry's new responsibility as a field worker and special projects troubleshooter was to help individuals and families find new places to live, arrange payments for moving expenses and property loss, and (for indigent people) negotiate a lump sum adjustment grant to help pay higher rent. Barry also wrote reports on instances of lead poisoning in tenement children (from ingesting paint) and on the use of Legal Aid lawyers for mortgage closings for low-income borrowers through the Federal Housing Authority (FHA) guaranteed mortgages program.

Barry's had many "eye-opening" experiences trying to obtain rentals for displaced persons. He discovered that many agencies and landlords refused to rent to minorities or people on welfare despite New Haven's anti-discrimination law. He wanted to file a legal test case on a lead paint removal issue, but he was warned about "rocking the boat." He recognized that his agency was swamped with people seeking relocation and needed the cooperation of the real estate agencies. He began to read widely on issues of poverty, housing, and public policy and did some research about the possibilities and implications of a negative income tax and a tax-sharing plan between the federal and state governments. He also followed the rise of Black Studies and Black Power on college campuses and in black communities and became convinced that black history should be an important component of the curriculum of all schools. He believed that black Americans needed to learn more about the positive side of their heritage so that they might better understand both their present status in American society and discover how they might improve their future prospects. He thought that the infusion of black history and cultural studies into the curriculum of all schools would reduce the alienation of black youth from American society. Previously he had urged Brewster to explore ways that Yale could sponsor or initiate a series of lectures on black history and culture. He subscribed to the widely shared view that pride in their heritage would enable black Americans to act in the traditional manner of ethnic politics, as a power bloc, to become a vital political force in the nation.

Racial rioting was rampant that summer in Newark and Detroit, and Barry observed Mayor Lee's preemptive strategy to avoid that scenario in New Haven. Lee's administration was hiring everyone available, especially "drop-outs" and kids on summer vacation, to rake, sweep and clean up the streets everyday. In addition Lee obtained federal grants for neighborhood associations to run day camps and playgrounds. But despite Lee's proactive strategies, New Haven still witnessed several days of violent disorders that summer.

Barry did not spend every day that summer working in New Haven's slums. He had a few dates in New Haven and spent one memorable weekend at the Kennedy compound at Hyannis Port. He was the guest of the daughter of a U.S. senator who was a close friend of the Kennedy clan. She invited him for a day of water-skiing with her father in the Kennedy family boat and introduced him to Bobby, Ethel, Eunice, and Pat Lawford. That day he also saw Jackie, Teddy, and Sarge Shriver. Still, he did not have much of a social life. He confessed to me. "I get pretty lonely at times but that is probably a function of the size of this house." When his summer employment terminated at the end of August he went to Philadelphia to help his Hackensack buddy and recently married fellow Yalie Tommy Blanck paint his living room. Tom was about to begin his second year at the University of Pennsylvania's Medical College. Barry wound up with only a three-day respite before he began Yale Law School.

Through a "Princeton in France" program Kevin had secured a position in Vannes, a small city in Brittany, on the northwestern coast of France. Although the Princeton agency normally restricted its internships to sophomores and juniors, an exception was made for Kevin because of his upcoming year-long Fulbright grant, which was scheduled to begin in September. He planned to study international economics at the University of Nancy, but he had also applied for a summer job in France, primarily to improve his French. Thus a few weeks after his triumphant Latin salutatorian speech at his Princeton graduation, Kevin began two months of employment by France's National Gas and Electric Company.

Vannes was an old, fortified town on the Gulf of Morbihan, less than ten miles from the Atlantic Ocean. Soon after his arrival there on June 21 his hosts warmly welcomed him and provided him with rent-free lodging in the three-story former home of the director of the French gas company, which he shared with another trainee from Czechoslovakia. They also entertained Kevin in their homes and took him on trips to the countryside, boating and swimming expeditions in the nearby gulf, and excursions to beaches (which resulted in a painful case of sunburn).

Kevin's work assignments sometimes required long hours, but overall his job proved not to be taxing. Among other tasks, he helped string wires for the electrification of the inhabited islands of the Gulf of Morbihan, explaining the meters to puzzled Breton peasants who had no prior experience with electricity. He thought that they must have been doubly perplexed by having to learn the basics of the new technology from an inexperienced young American. Kevin also helped survey the damage when Breton separatists seeking Brittany's independence from France blew up the electric company's relay stations. (They actually intended to attack the communications relay stations of the French post, telephone, and telegraph company, but sometimes they destroyed the electric company's facilities by mistake.) That summer the radicals also disabled the transatlantic cable.

In Vannes Kevin didn't meet many girls and did not have much of a social life. But he wrote to me that his life took "a rapid change for the better" over a weekend in Paris that at long last provided him with some material for a novel, which he described as "sort of a poor man's *The Sun Also Rises.* The elements of that memorable weekend included "no sleep, almost no food, too much booze, a girl, two guys, set in Paris and the Chateaux of the Loire." He never wrote that novel, but after four years of monk-like existence at Princeton he finally had a good taste of wine, women, and song.

Just prior to his return flight to the States, Kevin ate a meal of spoiled mussels and became violently ill. His misery continued throughout his trip home and ruined the first part of his vacation with his family and friends in Hackensack. By mid-September he had recovered sufficiently to join a boatload of Fulbright scholars who were sailing to Europe on the luxury liner *SS France.* After two extended trips to France he was now more fluent in French and had become a devoted lifelong Francophile.

On Sunday afternoon, June 18, 1967 I drove my Volvo five hours from my family's house in Hackensack to Suitland, Maryland, and an apartment shared with three other Cornellians. The next day I began my eight-week internship in the DC office of Senator Clifford Case, Republican of New Jersey. I was very fortunate in securing a plum appointment, which I gained mostly because of the glowing endorsement provided by Cornell's Public Affairs Summer Intern Program. I later learned that Senator Case had selected me out of about a hundred applicants. His policy was to rotate internships among students from several prominent universities and colleges. He chose me in part because he had never before hired a Cornell student. Case's office did not have the funds to pay me, but the Cornell program gave me $250 towards my living expenses, and my parents and I covered the remainder of my costs.

I knew two of my apartment mates quite well—Mark Green and Art Kaminsky. Mark was a graduate of Great Neck South High School on Long Island, an honor student in government, and a varsity college tennis and squash player. He had a kind heart, an incredible work ethic, and a huge ego. He had landed a prime internship in the office of Senator Jacob Javits, a New York Republican. Art was a year behind us at Cornell and was working as an intern for a Congressman representing a Long Island district. New to me was Ken Schanzer, who also had an internship with a Long Island member of the House of Representatives.

When I reported for duty on June 19 I was greeted warmly by Frances Henderson, the senator's administrative assistant and most senior staff member. She ran the office, controlled his schedule, and was his most trusted advisor. A single woman who devoted her entire life to public service, she owned a beautiful home on a lovely rural site overlooking a stream that fed into Chesapeake Bay, south of Washington, where she hosted a party for staff later that summer. Case's other senior staff member was his Legislative Assistant, William (Bill) Korns, who advised Case on foreign and domestic policy matters—especially pending legislation. He was a free spirit who rode a motorcycle to work. Gar Kaganowich and Ira Grayson were junior aides who took care of New Jersey political issues and problems and who supervised the clerical workers, secretaries, and student interns. We operated the duplicating machines, filed correspondence, read and sorted letters from constituents, sent out bulk mailings, and performed other clerical and menial tasks. One of my regular jobs was to run letters through two machines that signed Case's signature. One device inscribed his full name; the other (reserved for letters addressed to close friends and contributors) simply penned "Cliff." We were told not to tell people that the senator used machines to sign letters, although it was of course a common practice. I was also assigned to do basic research for Case's speeches and radio and television interviews. I actually wrote one address for him on a domestic policy issue that he delivered on a radio program in September.

After work a few days a week and on weekends I drove to my girlfriend Judy's house in the suburban section of northwest Washington. Her father owned a small construction company, and he and his family were members of a posh Jewish country club in nearby Maryland. On several occasions I was her guest at the club for swimming, but although I hinted to her dad that I would enjoy a round of golf, he never arranged it. I got along pretty well with her parents, but I also sensed that they did not want to know too much about how we spent our time together, especially back in my apartment in Suitland. In July our romance blossomed at concerts, parties, and especially on two dates a few weeks apart when we saw the French film *A Man and a Woman*. My car practically drove itself along the fifteen-mile, thirty-minute route from Suitland to her house. But as July turned to August our spring and summer fling simmered down, as she prepared for a year abroad in France and I looked ahead to graduate school at Columbia. In mid-August we said our goodbyes. One year later she visited New York for her brother's wedding, but by then I was engaged to Susan, so there was no chance of reviving our relationship.

George with Senator Clifford P. Case (R., N.J.) This photo was taken before Mark Green, Art Kaminsky, and I drafted the intern antiwar petition. Case did not object to my role in circulating it for signatures.

The highlight of that summer was my role in preparing and circulating a petition against the Vietnam War, addressed to President Lyndon Johnson. Mark Green drafted it and he, I, Art Kaminsky and a few others revised, edited, and circulated it among our fellow congressional interns for their signatures. That campaign would bring me, Art, and a few others our first fifteen minutes of fame. The letter would be far more important for Mark, as the media coverage it generated launched his long career in politics. Dated July 21, 1967, the document opened with an explanation and a disclaimer: "We believe the letter to be polite yet to the point. If you sign you do so as an individual and irrespective of office. The person for whom you work will not be implicated and will nowhere be mentioned. We feel that on such an enormously important issue as Vietnam it is essential that those who are informed and interested commit their names rather than silently sit back and fear involvement."

The main text explained that we congressional interns were "anxious to build a greater nation and a healthier world" but feared that the actions of the United States in Vietnam were "detracting from the achievement of these goals." We described U.S. policies in Vietnam as "self-defeating," and argued that our government "has turned a local struggle into an ideological war in which hundreds of thousands of people have died. . . . We are destroying the country we seek to liberate." We also expressed concern that the Vietnam conflict had turned world opinion against the United States, and that at home "usually responsible Americans" were ignoring the First Amendment and recommending that dissenters be handcuffed, chained with an anchor around their necks, and thrown overboard. We were alarmed that citizens would destroy democracy by adopting such tactics. We argued: "a nation in which one-third of its population lives in poverty, and which is faced with serious domestic disorders, should regard its own domestic situation as the highest priority. Yet we spend as much a month on the War in Vietnam as we do a year on the War on Poverty." We shared President Johnson's vision of the Great Society, but were disappointed that it was "being blurred by the billions being siphoned off to Vietnam." We concluded by emphasizing that the Vietnam War was alienating many of our generation—students who could not reconcile performance of military duty in Vietnam with their personal conscience. They faced "the alternatives of going to jail or killing for a cause they consider unjust." We called upon Johnson to "begin the de-escalation of the Vietnam War."

Our lobbying for signatures ignited a firestorm of controversy among both elective officials and their interns, as factions arose supporting or opposing our petition. One day before we launched our campaign, Representative Robert H. Michel, Republican of Illinois, learned of our plans and attacked our efforts and our letter in a speech in the House of Representatives, calling us "ringleaders" in a scheme to "undercut and embarrass the Administration." On July 27 a group of 150 House interns sent a pro-war petition to President Johnson; a similar one from Senate interns reached the White House on August 4.

In late July an Associated Press reporter released a story about the controversy that identified Mark as the leader of our protest movement. It gained him instant notoriety and also generated nationwide press coverage for our cause. Apart from the issue of protesting or supporting the Vietnam War, our campaign raised the related question of whether employees of Congress had the right to make public statements while working for the government. In some cases interns who were sympathetic to our antiwar sentiments told us that staff members in their offices had warned them that they would lose their jobs if they signed.

A *Washington Post* article featured criticism of us by Robert A. Martin, Jr., an intern in the office of Representative Donald E. Lukens (R. Ohio). Martin headed a committee that called for a boycott of our protest letter and all other petitions that included pronouncements on public issues unrelated to the intern program. He feared that the House of Representatives would react to our campaign by cutting funds in support of future intern programs. In our defense, Mark described our statement as an "honest letter of dissent." He added that Senator Javits's office had not objected when Mark revealed his intention to draft the letter, but explained that the senator took no position on the issue. He pointed out that the letter's introduction made it clear that its contents expressed "our opinion as individuals and the men we work for have nothing to do with it." When Martin suggested that Mark was a "radical," he replied: "The most radical thing about me is that I wrote a thesis on birth control in college." When a reporter asked me to comment on the pro-communist label that some congressmen pinned on the dissenters, I retorted: "Anyone who can say we're pro-communist after reading the letter certainly doesn't deserve a seat in Congress.. ..We don't want to be connected with hippies or peaceniks. In fact, not one of the drafters has ever participated in any type of anti-Vietnam War protest before. We are just trying to show that there can be a responsible dissent to this war by well-educated kids involved in the governmental process." On a radio interview we explained our purpose and goals in writing and circulating the letter, and defended ourselves as good middle-of-the-road American citizens who stood tall for democracy, not communism.

Of course, our protest letter did not convince President Johnson to withdraw U.S. troops from Vietnam. We therefore could not point to any positive outcome to our efforts, other than perhaps raising consciousness among our peers that middle-class students could participate in responsible democratic dissent. On the negative side, Johnson cancelled his annual social gathering with interns at the Washington Monument, Senator Javits became furious with Mark (although he did not fire him), and the House of Representatives voted to eliminate the internship program for the next three years. In 1999, when Mark was beginning his campaign for election as mayor of New York City, he told Elizabeth Kolbert of *The New Yorker* that this antiwar protest letter affair was his "first experience at the synapse of policy, media, and controversy." He added: "I loved it."

For me, the petition campaign crystallized my antiwar feelings and provided some welcome diversion from the dreary office work at Senator Case's office. My parents'—especially my mother's—reaction to my involvement with it was another story. She remembered the 1930s when students who had joined socialist groups or had been activists on campus were later fired or blacklisted during the McCarthy hysteria of the 1950s. Like most Jewish mothers, she was overprotective and implored me not to sign the petition, fearing that years later my words and deeds might be held against me.

I acted out of youthful idealism, belief in the cause, along with a touch of narcissism. I was not worried about the long-term consequences of my involvement with the antiwar intern petition campaign. I liked playing a role, albeit a small one, in the unfolding drama of the student revolts of the 1960s. I enjoyed the buzz in Washington that we generated. My participation also deepened my opposition to the war. If my name was recorded on a national list of dissidents or radicals it never caused a problem for me. However, recently Judy reminded me of an incident when we thought that a government office might be watching my actions. One evening she and I went out for ice cream and a man in a black car and a black suit followed us into the store. He ordered a pint of vanilla ice cream, and then stood there, leaning against the wall, holding his ice cream in a bag. He left when we did and then followed us a few more blocks before he peeled off. We joked about him being an FBI agent, but then attributed it to paranoia. Writing this memoir piqued my curiosity about whether the mysterious stranger was actually spying on us that night. Under the Freedom of Information Act I asked the Federal Bureau of Information to let me know if it had an investigative file on me. An official replied that while a search of the Central Records System produced no file records on me, "a manual search was not conducted due to the Headquarters manual indices have been transferred for electronic scanning and are not yet searchable." Therefore, the FBI "neither confirms nor denies the existence of [my name] on any watch lists."

As the conflict over U.S. policy in Vietnam heated up during that long, hot summer, urban riots in black ghettoes shifted public opinion from foreign to domestic policy. The outbreaks of burning, looting, destruction of property, and assaults on police in July in Newark, New Jersey, and Detroit shocked the nation. They also heightened public awareness that while the reform legislation of the civil rights revolution had raised expectations concerning equal opportunity and upward mobility for minorities, the laws had not yet generated many tangible results.

The violence in Newark and Detroit drew national attention to the persistent problems of urban poverty, unemployment, and despair in U.S. cities. Racism was still endemic throughout the nation, and especially in and around our nation's capital, despite the recent flurry of civil and voting rights laws passed by Congress and signed by President Johnson. My apartment mates and I experienced first hand evidence of the persistence of racism in suburban Maryland. Tom Jones, a black student who was about to begin his junior year at Cornell, stayed with us for a few days in midsummer. On a sweltering Sunday we took him to the apartment complex's common swimming pool. It never occurred to us that blacks were barred from both the apartments and the swimming pool. After a few ugly comments from other residents, we exited with Tom. The next day the manager of the apartments let us know that Tom had to leave immediately, and warned us that if we brought another black person into our rooms or the pool we would be evicted. As Jewish white liberals we were furious and also humiliated, but we also did not want to wind up on the street.

Tom was angry at the racist manager of the apartment complex and probably a little annoyed at us too. But he did not want to get us into more trouble and so he went on his way. The following year he turned more militant, grew an afro, and became a leader of a Black Power movement at Cornell. In April 1969 he joined the armed group that seized control of Williard Straight Hall, the student union building. A *Newsweek* story featured Tom as a prominent ringleader of the demonstration. He was not expelled, in part because he participated actively in the negotiations that brought the confrontation to a conclusion. Years later, with his radical phase behind him, he studied finance and became President, Chief Financial Officer, and Chief Operating Officer of the college teacher's pension fund, TIAA-CREF.

In mid-August my internship ended, and I drove back to Hackensack for a few weeks of relaxation with family and friends. I needed grounding for my transition to graduate school, which would begin early in September when Marty Leeds and I searched for an apartment in Greenwich Village. Barry Cohen and Henry, once again residents of Hackensack, planned to start Master's programs. Richard was about to begin medical school in Brooklyn. Barry Vasios was returning to New Haven for law school, and Kevin was preparing to sail off to France on his Fulbright fellowship. Years of postgraduate study lay ahead.

12. Meanwhile, Back in Hackensack

During our years away from home at college we were preoccupied with our academic work and social lives, but we also cared about the well-being of our middle-age parents, now in their fifties. They were all still employed, and for some of them retirement was beginning to loom on the horizon. That was not the case for my father, who was starting a new and challenging second career as a lawyer, which would lead to appointments as Hackensack's City Prosecutor and Municipal Court Judge.

Though we had not paid much attention to developments in our home town during the mid-1960s, Hackensack was undergoing major changes in its neighborhoods, schools, race relations, politics and municipal government, and business life. To begin with, the construction of Interstate Route 80 had an enormous impact on the residents, factories, and businesses in the southern end of the city. In addition, five major issues dominated the agenda of Hackensack's Board of Education and City Council: public schools, civil rights, the downtown business district (mostly Main Street); urban renewal, and residential and commercial development (especially new office and high-rise apartment buildings). Budget issues—especially efforts to boost tax revenues and limit spending—plagued municipal officials. The Chamber of Commerce and town officers continued to focus on the revival of Main Street, but also weighed commercial projects near the Bergen County Courthouse and across the Hackensack River from the Teaneck campus of Fairleigh Dickinson University. Most controversial was the rezoning of several blocks of Summit and Prospect Avenues to allow the construction of luxury high-rise apartment buildings there.

The predominantly Italian and Polish residents of Hackensack's south end bore the brunt of the disruptions caused by the building of the ten-lane I-80, including its entrance and exit ramps. By 1963, for the section of the new highway that traversed Hackensack, bulldozers and road crews had demolished and cleared away a substantial part of the First Ward residential area, including 45 two-family houses, a church convent, a parochial school, and several factories. Bureaucrats relocated many of the displaced and uprooted families and individuals to other parts of the city or neighboring suburbs, but a few wound up homeless. As the population of the First Ward declined, St. Joseph's and St. Mary's parishes were depleted and enrollments dropped at the Jackson Avenue elementary public school and the Immaculate Conception Catholic School. Italian and Polish farmers who had settled in the First Ward fifty years earlier were forced to move away, taking their children and grandchildren with them.

Residents were upset by the failure of local politicians to persuade federal and state officials to alter the new superhighway's route, and thus minimize the damage to their community. They organized to demand that the town fathers pay more attention to their needs. One second-generation

Italian-American expressed his frustration to a reporter for the *Record*: "We always got everything that was shouted out of the other parts of the City—a pool hall, the Jail Annex, a junk yard, oil tanks, and Route 80," adding: "This has been the down end of the City." Rev. Thomas Pietrantonio, a priest of the Capuchin Order of St. Francis Church and a spokesman for First Ward residents, remarked: "Just because the community was full of Italian and Polish-speaking persons who traditionally did not voice objections to City leaders [that] does not give others license to take advantage of them with improper or unrealistic zoning or numerous nonconforming uses."

The new unity in the town's First Ward yielded a few improvements, including the construction of the first garden apartments south of Essex Street and the widening and extension of River Street, which opened an additional 30 acres (the last vacant land in the city) to developers. Others with more grandiose schemes were dreaming about constructing high-rise apartment and office buildings along the banks of the Hackensack River.

Hackensack's government could do little to limit the havoc that the construction of I-80 wreaked on the south end of town, but its leading politicians believed it could be more proactive on other fronts. Mayor Kazmier Wysocki and his successor, Walter Nowakowski, were confident that Hackensack remained attractive as a business and legal center, but both realized that elected officials needed to be more aggressive in recruiting developers for projects. In April 1965 Wysocki affirmed: "Hackensack has all the ingredients for success as a central business location. There is a tremendous market for a city such as ours; all we need is the means to inform developers of our assets." After impatient taxpayers voted Wysocki out of office in May of 1965, the newly elected Councilmen chose Nowakowki as the new mayor. In his acceptance remarks he recognized that "the real solution to the tax problem in Hackensack lies in our ability to attract new ratables." Repeating Wysocki's message, he explained that the city remained part of a rich metropolitan region and had excellent transportation facilities. He concluded that Hackensack retained an appeal "far greater than is to be found elsewhere." He promised that "every possible means will be undertaken to prove to developers that Hackensack is right for them and that they are right for Hackensack."

The civil rights movement took a while to get going in Hackensack, but by the mid-1960s black community leaders were demanding the desegregation of the elementary schools, equal access to jobs and housing, and full participation in city government. Ten years had passed since Superintendent De Puyt and the Board of Education had aimed to create racial balance in the primary grades through a limited redistricting plan (that mandated only a slight adjustment of the school district boundaries) and the opening of the Beech Street School. The results were disappointing. Although more white students were assigned to Beech Street, its enrollment was still 70 percent black, while the other elementary schools remained overwhelmingly white.

Overt racism prohibited qualified middle-class black families from renting apartments or purchasing houses in white neighborhoods. Urban renewal projects often began with slum clearance that forced minority residents out of their living places, frequently leaving them homeless. Ambitious antipoverty programs typically financed community development projects that benefited community leaders, businessmen, and local politicians, but very little of the spending wound up in the pockets of the poor. For many years the town had hired a few blacks as teachers, policemen, firemen, and municipal employees, but prior to 1965 no black person had been elected to the City Council or appointed to the Board of Education.

In June 1963, while De Puyt, his staff, and consultants were still in the early stages of preparing a strategic plan for the school system, they realized it was imperative to decrease the percentage of black children in Beech Street by at least 10 percent. De Puyt chose the same tactic he had employed a decade earlier—moving the boundary lines of the sending districts for the Fairmount, Hillers, and State Street Schools. As a result, in September about 145 black children were reassigned from Beech Street School to either the Fairmount School in the northern end of town or Hillers in the south-central section. (The redistricting also relocated a few white children to those two schools.). The Board of Education also instructed De Puyt to maintain class sizes and educational programs at Beech Street at their present levels. Reaction from blacks to the new districting plan ranged from cautious acceptance of it as fair to rejection of the new scheme as "a waste of the taxpayer's money." Critics argued that while it increased the black population at Beech Street, it did not solve the larger problem of racial imbalance in the public schools and thus did not provide good educational opportunities for minority children.

In 1965 race relations again became a leading item on the agendas of the Boards of Education of Hackensack and Maywood when school officials from the latter town debated its options concerning which high school its students would attend. Maywood had been sending its secondary school students to Bogota, but its contract with that town was scheduled to expire in 1966 and would not be renewed. Maywood's Board weighed its options of sending the tenth through twelfth-grade pupils to Hackensack High School, building its own facility, or joining with Rochelle Park (which was already sending its seventh through twelfth graders to Hackensack) to construct a new regional high school.

At a Hackensack Board of Education meeting in early March, a white female resident first questioned whether Hackensack's schools had adequate space to absorb the newcomers from Maywood. Next, she raised the issue of race, stating:: "Maywood has no colored people. When they come to Hackensack they are going to go to school with colored children. This is going to cause friction. Some of the people who live in Maywood are the same ones who ran from Hackensack to avoid sending their kids to school with colored children." Richard C. Thiel, president of Hackensack's Board of

Education replied that neither school board expected any racial problems. He explained that the Maywood Board knew that Hackensack had an integrated high school and that negotiations had focused on facilities, programs, and finance, and not on race. He added that Maywood officials recognized the high quality of Hackensack's schools and that some Maywood parents were even asking about paying tuition personally to send their children to Hackensack. Board member Dr. John J. Kristal was more blunt, stating: "While they do not have mixed races in Maywood it would be an education for them to come to Hackensack and find out that mixed races do not mean contamination."

A few weeks later Maywood's Board of Education formally endorsed sending its teenagers to HHS, citing its high academic rating and the quality of its athletic programs (Hackensack's football team had just won another state championship). Also helpful were comments by Harold Bloom, a Maywood resident and a prominent HHS social studies teacher. In April Hackensack's Board of Education and City Council approved the agreement.

As Hackensack's black ministers and other prominent community leaders monitored the Board of Education's policies toward racial issues, they were organizing a campaign to increase the political involvement of their town's black residents. In 1964 Rev. James P. Coleman of the Mt. Olive Baptist Church and other black ministers formed the Citizens Leadership Committee (CLC). Their goal was the election of the first black member of Hackensack's City Council. Black candidates had run for election to the City Council before, but they had all failed, mainly because they had not been included on a party's ticket. So the CLC's strategy now was to choose a black candidate and then persuade one of the town's political factions to include him or her on its slate. After spending two months screening potential candidates, the CLC selected J. Herbert Leverett. Educated in the town's public schools, he was a graduate of the Newark College of Engineering, a naval officer, a supervising engineer with the U.S. Atomic Energy Commission, and vice president of the Neighborhood Civic Association.

The CLC lobbied Mayor Kazmier Wysocki to include Leverett on his ticket for the upcoming municipal election in May 1965. After waiting in vain for a positive response from Wysocki, the CLC responded to overtures from the opposing faction, the Citizens for Representative Government (CRG), led by Deputy Mayor Walter E. Nowakowski. He agreed to include Leverett on his party's ticket of five candidates, and also promised that if the slate was victorious, Leverett would get one-fifth of all municipal appointments that the new administration was entitled to make. Nowakowski was hoping that black voters would support his entire slate and not just Leverett, and that his inclusion would produce more than enough votes to offset the expected backlash among whites in the more upscale and exclusive neighborhoods of the Fifth Ward, in the northern and western sections of town.

Black support of Leverett and his running mates on the CRG ticket turned out to be decisive in the CRG's clean sweep victory. Citywide about half of Hackensack's voters cast ballots, but the turnout in predominantly black districts was about 75 percent, with those voters overwhelmingly in favor of Nowakowski and Leverett's ticket. Leverett saw the outcome as "a community effort which will allow the Negro to take his place beside the other ethnic groups of this city," adding, "The Negroes can no longer be ignored." An unidentified man on the street told the *Record:* "Uncle Tom is dead in the City of Hackensack."

The CRG's winning slate included Nowakowski, Frank A. Buono, Robert C. Sellarole, John A. Moss, and Leverett. The newly elected City Council then chose Nowakowski and Buono as Mayor and Deputy Mayor, respectively. In his acceptance speech at the City Council's Organizational and Inaugural Meeting Nowakowski celebrated the new governmental body as "unique in the City's history" because "for the first time, a Negro has become an equal partner in the city's government." He explained, rather disingenuously:

> Not because he is a Negro, mind you, but because he is an individual eminently qualified and devoted who will add immeasurably to the effectiveness of this council; and not because he is a Negro but because he is an individual who represents a large part of the city's population; and not because he is a Negro but because he is an individual whose concern for people goes far beyond their color.

Noting that "for the first time the Negro community became a full partner in the operation of this city," Leverett emphasized that "the effectiveness of that community's effort was shown by delivery of the largest single block of votes for the Council—a state and possibly nationwide record." He observed that his selection as councilman had generated more involvement by black citizens in municipal affairs and issues, along with more benefits for the entire city. Yet he also acknowledged that "there is still a long way to go before there is complete acceptance of the Negro in this City" and that much work remained to promote business and industry and to make Hackensack's government more efficient. Ten months after his election Leverett identified his continuing major areas of concern, which included the removal of blacks from their homes due to urban renewal projects, racial discrimination in housing, and continuing de facto segregation in the Beech Street School and throughout the educational system.

In the spring of 1965 the Board of Education's first goal was to renovate and expand the facilities at Hackensack High School. Its second mandate was to implement its long delayed "Blueprint for Progress," which aimed to end racial imbalance at Beech Street School and throughout the town's educational system. The death of Superintendent DePuyt and the appointment of his successor, George B. McClellan, was one of many factors that had impeded progress on this vexing issue.

The high school project's projected cost was $3.559 million, the largest single financial commitment in the history of the city's government to date. It entailed the addition of a dozen classrooms and special education rooms, a gymnasium, swimming pool, and library; the expansion of the neighboring Beech Street School, and the construction of a pedestrian ramp to be built over First Street that would link the high school and its athletic fields. The addition to Beech Street School anticipated future use of that building by both elementary and high school students, and became an integral part of the Board's new desegregation proposal.

The combined use of Beech Street School generated some opposition, but taxpayers complained mostly about the cost of the high school expansion and especially the inclusion of a swimming pool. A spokesman for the Hackensack town's Homeowners Association stressed that the need for renovation was far more critical at the Fairmount and Broadway elementary schools. As had been the case during the 1950s, opposition to the swimming pool was driven at least in part by racial concerns among white residents. Some feared that public pools encouraged intimate contact between blacks and whites. In rebutting critics, Marion Purbeck, assistant to the Superintendent, told a gathering of forty officials from sending-districts to HHS that the pool would be used for swimming instruction, lifesaving, boating safety, and survival courses. She further highlighted its value for intramural and interscholastic swim meets and regulated recreational community use. After a lengthy debate both the Board of Education and the City Council approved the school expansion plan.

The Board's new desegregation proposal also stirred up some opposition. In January 1966 it established a centralized middle school for sixth, seventh, and eighth graders at the existing State Street Junior High School building, and a four year High School at an expanded building complex on the sites of existing High School and Beech Street Schools. Moreover, only kindergarten and first grade pupils would remain at the predominately black (70 percent) Beech Street School. The remaining space at the Beech Street School would be used by the high school. Students enrolled in the second through fifth grades in the Beech Street School's sending district would be reassigned to the other three (overwhelming white) elementary schools.

The reaction of Hackensack's black population to this new scheme was mixed, with a few prominent leaders willing to give it a chance. Some dissidents accused Board members of viewing the city's black citizens as having a "high-class Uncle Tom nature" and were determined to prove them wrong by challenging the desegregation plan. In the spring of 1966 a few dozen parents and black church and community leaders filed a petition requesting that New Jersey's State Commissioner of Education review the plan. They objected to it because it maintained racial imbalance for the youngest children at Beech Street School and thus exposed them to disadvantages and inequities at the very onset of their formal education. They also charged that it was inequitable since it mandated only the transfer of black children to white schools, leaving white students "virtually unaffected." The group also doubted that the new plan could take effect in September of 1967, given anticipated delays in the completion of the renovation and reconstruction of the two schools.

As Hackensack's black community leaders became more vocal in their criticism of the Board of Education's commitment to its "Blueprint for Progress," they lobbied actively for the appointment of a black person to the Board. During the municipal campaign in the spring of 1965, Alexander A. McKenzie, a white former president of the Board of Education, had called for the selection of a Negro as soon as a seat became vacant. But in February 1966 Nowakowski chose instead to reappoint Richard C. Thiel. In the fall McKenzie resumed his plea in a statement he delivered at a Board meeting:: "We should no longer trade on the good will, patience, and dignity of the Negro people of Hackensack. They should have a representative on the Board of Education. Such an appointment will not serve merely as a sop to Negro pride. It will benefit the whole community. Just as no nation can survive half slave and half free, so no city can succeed half-dispossessed." But Hackensack's black citizens would have to wait until 1968 for the next chance to get a representative on the Board of Education. In the interim the Board displayed some good faith toward its black constituency by promoting Samuel S. Cameron, a black sixth-grade teacher at Hillers School, to the position of assistant principal at Fairmount, thereby designating him as the leading black administrator in the city's public schools.

When Dr. John J. Kristal resigned in January 1968 from the Board of Education Nowakowski finally if belatedly satisfied the demands of Leverett and other black community leaders by choosing a black clergyman, the Rev. Benjamin F. Keeling, to replace Kristal. At the annual Reorganization Meeting, Thiel warmly welcomed Keeling by recognizing that his appointment marked "a milestone in the city's history" which "reflects the proportion of Negroes in our population and indicates the community's total dedication to education." But he also felt compelled to add: "We do not decide issues by color. We decide things on their merits. This Board is sincerely color blind." Black residents now recognized that the election of Everett and the appointment of Keeling reflected the increasing assertiveness of their constituency.. Kenny Dixon, one of my black classmates, told me: "Once one of us got a foot in the door, now we have somebody to come back to tell the truth when they tell us a story, instead of just coming back with a line of b.s."

White and black reform-minded civic leaders also campaigned for equal opportunity in housing. In 1965 my father was a member of the minority housing subcommittee of Hackensack's Citizens' Advisory Committee that reviewed a federal government report on urban renewal, which indicated that nonwhites currently had access to at most only about 30 percent of the housing units in Hackensack. In August the committee's chairman, Alexander A. McKenzie, urged the Mayor and City Council "to take immediate action to provide equal treatment of all individuals by real estate brokers, banks, and other mortgage loan agencies." He argued that integrated housing not only benefited the economy, but also helped to remedy the racial imbalance problem in town, since he believed that "segregated housing leads to de facto segregation in the public schools." He was convinced that some older residents and many younger people "wish very much to find suitable homes in Hackensack outside the [segregated] neighborhoods in which they grew up," but found it difficult to do so. My father told a reporter from the *Bergen Evening Record* in December 1965 that the committee would recommend anti-discrimination legislation "if housing bias complaints were numerous," but he also believed that the city's minority groups were "more concerned about neighborhood improvements than open-housing practices."

During the summer of 1966 Councilman Leverett and other prominent black civic leaders applied increasing pressure on the City Council to create a Hackensack Human Rights Commission that would hear complaints concerning violation of civil rights in housing, education, employment, or city services. Advocates argued that it would address existing racial discrimination and also forestall potentially militant or violent protests in the future. Rev. Coleman of the Mt. Olive church told the councilmen that "Hackensack has long been protected by the good will of its Negro community from the sort of ugly incidents that have occurred elsewhere." Tellingly, he added: "However, although I know patience is a virtue, patience will eventually wear out." A black resident warned the Council that not establishing the Commission might invite "outside agitators" to take action in the town's Negro community. The *Record* printed a succinct yet insightful comment by an unidentified elderly black man: "When you're talking about starting a fire department, you don't go around asking if anybody saw any fires lately."

While many white civic leaders, including my father, also endorsed the establishment of a human rights commission, some doubted that it was necessary either because of the absence of evidence of racial bias in the city or because such a body would be redundant, since there were also existing state and federal laws that were already being enforced. But black leaders countered by insisting that racial discrimination in housing remained a serious problem that required action in Hackensack. Howard Williams, a prominent black community leader, noted that the proposed commission would provide reassurance for those who lived in the proposed Municipal Center Urban Renewal area, because "there is a great fear in the Negro community that residents displaced by this project may not be able to relocate in acceptable housing, and the commission would answer that fear." After considerable delays, in June 1967 the City Council finally founded the Hackensack

Committee on Human Rights, choosing eighteen members from the town's white and black civic and religious organizations. The Committee's goal was to "eliminate all types of discrimination based on race, creed, color, national origin, ancestry, or age." It created three subcommittees to concentrate on cases of discrimination in employment, education, and housing. These subcommittees would use persuasion and conciliation to resolve disputes and problems at the local level, but as a last resort would refer cases to the State Division of Civil Rights.

Hackensack's black leaders also founded a new organization that was dedicated to the principles of self-help. Rev. Coleman, James Trammell, Dorothy Stuart, and Chester W. Smith launched the Council for Democratic Action under the guiding philosophy "Let's do the job ourselves, no matter how tough it seems." The group's primary purpose was to identify and promote programs that would be most useful to the black community, such as providing mothers with classes in consumer spending and child care and offering talented children instruction in art and music. The organization also sought to expand the federal Head Start program for preschoolers and supplement the public schools' curriculum by offering courses in Negro history and culture that would "instill a pride in our people in both themselves and their community and race."

During the mid-1960s Hackensack's black leaders grew increasingly suspicious of slum clearance and urban renewal projects initiated by Mayor Nowakowski and the City Council. President Johnson's Great Society legislation included programs that invited large and small cities to apply for federal funds to demolish slum neighborhoods and replace dilapidated structures with modern residential and commercial buildings. To qualify for financial aid, local governments were required to complete a detailed and often costly survey of population and economic trends and submit a Community Action Program (CAP) for federal approval. Hackensack city officials prepared an ambitious CAP for the redevelopment of both downtown and the Third (central) Ward. Since blacks were concentrated in the Third Ward, slum clearance and urban renewal projects in that area were bound to affect them the most.

Although urban renewal projects had generated some early support in minority communities, by the mid-1960s black leaders at the national level and in towns like Hackensack concluded that "urban renewal means Negro removal." They argued that totally dilapidated structures could be bulldozed on a piecemeal, individual basis, cities should not demolish large slum areas. Instead, they supported applying for federal funds to upgrade substandard housing and to construct new apartment buildings for low-income and senior citizen residents.

In April 1966 the City Council launched a plan to expand and renovate Carver Park, the first project in a city-wide campaign to upgrade small neighborhood parks. Situated on Clay Street between First and Second

Streets in the heart of the predominantly black Third Ward, its basketball court and small recreational structure had had long been popular hangouts for young men. The city applied for grants of $105,325 from New Jersey's state Green Acres Program and $110,323 from the U.S. Housing and Urban Development Department's Open Space Program to expand tiny Carver Park into a three-acre recreational facility. The city's share of the cost would be less than $5,000. The Carver Park plan called for the municipal government to purchase 2.2 acres of land, remove ten buildings, and relocate twelve families, two other residents, and one small business. Three structures were in very poor condition, but most of the buildings targeted for demolition showed only limited signs of minor deterioration. The renovation would feature a playground for preschool children, a hard-surface area for basketball, volleyball, tennis, and shuffleboard, a "passive recreation" area with tree-shaded paths and benches, and a small building with bathroom facilities and a meeting room. Mayor Nowakowski acknowledged that the project would inevitably require the displacement of some citizens, but he promised that his administration would see that "persons affected are given every attention and assistance possible in making their relocation as convenient as possible."

While some of the town's black leaders had previously called for upgrading minority neighborhoods in 1964 when Hackensack's officials prepared the CAP report, sentiment had shifted dramatically by the spring and summer of 1966.. At City Council meetings Third Ward residents blasted away at the Carver plan. Their hostile reaction effectively killed not only the Carver Park project, but also any other city plans for neighborhood parks and recreational facilities. Black leaders and citizens complained that all of the displaced families were Negro and that because of their race they would have a very difficult time finding decent housing in Hackensack. They also pointed out that three of the seven houses designated for destruction were owned by elderly couples. Wells Manning, a community leader, stressed the inequity inherent in the plan: "I'm opposed to uprooting people—homeowners or tenants—in this fashion. They've been here years, and it's not fair to move them. This is what we've been fighting all along—the unfairness of these programs, whether you call it urban renewal or community renewal or Green Acres." Howard Williams added that the proposed preschool playground also raised a concern about the safety of the children, because it would be located at the northwest corner of Clay and First Streets—one of the city's busiest street intersections.

The Carver Park episode demonstrated that Hackensack's black leaders were willing and able to block projects proposed by the city that threatened to have negative effects on their residents. They were equally determined to resist efforts by outsiders who visited Hackensack to stir up support for more militant action. As my classmate Kenny Dixon told me, Hackensack's black people viewed their city as unique, a place that they would defend against outsiders, whether they were agitators or just young men looking for women to date:

> You couldn't come into our town and start anything, we defended it to the bitter end; matter of fact, black guys who wanted to come and visit some black girls from Hackensack basically had to ask permission to come into the town. Paterson never came into this town and overran it; Passaic never came into this town and overran it; Englewood never came into this town.

Dixon recalled that when members of militant groups like the Black Panthers came to Hackensack's playgrounds to promote violence and race revolution, the residents rejected them and their message. He remembered "a real togetherness; you knew everyone; everyone knew everyone else." Outside agitators were not welcome. When race riots exploded in many cities during the summer of 1967, including Newark in July, there were rumblings of discontent a few miles away in the ghetto blocks of Englewood. Hackensack's Third Ward remained calm.

During the 1960s Hackensack's businessmen worked hard to improve the economy of the downtown district. More vacant stores provided evidence of Main Street's continuing ordeal; in the summer of 1966 sixteen stores near the courthouse stood empty, including several that had been without a tenant for five years. While the town's retail sales continued to grow, the rate of increase lagged behind that of Paramus and other Bergen County and northern New Jersey cities. The popularity of the giant shopping malls partially explains Hackensack's sluggish performance, but internal problems were also contributing factors, especially for the stores located at the lower (southern) end of Main Street, near the Bergen County Courthouse. Among these challenges were the competition from Hackensack's own department stores at the northern end of Main Street and on Route 4; traffic and parking problems; repellant vistas that greeted motorists as they entered and exited the city. the shabbiness of the downtown district with a growing number of aging and dilapidated buildings; merchant rivalry; burdensome local taxes; and rising rents. Moreover, too many of the businessmen were unable or unwilling to offer quality merchandise at reasonable prices, and some were reluctant to adopt such retailing innovations as charge accounts and installment plans.

Hackensack's businessmen responded to these challenges in a number of ways, with at best only mixed results. A few of the merchants at the lower end of Main Street coped with the decline of business by relocating to the north. Willner's clothing store headed uptown after forty-eight years at its original spot, followed by the owners of Freeman's, who relocated after a half-century at two addresses downtown. Also, the police tried to alleviate traffic congestion by cracking down on teenagers who were "cruising the street" in their cars rather than shopping at the stores. Officers issued a warning to offending youths; if they were caught a second time, they would receive a summons for an appearance before the municipal court judge (with Harold Vasios as clerk and my father as City Prosecutor) and/or a fine. Parking remained a perennial problem, although by the mid-1960s the municipal government had assembled and purchased land to open five city-owned lots, and there were also a few private commercial facilities. Meters were installed in all of the municipal lots except for one that utilized parking attendants to collect fees. About half of Main Street's merchants could afford to pay for free parking by reimbursing shoppers or by providing off-street spaces behind or adjacent to their stores. The remaining shops, mostly at the southern end, either had no vacant land nearby or had public meters in the rear of their shops. Virtually every block contained some free parking and in many cases customers could actually park closer to their destinations than they could at the malls.

Many Main Street merchants invested in improvements. Construction projects ranged from installation of new fixtures to thorough renovations of interiors and exteriors. Merchandizing policies featured more attractive window and store displays of inventory, more personal customer relations (including a greater willingness to allow customers to look at merchandise without being accompanied by a salesperson), fair and consistent sales practices, extended weeknight hours, more free parking, and installment buying and credit accounts. Many of Hackensack's stores participated in the Community Charge Plan, which permitted customers to charge purchases at any member store in Bergen and Passaic counties. The account holder would then pay only one combined bill each month, with no fees or interest applied if the full amount was paid within thirty days. Individual proprietors regularly scheduled sales of discounted merchandise and ran advertisements in newspapers—especially the *Record*, the only daily in Bergen County. Merchants also joined together for collective advertising campaigns for the Christmas holiday season and regularly scheduled January and July seasonal festival sales.

The Bergen County Chamber of Commerce also supported the town's commercial community. The county organization attracted new industry to the city, improved transit facilities, and built better roads and recreational facilities. Hackensack's Chamber in 1967 developed a $30,000 Hackensack Endorses Progress (HEP) monthly promotional drive that featured fashion shows, sidewalk sale days, art and auto shows, contests with prizes for shoppers, and other attractions, all culminating in a huge Christmas festival complete with special holiday lighting and decorations, street caroling, and a Yule contest with a grand prize of an around-the-world trip for two. Merchants enthusiastically backed the new initiative and also were excited by the City Council's willingness to begin the preliminary work on the long-awaited Lower Main Street Urban Renewal Project.

Several affluent business leaders believed that entrepreneurs should take the lead in urban renewal through the development of private ventures. David Gelber, a local attorney, announced in 1967 that he intended to invest half a million dollars in a new three-story, 27,000 square foot office building. The *Record* called Gelber's proposal another example of his "continuing 1-man urban renewal project for the Lower Main Street area." He told a reporter: "My main intent is to improve the area so it may be used as a productive asset to the City." Gelber had a personal stake in the long-term economic viability of the downtown district; he already owned office buildings at 55 and 57 Main Street and was currently erecting another at 53 Main Street.

The demolition of large one-family homes and several mansions and their replacement by high-rise apartment buildings transformed the cityscape of the upscale hilltop section of Hackensack in the 1960s. The bulldozing of old and in some cases historic homes to make room for modern residential multi-story structures affected only a relatively small area of the city, but the change significantly altered the town's image. The streets most affected were Overlook Avenue (one block long, just west of Hackensack High School), Beech Street (between First Street and Prospect Avenue), and Prospect Avenue between Central Avenue and Passaic Street.

When the guys were growing up in the 1950s we often walked or rode our bikes along these streets, especially if our destination was Richie's house at 130 Prospect Avenue. A few blocks to the north were several sprawling, multi-acre estates—actual mansions with half-a-dozen bedrooms and bathrooms. Some even had carriage houses in the rear, the size of my family's house on Heath Place. The most famous of these was the William Brewster estate, at 300 Prospect Avenue. We and countless other Hackensack kids fantasized about life behind its front gates. Sometimes, late at night, it seemed haunted by ghosts. No one dared go there on Halloween.

The Brewster mansion was built in the 1920s and renovated in 1938 by one of the principal contractors for the George Washington Bridge. Though back in the day we never got inside, today we have descriptions of its grandeur that were published when it was demolished. Within its walls were a two-lane bowling alley; a movie room; a magnificently paneled dining room; a parlor; a library; and an ultra-modern kitchen with two walk-in refrigerators. A spiral back staircase rose from the kitchen area to the servant quarters on the third level. One of the family bathrooms had a Turkish bath cabinet that encased your body, exposing only your head. The mansion also had marble door trim, lead drain pipes, stained glass windows, a laundry chute, and electric buzzers to summon servants. Out back a large garage equipped with automatic motorized door openers housed automobiles and had space for an office. Behind the mansion and garage winding paths guided strollers past an ornamental pool, a wishing well, and well-kept scenic gardens.

But the Brewster mansion and property were showing signs of neglect and disrepair when the City Council granted one of the first variances in this pricey neighborhood for the construction of a high-rise building at 280 Prospect Ave, on the south side of the Brewster estate. Guidera and

Goodman, the firm that pioneered the real estate revolution in Hackensack, named the eleven-story apartment building "The Whitehall" in the rather tacky tradition of applying ostentatious, status-seeking European-sounding labels to apartment buildings. The Whitehall featured central heating and air-conditioning, an oval driveway to the front entrance, a spacious and easily accessible underground garage, and a large outdoor swimming pool bordered by sun deck, lawns and gardens. Prices ranged from $6,327 for a three-room apartment to $10,488 for a six-room layout. The Whitehall opened in the spring of 1961. One year later Rich's father rented space there for his medical office, and a few months later the whole family moved into another apartment a few floors above. That marked the end of our use of Rich's driveway for basketball and backyard for other games and bull sessions. But we were about to graduate from high school anyway. Dr. Prager sold the family homestead to a chiropractor. That house was demolished during the 1970s, and its land became part of the property assembled for the construction of the southern tower of the Excelsior buildings, diagonally across the street from my apartment in the "Eiffel Tower."

In 1966 Hackensack's Planning Board prepared a new zoning code for consideration by the town's City Council—the first major change in that ordinance since 1956. It acted in part because in May 1966 the U.S. government mandated revisions in the city's zoning laws to facilitate the implementation of the town's 1965 Land Use Plan, which it had submitted as part of its Community Renewal Program. The Planning Board recommended expanding the high-rise apartment zones in the hilltop section to include both sides of Prospect Avenue from Essex to Passaic Streets, both sides of Summit Ave from Essex Street to Beech Street, and properties fronting on Morningside Place and Overlook Avenue. According to Chief Building Inspector Wilbur H. Lind, the Planning Board wished to encourage high-rise apartment buildings in that district partly out of fear that the existing spacious private houses and manor-style residences could no longer be sold, and thus might be converted to four or five family dwellings or rooming houses. That in turn might soon lead to urban blight and a precipitous drop in property values and tax revenues. Town officials believed that luxury apartments were also desirable because they generated higher tax revenues overall. They also placed relatively lighter financial pressures on school budgets because the owners or renters of apartments tended to be older "empty-nester" senior citizens with grown children.

During the fall of 1966 irate homeowners organized a campaign to oppose the expansion of the high-rise zones. They suggested that the Planning Board had made corrupt deals with real estate agents and developers who stood to reap large profits from the construction of the high-rise buildings. Opponents of the new zoning code charged that the new apartments would tower over their homes, invade their privacy, ruin their property values, and endanger their children through the increase in traffic. By the beginning of 1967 they had accepted luxury high-rise buildings on

Prospect Avenue, but renewed the fight by targeting the proposal for high-rise apartments on Summit Avenue. They circulated a pamphlet that announced: "We settled in Hackensack to get away from the congestion, the crime, and the noise of the big city. Don't let the City Council destroy your homes... .Save your property! Protect your investment." A leader of the opposition proclaimed: "We don't want Hackensack turned into another Bronx." Another declared "We don't want our city turned into a concrete jungle." But other homeowners argued that rezoning Summit Avenue would be good for all of Hackensack's citizens. They predicted that property values would be doubled; ratables derived from apartment houses would raise more than seven times the taxes for the city; and as a result the tax burden on homeowners would decrease. For example, the property tax on the site of the Whitehall was formerly only $1,116; but since it opened the yearly tax paid to the city had risen to more than $84,000.

In July 1967 Mayor Nowakowski and the City Council approved the controversial new zoning code, maintaining the provision for future high-rise apartment buildings on both sides of Summit Avenue between Essex and Beech Streets, while incorporating a few changes. The revised ordinance kept the four corners of Summit and Passaic Streets under the one-family residential, 75 feet frontal zoning category, increased the parking requirement in the new high-rise buildings from 1.3 to 1.5 spaces per unit, expanded frontage setbacks from 25 to 40 feet, enlarged the minimum sizes of side yards, and limited a building's land coverage to only thirty percent of its lot. Perhaps most telling were remarks by Councilman Leverett, the first black to serve on that body, who resented the implication by some of the plan's opponents that it would result in an influx of minority groups into Hackensack. He argued that inaction by the governments of Newark and Paterson had compounded the problems of those cities, whereas proactive action by Hackensack's City Council would enable the town to avoid those problems.

As the construction of luxury high-rise apartment buildings transformed the landscape of Prospect Avenue between Essex and Passaic Avenues during the 1960s and 1970s, Summit Avenue enhanced its reputation as the preferred address for the town's wealthier residents. Because the City Council later decided not to permit high-rise buildings on that street, most of the private homes on the blocks between Essex and Central were converted into offices for physicians affiliated with nearby Hackensack Hospital. The largest and most elegant homes still stretched north of Central Avenue to Spring Valley Road, on both sides of the street.

During the 1960s Hackensack's Jewish community followed the example of many downtown Protestant and Catholic churches that moved their houses of worship to accommodate their members' migration. Hackensack's upwardly mobile Jewish families were relocating to the new high-rise apartments on Prospect Avenue or more upscale houses along Summit Avenue and in the Fairmount section at the north end of town. The officers of the Hackensack Hebrew Institute recognized the new trends in the residential distribution of its 350 families. In October 1966 Rabbi Jacob Kleinman and officers and members of the synagogue burned the mortgage on its building at the corner of State and Myer Streets, symbolically marking the end of an era that began in the early 1900s. Next, the HHI raised funds for a new modern edifice on Summit Avenue at the corner of Golf Place (just a few blocks from the Kirsch homestead on Heath Place). Plans for the new structure included a combined auditorium and ballroom, classrooms, conference rooms, a kitchen, offices, and an expandable sanctuary to accommodate attendance for High Holiday Services. It also featured stained glass windows depicting the Tribes of Israel. The congregation held a ground-breaking ceremony in June 1968 and dedicated their new building in 1971. It retained its religious affiliation with Conservative Judaism but also renamed itself Temple Beth-El.

As my father's businesses prospered during the 1960s, he also achieved professional success and recognition as a lawyer, City Prosecutor, and Municipal Court Magistrate. After he earned his law degree from NYU in the summer of 1964 it did not take him long to establish himself in Hackensack's legal community and its municipal government. A friend, Arthur Lesemann, rented him a room in his suite of offices. He opened a small practice even as he ran his small chain of bridal and junior women's wear stores. He gained experience through part-time employment with an up-and-coming young attorney and fellow member of the Hackensack Chamber of Commerce, Seymour ("Sy") Chase. When Sy traveled to Europe for his summer vacations he hired my dad to oversee his law practice while he was away. After Sy was appointed City Attorney by Mayor Nowakowski in 1965 he needed help with his municipal cases, so he hired him as a part-time assistant to represent the city in municipal court. In May 1966 Nowakowski appointed my father to serve as City Prosecutor for a one year term. The city's policy was to rotate that post among local attorneys, so in the spring of 1967 my father received an honorary plaque commending his "devotion and dedication" and thanking him for his "personal desire that justice be done; that the rights of the individual be upheld; that the dignity of the judicial processes be maintained." But he earned the respect of prominent politicians who opposed Nowakowski's faction and returned to public office in May 1969 when a rival group triumphed in the municipal election. The new Mayor, Kasmir Wysocki, appointed him City Prosecutor, this time for a two year term.

As City Prosecutor and as Municipal Court Magistrate beginning in 1971, my father benefited enormously from the expertise and advice of Barry's father, Harold Vasios, clerk of the Violations Office and the Municipal Court. Harold and Nate had known each other for a decade through my friendship with Barry, so it was not surprising that they bonded so well together. Harold was strict but helpful to those who had received a summons to appear in court. "One has to have patience and be a good listener to handle traffic violators," he told the *Record* in 1961, adding: "They all come in and tell you their problems." After Harold died in 2011 at the age of 93, his son Barry remembered him as "a frustrated lawyer," recalling: "He always talked about the judges he worked with, the kind of cases that would come up in court. My brother and I got a real feeling from him about not just the law, but about the lawyers appearing before the judges." Harold also assisted my dad in implementing an innovative policy that my father initiated, which required that persons convicted of drunk driving participate in Alcoholics Anonymous meeting. Harold also worked closely with City Attorney Sy Chase, who remembered him as a hard worker with a great attitude, very competent and an all-around "good guy."

In 1973 my parents bought two "statement" houses that symbolized their ascent into the town's upper class. They sold their Heath Place house to my brother and sister-in-law, who were raising their three young daughters, and they purchased an elegant three-story home at 565 Summit Avenue. The dining room had a hand-painted mural of pastoral scenes, there was a paneled library and sun porch, and a grand, winding staircase to the second floor and four bedrooms. A back staircase rose from the rear of the kitchen to the second level, and continued up to the third floor, which had servant's quarters of a small bedroom and bath, plus plenty of storage space. The finished basement had a dart board, full-size billiard table, and a wet bar. The previous owner, an elderly and infirm woman, had installed an elevator that ran from the basement to the upper stories. A three-car detached garage stood at the rear of the backyard, in front of a wooded area that extended down a steep slope to the Maywood border. Known locally as "Borg's Woods," this property was a nature preserve, with subdivision and development prohibited. That restriction enhanced both my parents' privacy and the value of the property.

My parents could also afford a summer vacation home. After looking at properties in the mountains of western New Jersey and the Poconos as well as beach houses on the Jersey shore and on eastern Long Island, they bought a house on Crescent (or "C") Street in Seaview on Fire Island. It was a two story wooden frame structure situated about one hundred yards from the Atlantic Ocean on the south side of the island. My dad also bought a small cabin cruiser for boating, fishing, and clamming. My mother was not thrilled by his choice of a summer residence, for she remained a New York City lover throughout her life. She spent her happiest summer days at Fire Island when she entertained her former students from Julia Richmond High School there after her retirement from teaching in 1972. My father loved sun bathing and reading on the beach, swimming in the ocean, boating, and digging up clams and mussels on the Great South Bay, playing with his grandchildren on the beach or the deck behind the kitchen, and walking a few blocks to the village of Ocean Beach for dinner or ice cream cones. Each winter for the remaining twenty-five years of his life he looked forward to opening up his Seaview house in April.

Judge James I. Toscano swearing in my father, Nathan S. Kirsch, as Magistrate of Hackensack's Municipal Court. My mother, Anne R. Kirsch, holds the Bible.

13. Susan and Columbia

The dark clouds of a deteriorating economy, rising rates of crime and drug addiction, a dysfunctional public school system, and an ineffective and nearly bankrupt municipal government that hovered over New York City in early September of 1967 did not dampen the spirits of Marty Leeds and me as we moved into a small one-bedroom ("junior three") apartment in the "Victoria," a high-rise apartment building at 7 East Fourteenth Street in Manhattan. We were ready for graduate school and were excited about the prospects of meeting attractive young women. After all, you did not need an Ivy League diploma to decode the message on the cover of *Cosmopolitan* magazine. Manhattan was at the epicenter of the new lifestyle of "Sex and the Single Girl," and Marty and I were eager to explore the possibilities.

That very week as I walked into one of the Victoria's elevators I found myself facing a young woman wearing a University of Michigan sweatshirt. At that precise moment I recalled that Tom Lieder, one of my Cornell roommates, had given me the names of a few girls from his hometown who had just moved to Manhattan after their graduation from the University of Michigan. I blurted out, "You must be Jackie Sand, from Shaker Heights." What were the odds that she was that person? A hundred thousand to one? A million to one? Amazingly, she *actually was* Jackie Sand. She stared at me, dumbfounded—and a little freaked out. I explained that Tom was our mutual friend and then she realized who I was. Jackie then invited me and Marty to a party she and two of her roommates had planned for September 19 to celebrate the twenty-first birthday of the fourth person in their apartment, Susan Lavitt.

Susan was a smart, cute, lively young woman who had grown up in the affluent Kings Point section of Great Neck, on the north shore of Long Island. It was not exactly love at first sight—Susan had recently broken up with a boyfriend who was a law student at Michigan, and I still missed my Cornell girlfriend who had sailed off to France for a year. Marty and I enjoyed hanging out at our new friends' apartment (just three stories above our place) and getting to know all four of them. I was shy about asking her out on a Saturday night, but when she started appearing unannounced at our door with some lame request or just to say hello I became emboldened. On our first real date, in early December, we saw the romantic *Elvira Madigan* at the arty Cinema One on the Upper East Side. The evening had begun awkwardly when Susan spilled the contents of her purse on Fourteenth Street as we walked to the Lexington Avenue subway. We laughed as we scooped up her makeup, wallet, keys, tissues, and other assorted girl stuff. After perhaps three or four more dates over the next two weeks I was lovesick, to the point that while visiting my parents during Christmas vacation I could not stop thinking about her. Luckily she seemed to feel the same way about me, and in January we knew it was the real thing. She was The Girl.

George and Susan in love, 1968

I plunged into graduate work in U.S. history at Columbia. Although I had been awarded a financially generous merit four-year Faculty Fellowship, only the first year was guaranteed. I was one of about 150 candidates for a Master's degree (although I was one of only a dozen students with full financial aid). A committee of Columbia's History faculty would decide whether I would continue as a doctoral candidate after I received my Master's degree. My courses included a seminar in which each student began preliminary work on a thesis. By chance I was assigned to a section taught by a young scholar of early America, Alden Vaughan. Thus I was required to choose a topic on the colonial or Revolutionary periods of U.S. history. Given my prior study of American literature at Cornell, I looked for a topic in literary or cultural history or American Studies.

I wrote my Masters thesis during the spring term of 1968. Entitled "The American Revolution in Early American Fiction," it was a study of the first attempts by American novelists to interpret the political and cultural meaning of the colonists' break with Great Britain. I examined a few sentimental and didactic works, a political allegory by Jeremy Belknap, *The Foresters*, and several tales by James Fenimore Cooper, including *The Spy: A Tale of the Neutral Ground*. Today my eighty-page essay reads like an archetypal example of the old-fashioned literary approach to American Studies, which was discredited in the 1980s and replaced by sociological and anthropological interpretations of American culture, which were in turn challenged by deconstructionist theories of literature. But my Master's research did provide me with a topic for my doctoral dissertation—a biography of the revolutionary war Patriot preacher, pioneer historian and man of letters, Jeremy Belknap.

As a candidate for a Master's in U.S history I enrolled in small classes offered by professors who ranked among the most accomplished teachers and scholars in the country. They included James Shenton for the Age of Jackson, Stuart Bruchey for American Economic History, and Eric McKitrick for the era of Civil War and Reconstruction. Shenton was a legendary character who was beloved by both undergraduates and graduate students for his passion for his subjects and his engaging and entertaining teaching style. A bachelor, he enjoyed entertaining a select few of them at restaurants after class and on weekends. He had gained tenure despite a rather meager record of publications. Bruchey was more of a scholar. Modest and soft-spoken, he had the gift of making a dry and difficult subject interesting. I admired McKitrick the most because of his intellect and command of the political, economic, military, social, and cultural aspects of U.S. history from the American Revolution to the late nineteenth century. I also thoroughly enjoyed taking two semesters of Nineteenth Century American Literature (reviewing texts I had read at Cornell) in preparation for my minor field in my doctoral oral examination.

Sports remained an important part of my life, both as a recreational athlete and as an avid fan of collegiate and especially professional sports. Marty Leeds and I journeyed up to Central Park for pickup touch football in the fall and softball in the spring. In the winter at Columbia I continued my Cornell habit of going to the college gym to play basketball. On many Saturday mornings I traveled to a dorm at Cornell's Medical College on the East Side, where I knew a few medical students who could get me into their game in the basement court. On other Saturdays Barry Cohen came into the city and we took a subway to Downstate Medical College in Brooklyn, where we played basketball with Richard and a few of his classmates in a brand-new facility.

In September 1967 I was captivated by the pennant drive of the Boston Red Sox "Impossible Dream" team, which trailed the Minnesota Twins by one game with two contests remaining against them, scheduled for the final weekend of the season. The Red Sox won both and finished one game ahead of both the Twins and the Detroit Tigers, who cooperated by losing their final two games. Incredibly, the Boston Red Sox had won the American League championship after finishing ninth in 1966. My euphoria was diminished only slightly by the Cardinals' seven-game victory over the Red Sox in the World Series, despite a stellar performance by the triple crown winner, Carl Yastrzemski ("Yaz"), and a supporting cast that featured Ken Harrelson in right field, Reggie Smith in center field, Rico Petrocelli at shortstop, and Jim Lonborg on the mound. It was the second time that the Cardinals had defeated the Red Sox in the deciding game of the World Series.

In February I met Susan's parents for the first time. Her father, Julian Lavitt, was the son of a lawyer who had barely survived financial ruin during the Great Depression of the 1930s. A Phi Beta Kappa graduate from the City College of New York (class of 1936—a few years ahead of my father), he earned an M.BA (with distinction) from Harvard Business School in 1938. He then began a long career with Interstate Department Stores, interrupted by three years of military service. A Naval Supply Officer (Lieutenant JG) from October 1943 to January 1946, he spent several months on a supply ship in the Pacific during World War II. After his honorable discharge he rose through the executive ranks at Interstate, becoming president of Interstate's White Front Division in 1968, a promotion that required him and his wife Lorraine (Lolly) to relocate to Los Angeles, where they rented a house in the Hollywood Hills..

The move proved troublesome to Lolly. A graduate of New York University with a degree in nutrition, she had been a housewife for most of their marriage, primarily because Julian did not want her to work at a paid job. A bright woman who was not content with housekeeping and raising her daughters, she was a prototype of the frustrated woman that Betty Friedan profiled in *The Feminine Mystique*. Lolly had found some satisfaction (and self-esteem) in volunteer work in her Great Neck temple's Sisterhood and Hadassah organizations, serving as president of both organizations. But she could not transfer her hard-earned seniority to the Jewish community of Beverly Hills. She was frustrated that she had to start all over to earn the respect of her peers and a leadership position in her new community.

By the spring of 1968 Susan was enjoying her independence and had adjusted to her parents' relocation to the West Coast. Although she was a year younger than I (and thus a true "baby boomer"), she had completed her B.A. at Michigan as an economics major in only three years, because of extra credits earned at Michigan and at summer sessions of Adelphi University on Long Island. She chose economics not because of any passion for the subject, but because Julian insisted that she major in a subject that might have some practical value in landing her a job after graduation.

In Manhattan Susan followed the advice of her older sister Louise and looked for a position in the new field of computer programming. Louise was also a graduate of the University of Michigan, and in 1965 she had married her college boyfriend Richard (Rick) Crandall, an entrepreneur who had founded a very successful company that enabled small and middle-size companies to share time on large mainframe computers. Louise had mastered the basics of computer programming and gave Susan a practice test to help her prepare for interviews at employment agencies. On one of her first appointments Susan was given the same test that Louise had shown her. To avoid suspicion Susan marked a few incorrect responses on the answer sheet. The supervisor was so impressed by Susan's aptitude that she placed her in an entry-level position as a programmer for Sealtest Foods. Her office was on the northwest corner of Fifth Avenue and Forty-Second Street, diagonally across the street from the main branch of the New York Public Library. Susan's first job was right in the heart of midtown Manhattan—a shopper's paradise during her lunch hour.

1968 would certainly make any historian's list of the top ten worst years in American history. It witnessed the deepening abyss and horror of the Vietnam War, two shocking political assassinations, race riots, student disorders, bitter partisan tensions in a presidential election campaign, increasing demands by feminists, and cultural turmoil. There seemed to be an unending stream of "bad news on the doorstep."

The year began with some cautious optimism by the Johnson administration concerning progress by U.S. and South Vietnamese military forces against North Vietnamese invaders and Viet Cong insurgents. But those hopes were dashed by the Tet Offensive launched by the communists on January 31. The battles raged for several months and included a Viet Cong assault on the U.S. Embassy in Saigon. Although U.S. and South Vietnam troops ultimately prevailed, the Tet Offensive profoundly undermined public confidence in President Johnson's management of the Vietnam War.

Reports of casualties suffered by American soldiers included heart breaking news for Sylvia Lewis's family. When Sylvia's mother, Clara, saw Navy officers in full dress uniform approach her window she knew that her worst nightmare had just become a reality. Her son Stanley, a lieutenant and naval flight surgeon serving in a hospital unit in South Vietnam, had been killed in a rocket attack on a bunker in Chu Lai on the first day of the Tet Offensive. When Sylvia called to tell me the grim news my first thoughts were whether her mother would once again be able to summon the strength to cope with yet another family tragedy. More than a decade earlier she had suffered the loss of another son and her middle-age husband.

I called my friends to convey the chilling news. Stan's death provided a sobering reminder that we might also be called to duty in Vietnam, since graduate school deferments from the draft had just been abolished. I took a bus to Hackensack on a cold February afternoon to pay a condolence call to Sylvia and her mom, at Clara's apartment on American Legion Drive, one block from the high school. After about an hour's conversation with Clara, during which we discussed developments in my life as a diversion from the sad news about Stan, Sylvia and I took a long walk in the freezing cold around the local streets. All I could do was stammer some lame comments about how proud they must be of Stan's achievements in his all-too-short life. We all understood that his death was a tragic waste of a brilliant young man—a Cornell graduate with an M.D. from Albert Einstein College of Medicine—in a senseless war. I knew that given Sylvia's spirit she would find some way of comforting her mother and sister, Harriet.

In March the antiwar movement got a boost from the candidacy of Senator Eugene McCarthy of Minnesota for the Democratic Party's nomination for the presidency in the November election. Although Johnson defeated McCarthy in the New Hampshire primary, his surprisingly narrow margin of victory (49 to 42 percent) demonstrated both the credibility of McCarthy's campaign and the incumbent president's shaky support. Johnson soon faced an even more formidable opponent a few days after the New Hampshire primary, when Senator Robert F. Kennedy of New York entered the race. McCarthy's devoted volunteer corps of liberals and college students (including many young men who shaved their beards and cut their long hair to "Get Clean for Gene") were enraged that Kennedy entered the fray only after McCarthy had exposed Johnson's vulnerability. After my dad decided to enter the New Jersey Democratic Party's primary election in June as a McCarthy delegate I volunteered to help out with door-to-door canvassing (but I did not shave off my mustache).

On March 31 Johnson delivered an address to the nation in which he announced the suspension of bombing in North Vietnam, along with plans for peace negotiations that would include delegates from both North Vietnam and the National Liberation Front (Viet Cong). At the very end of his somber talk he stunned the American people by announcing that he would not seek another term as president of the United States. Shortly after Johnson's withdrawal Vice President Hubert Humphrey entered the competition for the Democratic presidential nomination. He did not enter the primaries, counting on longtime party supporters to act as surrogate "favorite son" candidates in several states. They pledged their delegates to Humphrey in the Democratic National Convention.

Just a few days later, on April 4, 1968, the American nation sustained another shock when James Earl Ray shot and killed Martin Luther King Jr. in Memphis. Robert Kennedy delivered a moving tribute to King shortly after he learned of his death, urging all to honor King's commitment to nonviolence as they mourned his passing. But despite Kennedy's pleas for restraint, rage engulfed many black communities and exploded into rioting, most notably in Washington, Baltimore, Louisville, and Kansas City. Given the black uprisings in Newark and Detroit the previous summer, New York residents feared a renewal of racial tensions and perhaps widespread disorders. But except for a few local incidents, most of the city remained calm. Moderate leaders of the black community urged respect for King's message and legacy of nonviolent resistance to injustice, but more radical activists urged blacks to arm themselves for protection and to gain their rights by force if necessary.

A few weeks after the King riots a different kind of rebellion broke out in Morningside Heights, on the campus of Columbia University. Several groups of militant students, including members of Students for a Democratic Society (SDS) and black undergraduates, orchestrated a series of demonstrations and occupations of buildings that precipitated a major crisis for the university's President, Grayson Kirk, and its administration and Board of Trustees. The antiwar petition that Mark Green, I, and other congressional interns had organized in Washington the previous summer paled in comparison to the tactics and goals of the SDS crowd in April 1968.

Student activist Mark Rudd and other members of Columbia's chapter of SDS viewed themselves as a different breed of revolutionaries than the "Old Left" Marxists of the Great Depression and post-World War II eras. The "New Left" of the 1960s had little interest in the fine points of communist or socialist ideology. They also dismissed the examples of the Soviet Union and the People's Republic of China as irrelevant to the American experience. They portrayed the United States as a hypocritical and sick society, supposedly founded on the principles of morality, justice, democracy, freedom and equality for all, but actually ruled by power-hungry politicians and greedy capitalists and imperialists who exploited the poor at home and aimed at world domination abroad. For SDS only a true revolution, and not liberal piecemeal reform, would restore "power to the people" and cure the ills of this country.

The "radicalization" of students like me was an essential part of Rudd's plan for radical action at Columbia. In a "position paper" he wrote in the fall of 1967, he estimated that over half of Columbia's students were against the war, but believed "we will need real organizational strength to mobilize these people."

Rudd and his fellow SDS revolutionaries believed that major universities like Columbia played a central role in a conspiracy of the ruling class to maintain their power at home and extend America imperialism around the globe. They focused on four issues. The first was local—Columbia's plan to build a new gymnasium on public land adjacent to the campus in Morningside Park. SDS knew that black community leaders from Harlem strenuously opposed this project, in part because of the stipulation that the new facility would have a separate entrance and limited hours for local residents who were not Columbia students. Second, SDS demanded that Columbia sever all its ties with the federal government's Institute for Defense

Analysis (IDA), a think tank created in 1956 as a private nonprofit corporation that provided grants to leading universities for research on matters of national security. Third, the radicals called for Columbia to cut off all support for the Vietnam War by prohibiting campus recruiting by the Central Intelligence Agency and by Reserve Officer Training Corps (ROTC) units. Finally, SDS sought a democratization of the university through a reformed governmental system that would give much more power to faculty and students. In short, SDS attacked Columbia University as an evil institution that facilitated injustice at home and American imperialism and militarism overseas. In a manifesto the organization added a personal explanation of their motivation: "We can point to. . .our meaningless studies, our identity crises, and our revulsion to being cogs in your corporate machines as a product of and reaction to a basically sick society." In mocking liberals (like me) they chanted: "Work, Study, Get Ahead, Kill."

The student demonstrations at Columbia began on April 23. Early that day police drove the activists away from the gymnasium's construction site in Morningside Park. Soon afterward university security guards denied them access to the President's office in Low Library. Three hundred chanting protesters then occupied Hamilton Hall. They seized Henry S. Coleman, Dean of Columbia College, as a hostage and barricaded themselves in his office. About sixty black students joined them, claiming that they represented Harlem community leaders who opposed the construction of the gymnasium. However, the black contingent was uncomfortable sharing the occupation with the white radicals, partly because they questioned their degree of commitment to the cause, and partly because their social class and racial backgrounds were poles apart. (Many if not most of the Columbia SDS crowd were from middle-class suburban Jewish families, while most of the black militants were raised in the ghetto.) A few days later the SDS group left Hamilton Hall to join hundreds of protesters who had seized control of Grayson Kirk's office in Low Library, Avery and Fayerweather Halls, and the Mathematics building.

Meanwhile, during these first days of student disorders, hundreds of student counterdemonstrators, including many athletes and members of fraternities, gathered around the occupied buildings. They tried to prevent the delivery of food, water, and other supplies to the radicals who had taken control of the five buildings. Security guards and some faculty members tried to keep the radicals and the opposing groups apart to avoid violence among students. In an effort to diffuse the volatile situation, Columbia's administration temporarily halted construction of the gymnasium, suspended classes, and closed the campus to outsiders. Kirk also authorized faculty committees to attempt mediation of the dispute and to propose reforms in university governance that would give more power to the faculty and students.

The standoff among student activists, counterdemonstrators, university security guards, faculty members, and New York City police lasted one week. Shortly after midnight on April 30 President Kirk officially asked the NYPD to evict all students from the five occupied offices and buildings. To avoid any ugly incidents that might spark a riot in Harlem, the police deployed a special squad of black officers to clear black students from Hamilton Hall, along with black lawyers who were present to provide legal counsel to those who were arrested. The eviction of these black protesters proceeded peacefully, but that was not the case with the removal of the white SDS militants from the other buildings. Police beat and dragged dozens of bloodied and bruised students out to waiting vans. At least 148 of them sustained injuries, most of which were minor, and 720 people were arraigned, mostly on charges of criminal trespassing. The deployment of the police and the arrests stunned the Columbia community but brought a temporary calm to the campus.

Within a few days, police brutality and the treatment of the students by the criminal courts and the university replaced the gymnasium and the Institute for Defense Analysis as the central issues of the crisis. The following week the administration cancelled all classes and final examinations for the remainder of the spring semester, and permitted faculty and students to decide on grading policies for courses. But violence returned to the campus on May 21-22, when new occupations of buildings by SDS prompted another round of police evictions of student protestors and more injuries.

At my safe haven apartment on Fourteenth Street I was physically removed from the battle scenes at the height of the protests. I sympathized with SDS's campaign to stop the construction of the gymnasium and I supported the antiwar message and opposition to the draft. I was indifferent to the fate of Columbia's ties with IDA, but I was agitated by the scenes of police beating up fellow students. On the other hand, I was opposed to the tactics of holding a Dean hostage and occupying administration offices and academic buildings. In principle, I resented how the radicals justified shutting down the university, thereby sacrificing students' rights as a means to achieve their primary goal of undermining the university's role as a pillar of the establishment. On a practical—and somewhat selfish—level, I was annoyed by the inconvenience and uncertainty of cancelled classes and examinations, as well as grading policies. Even though the chaos in May reduced my workload at the end of the semester, I was angry that the SDS crowd demonstrations put in doubt the timely completion of the requirements for my Master's degree.

During the crisis I traveled to campus most days to try to attend classes, most of which did not meet. However, I was able to use the library (which mostly remained open) and I finished my Master's thesis on time. I had a few tense confrontations with radicals when I delivered photocopies of my thesis to my advisor, Alden Vaughan. But I received credit for all my required courses, and I was awarded a Master of Arts degree at the Columbia graduation, on June 4, 1968, which I did not attend. Nor did President Kirk, who was concerned that his presence might cause more trouble. For security reasons the Columbia administration moved its commencement exercises from the traditional location on the steps and Plaza in front of Low Memorial Library to the Cathedral Church of St. John the Divine, a few blocks away. Pulitzer Prize-winning historian Richard Hofstadter replaced Kirk as the leading commencement speaker. Just as he began his remarks about three hundred graduates of the class of 1968 staged a peaceful protest against Columbia's treatment of Harlem residents and its complicity in the Vietnam War. The dissidents filed out of the Cathedral and held a counter-commencement on Low Plaza. They later joined a small group of Harlem residents for a picnic in Morningside Park. About 1,600 candidates for undergraduate and graduate degrees remained in their seats in the Cathedral.

Overall, although SDS did not convert many liberals (like me) into revolutionaries, they did achieve several goals. The gymnasium project was abandoned and Columbia cut its ties with IDA. Grayson Kirk resigned at the end of the summer, and a new system of university governance gave faculty and students more influence over administrative policies and procedures. At least thirty Columbia students were suspended by the administration for their participation in the demonstrations, occupations of buildings, and the damages they caused in offices and classrooms. Mark Rudd was expelled from Columbia and soon thereafter joined the radical Weatherman underground movement. As for Columbia University, over the next few decades the riots of 1968 had a negative impact on admissions, alumni support, and faculty morale. But by 2000 Columbia had reclaimed its rightful place as one of the great educational institutions of the world.

One fine day in June, while lying in bed next to Susan, I whispered in her ear that I thought that we should get married. Not exactly the traditional means of popping the question, but it achieved its objective. Susan said "yes"—or maybe it was just "Really? . . . OK." A few days later she suggested that perhaps we should live together for a while to see if we were compatible enough for a lasting marriage. I thought about it, but decided I wanted a greater commitment. She agreed, and we proceeded to plan our wedding.

Susan was hardworking and compassionate, with many wonderful qualities that elevated her far above the stereotypical Long Island Jewish Princess. But she still expected her parents to pay for a big Jewish wedding, especially since they had provided one for her sister Louise. Time was of the essence, since the draft clouded my future. I was trying to obtain a deferment, but the outcome of my appeal was still very much in doubt. As a backup plan I had applied for a place in the Army Reserves. We thought it would be better for us if we were married before I started my military service, which would probably involve a few months of basic training in a Reserve unit. Fleeing to Canada was still an option as far as I was concerned, but was not appealing to Susan. I told her that if I went into the Army she could live with my parents, but she did not even dignify that idea with an answer. Perhaps subconsciously I feared that if we waited until my return from basic training,

Susan might lose interest in me and find another boyfriend. I did not want to lose her.

We called Susan's parents to share the good news with them. Julian and Lolly were a bit surprised but seemed happy for us. Together we decided on a date that was less than three months away—September 8, 1968. Susan promptly summoned her mother back to New York to help with the wedding arrangements. I tagged along as they visited a few venues in luxury hotels near Central Park, before selecting the Baroque Room at the Plaza.

In mid-July I greeted my mother and father, back from vacation in Europe, when they disembarked from the luxury liner, the SS France. Kevin was also a passenger on that voyage, returning from his year-long Fulbright grant in France. My parents were initially less than thrilled at the news of our wedding, although they had gotten to know Susan at several family events and seemed to like her. Of course it was not unusual for a Jewish mother to be skeptical about her son's choice of a wife, and my mother was no exception. But she and my father did suggest that perhaps we were a little young to get married.

Later in the summer Susan and I flew to Los Angeles for a week's vacation at her parent's rental home in the Hollywood hills overlooking West Los Angeles. It was my first trip to the West Coast, and Los Angeles seemed to me to be a giant version of Nassau County, with its endless stretch of freeways and wide streets designed for automobiles, office skyscrapers in downtown business districts, industrial parks, residential zones of single-family homes and low-rise apartment buildings, shopping centers and strip malls. Julian and Lolly lived a few miles from the upscale shops of Rodeo Drive in Beverly Hills and the mansions of Hollywood producers, directors, and film stars. Susan and I attended parties given by her parents' new friends where the hosts and most of the guests seemed to be transplanted New Yorkers or midwesterners who were obsessed with justifying their relocation to L.A. It amused us that they could not stop talking about how happy they were in their new surroundings and how we should move to the sunshine and good life of the West Coast as soon as possible. We did some sightseeing and even enjoyed Disneyland, but we much preferred New York.

After returning to New York we were excited about the upcoming Democratic National Convention, scheduled for the last week in August in Chicago. My father would be attending as a delegate for Eugene McCarthy, with my mother accompanying him. In June the assassination of Robert F. Kennedy in Los Angeles after his victory in the California Primary profoundly altered the competition for the Democratic Party's presidential nomination. I remained hopeful that McCarthy could still find a way to defeat Humphrey.

The convention attracted thousands of radical activists, many of them college students, gathered to protest the Vietnam War. On Wednesday, August 28, (my twenty-third birthday), Chicago's mayor, Richard J. Daley, ordered the city's police to break up the demonstrations, drive the protesters off the city's streets, and arrest all who resisted. A national television audience witnessed live confrontations between the Chicago cops and dissidents. The crowds chanted "The whole world is watching" as the officers pelted them with tear gas and beat them with clubs, leaving many of the radicals dazed, bloodied, and bruised. On the convention floor Senator Abraham Ribicoff (D., CT) denounced the excesses of Daley's crackdown on the protesters; later the telecast captured the mayor as he angrily cursed Ribicoff in reply.

In the midst of this chaos my mother called me in New York from her hotel room. She was alarmed by the smell of tear gas that was wafting by her window and by the violent clashes on the streets below that I was simultaneously witnessing on my small black and white television. She was also worried sick about the safety of my father, who of course was perfectly secure a few blocks away at the convention center. It was a surreal scene and a bizarre telephone conversation. I tried to calm my mother by distracting her with a reminder that our wedding was just eleven days away. But that just seemed to make her more anxious.

Hubert Humphrey won the Democratic nomination easily that night, but the violent clashes on the streets of Chicago severely damaged his chances of winning the presidency. In the November election Richard M. Nixon, the Republican nominee, edged out Humphrey by a very narrow margin in the popular vote, but piled up a decisive victory in the Electoral College, thanks to the strong showing of the third-party American Independent candidate, the segregationist George Wallace, who won five southern states.

September 8, 1968 was a beautiful day in New York City, with clear blue skies, comfortable temperatures, and low humidity. The rabbi of Susan's Great Neck temple conducted the traditional wedding ceremony. I was nervous about breaking the glass (actually a light bulb) at the ritual's end, but I stomped it to pieces, and the partying began. All of the guys were there, except for Kevin, who was still recovering from illnesses he had contracted just before he returned from France. Susan and I danced to our favorite songs, especially the Supremes' hit "I'm Going to Make You Love Me." We spent our wedding night in another fancy hotel on Central Park South, because I was annoyed that the Plaza's management did not include an overnight room in its wedding package. The next morning we moved our gifts back to our apartment, deposited dozens of checks, and drove out to East Hampton for our honeymoon—a week's stay at the historic "1770 House." The weather was still warm, and the beaches were deserted. It was a romantic way of launching a marriage that lasted for nearly forty years, "for better or for worse, in sickness and in health," until death parted us.

A few weeks before our wedding I received official confirmation that Columbia's Committee on Doctoral Candidates approved my application to complete the requirements for a Ph.D. in History. My Faculty Fellowship ($1,900 to cover tuition and fees plus $2,200 for a living stipend) was also renewed. My second year of graduate work proved to be less stressful than my first, since I only had to pass a few courses each semester, and there was no thesis to write. In the fall I devoted much time and energy to a course taught by Professor Vaughan on Colonial American Puritanism, which turned out to be useful for my dissertation. In the spring I ventured into twentieth century topics with a course on the Progressive Era taught by John Garraty and another on the New Deal offered by Joseph Huthmacher. I got to know Garraty and gained some research experience by contributing to the revised edition of the *Dictionary of American Biography* that he was then editing. Huthmacher was a visiting professor substituting for William Leuchtenburg. His course was worthwhile, but I regretted that I missed the chance to study under Leuchtenburg—one of Columbia's premier professors.

Susan and George, newlyweds at the Plaza Hotel

Guests at the wedding of George and Susan. Clockwise from center couple Dan and Laura Kirsch, Barry Vasios, Ruth Heiferman, Richard, Sylvia Lewis, Betty, Henry, Barry Cohen.

During the spring of 1969 Nixon pursued a dual policy of war and peace talks in Vietnam. To diffuse growing popular frustration and dissatisfaction with American military efforts, he announced a new strategy of Vietnamization, which projected a phased withdrawal of hundreds of thousands of U.S. soldiers, along with increased responsibility by the South Vietnamese government for its national security. But the continuing bombing of North Vietnam, along with stalled peace negotiations, generated renewed protests by both moderates and radicals. In the spring a new round of student demonstrations and occupations of buildings disrupted classes on several college campuses. At Columbia black students renewed their demands for the admission of more African-American students and the expansion of courses and programs in Black Studies. White radicals intensified their campaign against Nixon's prosecution of the Vietnam War. I paid little attention to these incidents and was only slightly annoyed and inconvenienced by disruptions, cancellations, and relocations of classes and final examinations from late April through mid-May, 1969.

Susan and I settled into our first year of marriage in our new apartment in the same building. Living with a person of the opposite sex was new to both of us, and we quickly discovered that it was different than cohabiting with roommates, but we bonded. Susan disliked her job (and especially her female boss) at Sealtest Foods, so she found another at Health Insurance Plan (HIP). Her main task involved programming a lengthy health information questionnaire required for all employees of companies insured by HIP. Her hours were usually not very long, but occasionally on weekends a supervisor would call and summon her to her office to "debug" a program.

For fun we went to concerts and movies, had dinner with friends, or smoked marijuana. We even grew our own plants, but the product we purchased from friends was much more potent than our own crop. Our recreational "drug phase" lasted only about a year or two. Smoking grass never did very much for me. Maybe that was because, like Bill Clinton, I never learned how to inhale.

I remained close to Marty Leeds. After our wedding Marty chose to live alone for another year in our apartment on Fourteenth Street before moving up to a building his father owned on the upper East Side. Marty replaced me with an Irish red setter named "Max," a beautiful dog that needed a lot of exercise and thus was not well suited for the Village environment. I had always loved dogs, but they were banned from the Kirsch household in Hackensack because my mother was terrified of them. So I enjoyed taking Max for a walk around the Union Square neighborhood when Marty was in class or at his internship at a Veterans hospital in East Orange. Max's life improved dramatically when Marty moved uptown, three blocks from lots of running room in Central Park.

For a resident of New York City and a fan of its professional sports teams, the period between 1968 and 1970 was "the worst of times; and the best of times," to borrow a phrase from Charles Dickens. Living conditions in the Big Apple remained pretty miserable during those years, but over a brief fourteen-month period New York teams won championships in three of the four major sports. I was more a Giants than a Jets fan, but in January 1969 I rooted hard for Joe Willie Namath and his teammates from the American Football League to make good on his "guarantee" of an upset victory in Super Bowl III over the mighty Baltimore Colts of the National Football League. After the Jets defeated the Colts euphoria swept across the New York metropolitan region. Nine months later the "Miracle Mets" completed an "Impossible Dream" season that was even more amazing than the one recorded by my beloved 1967 Red Sox. In October 1969 the Mets shocked another Baltimore powerhouse, the Orioles, four games to one, in Major League Baseball's World Series. Laughable incompetents since their comical inaugural season in 1962, the Mets had completed their improbable journey from worst to first in just eight seasons.

Other than the Boston Red Sox, I was emotionally most connected with the New York Knickerbockers of the National Basketball Association. . In March 1969 Marty Leeds and I attended a semifinal playoff game that the Knicks lost to the Boston Celtics, but in the following spring they finally advanced to the championship round against the awesome Los Angeles Lakers, led by its superstars Wilt Chamberlain and Jerry West. In the pivotal fifth game the Knicks weathered a severe knee injury suffered by their captain, Willis Reed, and won the championship in a decisive seventh game at Madison Square Garden. That epic contest began with a heroic first few minutes sparked by a hobbled Reed, who had emerged from the locker room just a few moments before the opening tip-off. A magnificent performance by guard Walt Frazier highlighted the Knicks surprising victory and their first National Basketball Association title. It was the sweetest victory by one of my favorite teams that I had ever enjoyed. I would have to wait until the Red Sox won the 2004 World Series for a more satisfying championship experience.

Even though President Johnson had ordered the end of all graduate student deferments, there was a loophole for me that bought me more time. Because of a delay in my reclassification, any induction notice received during the 1968-69 academic year would be cancelled. So I did not panic when the Hackensack draft board ordered me to report for induction into the Army on December 6, 1968, but I had to sweat for a few weeks until that notice was officially voided. Six months later the Hackensack draft board reclassified me as "available for military service." I immediately filed an appeal and also applied for a place on the waiting lists of a Manhattan Army Reserve unit and a Brooklyn Naval Reserve unit.

Then President Nixon provided some breathing room for me and 10,000 other graduate students when he ordered the Selective Service System to allow us to finish the school year (not just the fall semester) before being inducted into military service. Nixon also suspended the draft for the final two months of 1969 and asked Congress to replace the conscription system with all-volunteer armed forces. While waiting for Congress to act on that proposal he signed a law that established a random selection lottery based on birth dates to determine the order of conscription. All of these actions were Nixon's attempts to reduce student dissent and demonstrations against U.S. involvement in the Vietnam War. In the lottery drawing held on December 1, 1969 my birth date was assigned the number 167. The unofficial projection was that young men with numbers lower than 195 were likely to be called for induction.

So I kept my applications to the Army and Navy Reserve units active, but I also sought reclassification through an occupational deferment, since for the previous eighteen months I had been working as an instructor at the Manhattan Reading Institute (MRI), located on the corner of Fourteenth Street and Seventh Avenue. I taught disabled and disadvantaged adults mathematics, from simple arithmetic through algebra.. The school's Director, Doris C. Schneider, had been one of my mother's colleagues at James Monroe High School in the Bronx. Mrs. Schneider wrote several letters in support of my request for reclassification, arguing that I was performing a vital service in the rehabilitation of the disabled and that "it would be a serious loss to our program should we be deprived of Mr. Kirsch's services."

I was granted appearances before the local Hackensack Selective Service Board on November 6, 1969 and on April 15, 1970. A few days after my final interview I received official notification that the Board had approved my request for a vocational deferment and reclassification into Class II-A. I withdrew my applications to the Reserve units, and breathed a sigh of relief. I could now focus on finishing my requirements for my Ph.D. I wondered at that time whether it was Mrs. Schneider's letters and my testimony that persuaded the Board to rule in my favor, or whether my father's status as City Prosecutor had also influenced the outcome. Years later, when I asked him directly if he had intervened in any way on my behalf, he told me that he had not. But then again, sometimes my dad did not always tell the whole truth.

While I waited for the draft board to rule on my status I completed my course work for my doctorate and studied for my oral examination on my major subject of U.S. history and my minor field of American literature. If I passed that two-hour test, scheduled for December 19, 1969, the History Department would certify me to begin work on my Ph.D. dissertation. I anticipated an intimidating session as four professors fired questions at me on the entire scope of American history and literature.

I had been preparing for this doctoral rite of passage since I began my work for a Master's degree in the fall of 1967. When the long anticipated date finally arrived, I was confident that I knew enough to pass, especially considering the additional knowledge I gained that fall as a teaching assistant for Alden Vaughan in a U.S. history survey in Columbia's School of General Studies.

My committee consisted of Professors Vaughan, McKitrick, Henry Graff, and a specialist in American Literature. Vaughan and McKitrick were professional but also friendly and supportive. The two hours passed very quickly with only a few awkward moments. Graff gave me a hard time on a few questions that dealt with U.S. foreign policy during the 1890s—he did not agree with revisionist interpretations I had learned from LaFeber at Cornell. I sailed through the part on American literature, except for one inquiry about an Emily Dickinson poem. Afterward Professor McKitrick congratulated me on my performance (He told me that I passed with some level of distinction, but I sensed that there was some disagreement about their evaluation of my performance.) I then raced, high on adrenaline, to the Riverside Drive apartment of my classmate Peter Decker to share the good news, before joining Susan at her office Christmas Party.

During the first quarter of 1970 I took a break from graduate work to try my hand at playwriting. My topic was the troubled life of the Pennsylvania abolitionist Thaddeus Stevens, who had a clubfoot and who was rumored to have had an affair with his mulatto housekeeper. But by the middle of March it dawned on me that I had neither the talent nor the inclination to be a successful dramatist, so I got back on track and started searching for a topic for my dissertation. In researching my Master's thesis I had become intrigued by the life of Jeremy Belknap, a Congregational minister in Dover, New Hampshire, who was an active Patriot preacher during the American Revolution. Later he relocated to Boston and became a historian of colonial America and founder of the Massachusetts Historical Society. I was wary of the reputations of several of Columbia's history faculty, who were notorious for neglecting their obligations as sponsors of theses. I asked Professors McKitrick and Vaughan to be my advisors because I believed that I could trust them for guidance, encouragement, and cooperation. Both agreed to supervise my research on Belknap.

Although my decision to write a scholarly biography of Belknap had positive short-term consequences, in the long run it limited my prospects to secure an appointment at a major research university. On the plus side, no one had written a comprehensive academic study of Belknap's life, historical works, and contributions to the field of history. I was eager to start my career in college teaching, and I knew that my Belknap project would be relatively straightforward and could be completed within two years. I thought that at the very least I could mine it for scholarly articles, and with some luck I might find a publisher for it. I was right on both counts—over the next decade I adapted sections of my dissertation for three articles that appeared in *Historical New Hampshire* and the *New England Quarterly,* and Arno Press produced a revised and condensed version in book form in 1982. (It was favorably reviewed, but sold fewer than 500 copies, mostly to libraries and specialists in colonial America.) In the end, my Belknap biography and related journal articles help me gain tenure and promotion at Manhattan College and enhanced my reputation as a scholar of colonial and revolutionary America.

On the other had, my Belknap dissertation was a traditional if not old-fashioned project that would not be viewed as a groundbreaking or pioneering scholarly work in either its subject matter or methodology. It had little relevance for the new field of social history, since it did not delve very deeply into issues of social class, ethnicity, race, or gender. While it would be grounded in archival sources, it would not require statistical analysis of a database. In short, it was a safe research subject but not one that was likely to establish me as a rising young star in the field of American history.

On November 17, 1970 Columbia's American History Faculty Group accepted my proposal for a doctoral thesis on Belknap, so I intensified my research at the Columbia library, the New York Public Library, and the extensive Belknap collections at the Massachusetts Historical Society (MHS) in Boston. On my monthly three-day trips to Boston I boarded a Wednesday early morning shuttle flight to Boston, traveled directly to the MHS on Boylston Street, worked there until it closed, and then took a bus to Kevin's dorm room at Harvard Law School. I saved money by eating dinner as a guest in the Harvard dining halls and by sleeping on the couch in his room. I flew back to New York on Friday evenings.

Susan and I spent the summer of 1971 in Cambridge, which enabled me to complete the bulk of my research in the Belknap collections at the MHS. Gayle Rubin, one of Susan's sorority sisters at Michigan, found us an apartment to sublet (Susan's boss gave her permission to take the summer off). Susan and I had a wonderful summer touring the historic sites of Boston, including a long but successful search for the Belknap family gravesite in an old burial ground on the Freedom Trail. Kevin was also still in

Cambridge, finishing some research for a Harvard Law professor until his clerkship for a federal judge began in September. He and I played golf once a week and several times Gayle, Susan, Kevin and I met for dinner. On a few warm evenings I dragged Susan to Red Sox games at Fenway Park. I had not fully recovered from the excitement and ultimate disappointment of the 1967 "Impossible Dream" season. In those days decent reserved seats were still reasonably priced, and only a few dates were sellouts.

As I labored on writing my biography of Belknap, Susan was becoming increasingly unhappy with her work as a computer programmer for HIP. She was smart and good at her job, but it was becoming more and more obvious that she was in the wrong profession. Her father and sister had steered her into the computer science field, but she now craved a position that involved more contact with people, perhaps something in social work or psychology. But since she had only taken a few undergraduate courses in Psychology at Michigan, she signed up for several more at Columbia's School of General Studies so she could apply to graduate programs. Two years later she earned a Master's in Developmental Psychology from Columbia's Teachers College. In 1978 she completed her doctoral work in Educational Psychology at Yeshiva University.

In mid-January 1972 Susan received a late night phone call from a Los Angeles family acquaintance who told her that her mother, Lolly, had been diagnosed with a deadly form of lymphoma. Susan's father had known about the gravity of his wife's illness for a few months, but he was emotionally unable to tell his daughters. A few days later Susan and I flew to Los Angeles to be at her mother's bedside, believing that her death was imminent. But instead, she rallied.

That spring we made one more extended trip to LA. I used the UCLA library to finish my revisions on my doctoral thesis. I still intended to defend my dissertation in May and receive my Ph.D. at the June commencement ceremony. But yet another round of student protest marches nearly prevented me from graduating. In April I had to smuggle eight photocopies of my thesis out of the copying room of Fayerweather Hall and evade the corps of SDS protestors who were again trying to shut down all of Columbia's academic programs. By then I had little sympathy for their goals; all I cared about was finishing my requirements and finding a position as a college professor. Despite the campus disorders Professors Vaughan and McKitrick honored my request to defend my thesis before the May deadline. During my defense I survived some eleventh hour criticism from a colonialist on the Barnard faculty and a professor from Union Theological Seminary, who criticized my interpretation of Belknap's changing religious beliefs. But Vaughan and McKitrick supported me, and I was certified as a Ph.D. Once again I chose not to attend the June commencement exercises due to ongoing student protests.

Three weeks after commencement Susan's mother died of cancer in a Los Angeles hospital. Lolly was fifty-five years old; Susan was twenty-five. Julian arranged for Lolly's shivah and funeral to be held in Great Neck, with interment in a Jewish cemetery in Queens. Julian then told Lolly's father, who was then in his mid-nineties and had been living with them in their Beverly Hills house, that he would have to move into a nursing home. One year later he passed away.

A few days after Lolly's funeral I mailed about two hundred applications for a teaching position in history to a variety of junior colleges and public and private colleges and universities on the West and East Coasts. In early August, Brother Patrick McGarry, head of the History Department at Manhattan College, invited me to its Riverdale campus for an interview. An Assistant Professor position had unexpectedly become open because a colleague who had been denied tenure had found a new job in Pittsburgh. He had the option of spending his terminal year at Manhattan but chose to start his new position right away. Br. Patrick did not care that Manhattan's history department already had a specialist in colonial and Revolutionary America—Robert Christen. He liked my credentials and especially my graduate degrees, since most of the history faculty held either an M.A. or a Ph.D. from Columbia. Br. Patrick offered me a contract as an Assistant Professor of History, with an annual salary of $11,000, plus medical benefits. The professor who had departed was scheduled to teach three sections of the first half of the survey course on American History, plus an upper-division elective on American Foreign Relations from the Revolution to 1900. I assured Brother Patrick that I was qualified to teach American diplomatic history even though my limited knowledge of that topic derived solely from my two classes with Professor LaFeber during my senior year at Cornell. Thus my long career at Manhattan College did not result from a national search for the most qualified candidate, or through any affirmative action process to bring diversity to the college faculty. (Although I became one of the few Jews on the faculty at Manhattan—an Irish Catholic college run by the Lasallian order of Christian Brothers.) Frankly, I owe my teaching career to good timing and luck. My résumé crossed Brother Patrick's desk at just the right time.

14. The Professionals

As I earned a Ph.D. in History at Columbia, prepared for a career as a college professor, and fell in love with Susan and got married, the other guys sought full time employment and/or began postgraduate studies. Henry landed a very good position as a research chemist in a consumer goods and pharmaceutical company and he and Barry Cohen enrolled in Master's programs. Barry Vasios and Kevin entered law school, while Richard started medical school. All had to deal with the draft. Finding a romantic partner was important to Barry Vasios and Kevin, but not a high priority for Barry Cohen or Richard. Henry would soon become engaged to Betty; the other guys would remain bachelors for several more years.

A Scientist and Businessman

In June 1967 Henry began his long career in the consumer goods and pharmaceutical industry when he accepted an offer of employment from the Shulton Corporation. He was assigned to its corporate headquarters on Route 46 in Clifton. He chose Shulton because its package included full payment for graduate work. Accordingly, that fall he started a Masters program in Applied Pharmaceutical Sciences at the Columbia College of Pharmacy. It took him two and a half years to earn that degree. Henry later added an MBA from Fairleigh Dickinson University.

Henry's first job assignment was in product development for women's makeup—specifically pressed powder in ladies' compacts. His research involved analyzing the degree of absorption of oil on the face. His experimentation led to patents on the processing of corn cob dust and its application in ladies' makeup. He remained with Shulton until 1971, when he accepted a position with the Avon Corporation in Manhattan. But he soon tired of the company culture and returned to Shulton in 1972.

In the fall of 1967, with no more worries about the draft, Henry and Betty became engaged to be married. They planned their wedding ceremony for Saturday afternoon, August 31, 1968, in the Reformed Church of Westwood. Henry's mother, Pauline, would have greatly preferred to see her son married in a Roman Catholic Church, according to the sacred traditions of the Church of Rome. To put Pauline's mind at ease and to comfort both her and her husband Enrico, the betrothed couple met with a Roman Catholic priest who provided appropriate blessings for their marriage. The first of our group to marry, the newlyweds returned from a brief honeymoon in the Poconos in time to attend my wedding to Susan the following Sunday in Manhattan at the Plaza Hotel. They soon settled into their new apartment on Coles Ave. in North Hackensack.

After their wedding Betty completed her student teacher's training in Teaneck and received her Bachelor's degree in Elementary Education in January 1969. The principal of a New Milford elementary school who observed her practice teaching was so impressed with her work that she offered Betty a position to begin in February. It was a good start to a career as an elementary school teacher that would last for thirty-two-and-a-half-years.

Betty and Henry were both goal-driven, with a top priority of saving enough money for a down payment on a house. It took them seven years to accomplish that task. Sufficient funds remained for a delayed but satisfying honeymoon in Bermuda.

Henry and Betty had been married for less than four years when Henry lost his father. Enrico had survived heart attacks in 1961 and 1962, but his third episode proved to be fatal. On August 2, 1972 Enrico went for a routine medical examination and an electrocardiogram (EKG). Since he did not drive a car he did not have a driver's license, and he did not generally carry any other form of identification with him. He usually traveled by bus, except when Henry or another relative or friend drove him. He was stricken at the Hackensack bus terminal on River Street, where he died. Since the police and coroner's office were unable to identify him, they moved his body to the city morgue and listed his remains as a "John Doe." Pauline naturally was alarmed when her husband did not return home, but it took a day before a cousin discovered that the morgue was holding an unidentified body. Henry and Betty were on vacation on Cape Cod, and his mother Pauline did not have a telephone number for them there. Eventually, Henry's colleagues at work and Betty's father were able to track them down on Cape Cod. They rushed home to a funeral mass for Enrico. He was buried in a Roman Catholic cemetery in Hackensack. Pauline was distraught. In Betty's words, Enrico's death left the memory of a "beautiful, loving marriage" that was "simple, kind, and pure."

An Educator

After his graduation from Rutgers, Barry Cohen enrolled as a full-time student in a Master's of Education program at the University of Maryland. But when his father, Rudy, was diagnosed with colon cancer, Barry returned home to help his mother operate the family's leather goods store on Lexington Avenue in Passaic. It was difficult enough dealing with the gravity of his dad's medical condition, but working at the store was no easy assignment considering the deteriorating economy of Passaic in general and its downtown shopping district in particular.

During the postwar period and through the 1950s the Cohen family business had been moderately profitable, but by the late 1960s sales had declined significantly. The closing of several local rubber and textile factories had weakened the city's economic base, and competition from nearby Willowbrook Mall hurt retail sales in town. Like the merchants on Main Street in Hackensack, the shopkeepers on Passaic's Lexington Avenue could not compete with Willowbrook and the Bergen County malls, which offered shoppers ample free parking and cleaner and fancier environments.

Rudy had an operation to treat his cancer, and by the spring of 1968 he had recovered sufficiently to permit Barry to resume his graduate work. But Barry was still concerned about his father's health and felt obligated to work part-time in the Passaic store, and thus could not return to Maryland for graduate school. Instead he enrolled in a Master's of Arts in History program at Rutgers, earning twelve credits while attending classes at both the Newark and New Brunswick campuses. He also earned extra money as a substitute teacher and began his search for a full-time faculty position.

In September of 1968 Barry secured a one-year job as a replacement for a faculty member on leave at Mahwah High School. His year at Mahwah boosted his confidence and reaffirmed his belief that he had chosen the right career path. But it was also a trying year, because of the failing health of his father.

Mahwah's environment and student demographic composition were unique. The high school was more like a college campus, with separate buildings dedicated to each of the academic disciplines. School administrators and taxpayers discovered that the school's architectural and energy designs were inefficient, especially considering the cold winters and the need to heat each of the buildings separately. The mixture of students was also exceptional, ranging from middle-and upper-class white suburban adolescents to the offspring of the "Jackson Whites" of the Ramapo Mountains. The Jackson Whites claim to be mixed descendents of Native American Indians, Dutch colonial settlers, runaway slaves, and Hessian soldiers who fought for the British during the Revolutionary War. Anthropologists argue that there is little or no proof to support this genealogy, describing them instead as an isolated and inbred people who are very protective of their cultural identity and traditions. Jackson Whites who attended public schools in Mahwah or other neighboring towns had literacy rates far below that of their peers. Consequently they experienced academic problems and had high dropout rates. The few who did manage to graduate struggled to assimilate into the mainstream suburban culture.

After that year of teaching Barry was no longer eligible for a student deferment, and he was notified by the Selective Service system that it was likely he would be called for active duty in the summer of 1969. This was several months before the federal government announced that a lottery would be held on December 1, 1969 to select inductees for 1970. If Barry had not acted he probably would have drafted in 1969 before the new lottery system went into effect. So he put his name on a waiting list for induction into the U.S. Army Reserves. Soon thereafter he was notified that he had been accepted. He was sworn in for a six year commitment on June 3, 1969.

Although he had signed up for the active Army Reserves, it was highly unlikely that his unit would ever be assigned to Vietnam because it was a training unit whose mission was to prepare other soldiers for military duty.

Rudy Cohen's period of remission from colon cancer did not last very long, and he passed away in late August 1969. Barry could spend only a few days with his grieving mother and brother before he had to report for basic training. In early September he flew to Fort Knox, Kentucky for his 120 days of boot camp. He attended orientation sessions, received his uniforms, and got his haircut. (The Army had recently reduced the length of basic training from 180 consecutive days to 120 consecutive days so that the U.S. government could avoid paying the new recruits costly future veterans' benefits, including college tuition and mortgage assistance.)

Most of the other recruits were southerners and midwesterners. Some appeared to be backwoods rednecks, eager to join the Army because it provided them with three meals a day and/or a job. One recruit had difficulty hitting targets during rifle practice, until he went for an eye exam and learned he was nearsighted. The Army gave him eyeglasses and he passed the rifle test. He had assumed his blurred vision was normal.

When Barry arrived in Kentucky he weighed about 170 pounds, perhaps 20-30 pounds over the norm for his height of five feet seven inches. Although he thought he had kept in decent shape through pickup basketball and baseball games, he was totally unprepared for the intense physical training regimen of boot camp. Each day began with a wake-up call at 4:30 a.m., followed at five by a physical training session before breakfast. Fitness drills, which included lots of calisthenics and exercises to strengthen the arms and upper body, occupied most of the rest of the day. He had to pass timed tests that included climbing bars, carrying a heavier partner for at least 100 yards, and running a mile in under ten minutes. Instructors taught him how to kill people with guns, knives, hand grenades, and other deadly devices. The food was plentiful but awful. Even though Barry forced himself to eat, he could not maintain his body weight. The only relief was overnight sleep (lights out at 9:00p.m. plus Sundays off).

Barry encountered little or no anti-Semitism at Fort Knox. In fact, indeed Jewish soldiers actually benefited from special treatment, in that they were permitted to attend services in Louisville on Friday evenings and Saturday mornings. Barry thus became religious throughout his time in Kentucky, attending weekend services and the Louisville Jewish Center on Sundays. He appreciated the kindness of the local rabbi, who told the recruits it was okay with him if they fell asleep on Friday nights. The sounds of explosions from nearby Fort Knox were a constant backdrop as Barry chanted Hebrew prayers.

When Barry returned to Hackensack after basic training he tipped the scales at 130 pounds—about forty below his pre-induction weight. He still faced five years and eight months service in the Reserves. He was required to attend Reserve unit sessions two Sundays a month and summer camp at Fort Dix, New Jersey, two weeks each year. Trained to be both an infantryman and a clerk typist, he did a lot of paperwork (typing up orders, food lists, and job notices). At those meetings he got to know lawyers, accountants, and businessmen who, like Barry, had joined the Reserves to avoid the draft. Conversing with them helped Barry get through the extensive dead time.

Barry was now able to resume his course work for a Master's of Arts in History as a part-time student at Newark Rutgers. In the spring of 1970 he continued to live at home and work part time in the leather goods store in Passaic. His main focus was to find a suitable position as a secondary school Social Studies teacher. His prospects seemed good, despite some concerns about the health of the economy and the continuing unrest on college campuses and on many city streets over President Nixon's Vietnam policies. But there were still many pockets of affluence in the country, especially in Bergen County. Public school enrollment was growing in the upscale town of Park Ridge. Its high school offered Barry a contract to begin work as a Social Studies teacher in September 1970. He would remain there for thirty-two years.

At Park Ridge High School Barry perfected a style of instruction that made him one of the most popular teachers in his school. He credits the influence of Hackensack High School's Social Studies teacher, Harold Bloom, his role model. Barry incorporated much of Bloom's method and message into his own classroom in his world history and U.S. history courses. His approach was strictly "old school." He began each class by writing a brief outline of the day's lesson on the blackboard. He occasionally employed the Socratic Method to grill students on the topic at hand, but mostly he delivered standard lectures. Although this teaching style was traditional if not downright conservative, his perspectives on the subject matter reflected his (and Bloom's) liberal bias. His teaching reflected the revisionist views of U.S. history that emphasized the participation and contributions of Native Americans, blacks, Hispanics, Asians, and women, along with the conflict between labor and capital and the rise of American imperialism at home and abroad.

Beginning with his first year of full-time teaching at Mahwah High School and continuing at Park Ridge High School, Barry excelled in exploring differing interpretations and conveying the basic facts of American history. He also experimented with team teaching and helped to develop special one-semester electives in world cultures and other social science fields. He soon realized that to be an effective high school teacher he also had to master certain "people skills." This entailed learning how to keep order in a classroom, discipline unruly students, and develop engaging, topical lesson plans that encouraged reticent students to participate in class.

Between 1967 and 1972 Barry lived with his mother in the family apartment on Beech Street. His life became quite hectic as he balanced the demands of his teaching position, part-time work in the Passaic store, and completion of his Master's in History at Rutgers. For that degree he wrote a 25 page research essay for a course in American Economic History titled "A Study of Slavery in Bergen County, New Jersey." He continued to attend weekly and monthly Army Reserve meetings. He somehow found time to commute to Manhattan's Central Park for sandlot softball games with me and Marty, or to Downstate Medical Center to play basketball with me and Rich. He also joined a faculty basketball team that competed against faculty squads from other high schools in charity games.

He even got lucky with the ladies. A major benefit of his Army basic training was losing weight. His lighter body enhanced his self esteem and motivated him to pursue a more active social life. A few of his Rutgers College buddies and some new friends he met at the weekly and monthly Army Reserve meetings encouraged him to attend mixers for Jewish singles in banquet halls, hotels, and temples in Bergen County. He dated plenty of women after that.

A Lawyer from Yale

When Barry Vasios started his first semester at Yale Law School he became a member of the Class of 1970—the group that experienced the full impact of the Sixties, and especially the effects of the Vietnam War. Accordingly, his major concern became the Selective Service system. The draft forced him to take a leave of absence after his first year, a three-semester interruption of his studies.

Many in the legal community of the late 1960s viewed Yale's law school as second best in the nation, trailing only Harvard Law. But Yale was clearly the first choice of many applicants, like Barry, who were accepted by both institutions. They preferred Yale over Harvard because of its much smaller size (and thus its much more favorable faculty-student ratio) and its guiding philosophy of "legal realism," which stressed the integration of law with the social sciences and especially its application as an instrument of social justice. Yale's law curriculum included clinical legal education courses and assigned casebooks emphasized the law's practical effects on society. Sidney Stein, a classmate of both Kevin at Princeton and Barry at Yale Law School, recalls that most Princetonians who were admitted to both law schools chose Yale. That outcome so troubled Harvard's admission office that it sent a delegation down to Princeton to interview Stein and others who favored Yale to discover their reasons. (Kevin did not apply to Yale Law School because a career in law was then his backup plan to a career in business, and the Harvard Law School application was much shorter and simpler than Yale's form, which required writing longer essays.)

Barry chose Yale Law School partly because of his affection for Yale College, but mostly because of its reputation as being more socially progressive than Harvard Law. Barry had been disturbed by racial rioting in

Harlem and Watts in 1964 and 1965, and a city planning course he took as a senior piqued his interest in urban renewal. Working for New Haven's Redevelopment Office during the summer of 1967 convinced him that the law could be a useful tool to improve society. Just twenty-two years old, he was still fired up with the idealism of youth. Spending four years at Yale College also exposed him to its two traditions. One was rooted in capitalism and promoted the accumulation of wealth; the other derived from the university's Congregational heritage and stressed doing good works. Barry was determined to follow the latter path. One way he did so as a first-year law student was to assist Yale College's admissions office in recruiting applicants who were underprivileged minority and white working-class high school students.

The vast majority of Yale Law School's Class of 1970 were white males from privileged, affluent families. Their ranks included only seven women and about the same number of blacks. The social upheavals generated by the Vietnam War, civil rights movement, women's liberation, and the flowering of the counterculture motivated many of them to become social reform activists as undergraduates. Some also condemned the Socratic Method of legal education still applied by most of Yale's professors, as presented in the popular 1973 film about Harvard Law School, *The Paper Chase*. In this form of instruction, the professor interrogated students on assigned cases, using techniques that critics thought were sterile, mean-spirited, and needlessly competitive. Many students also lobbied to democratize the school's governance and administration through expanded student representation on faculty, staff, and executive committees.

During his first year Barry felt the full pressure of the Socratic Method as professors grilled students, ridiculing those who were unprepared. At one memorable meeting of a contracts course the professor assigned a classic case from World War II, *Batsakis v. Demotsis*, in which one Greek sued another for payment of a loan in drachmas made in 1941. The question was whether the debt should be paid after the war in the same amount of drachmas (now at a much reduced value due to inflation) or in an amount that was equivalent to the original uninflated value of the 1941 drachmas. The atmosphere in the classroom grew increasingly tense as the professor called on a series of students, none of whom were prepared for the class. (Stating that you were unprepared was viewed as an insult to the professor, and if repeated could lower your grade). Finally the teacher asked Barry to state the ruling in the case. Drawing upon his Greek heritage, Barry answered that the decision was based on an ancient Armenian saying: "Always count your fingers after you shake hands with a Greek." His response cracked up the class and broke the tension; and the professor laughed so heartily that he stepped off the platform. Decades later, whenever Barry bumped into a classmate who attended that session, he would be saluted with the call: *Batsakis v. Demotsis!*

In the fall of 1967 student activists at Yale Law School had the Vietnam War, civil rights, and poverty on their minds, but they decided to begin their reform campaign with a more mundane institutional issue—the eight-point grading scale that ranged from A downward. First-year students felt the intense pressure to perform well on their final exams at the end of the fall and spring terms, especially since the tests were the major means used to select editors of the prestigious Yale Law Journal. (Yale, Harvard, and other prominent law schools were just beginning to use essay competitions to select editors of their law journals.) One year later Yale pioneered grade reform across the nation's law schools and many law journals viewed the outcome as a victory for the students. For Barry the significance of the new grading system was that it placed most of the law students in the great middle category of "Pass" and reduced the number who earned "Honors." He thought that outcome pleased reformers whose primary goal was the democratization of Yale Law School. Furthermore, its administration attempted to lessen student anxiety by giving them the option of taking courses taught either through the traditional Socratic Method or through lectures with no interrogation of students. Since Barry was nearly always prepared for class and was comfortable with the Socratic format, he generally signed up for those sections.

Barry found his first year courses to be very demanding, but nonetheless they provided him with "an incredible learning experience." Thus he was not much disturbed by the arrival of members of the Hog Farm Commune on campus. Representing the more light-hearted side of the Sixties, the Hog Farm was affiliated with Ken Kesey's "Merry Pranksters." They arrived in a psychedelic bus, wore colorful jumpsuits, and crashed with students who lived in the Sterling Law dorms. Barry, determined to get a first class legal education at Yale, saw the hippie scene as alien to his values. He was uncomfortable hanging out with students who smoked pot and championed alternative lifestyles

In the fall of 1968 Barry began an extended leave of absence from Yale Law School, in order to delay or avoid being drafted. Once the federal government ended graduate student deferments for the draft in the spring of 1968, 70 out of the 165 members of Barry's class of 1970 dropped out of school. They enrolled in programs that enabled them to avoid immediate induction into the U.S. Army either by signing up for the National Guard Reserves or by joining the federally funded Peace Corps or Volunteers in Service to America (VISTA, also known as the domestic Peace Corps), or local teacher trainee programs. Before the Johnson administration ended graduate student deferments, Barry had accepted an offer to work in an elite program for a select number of law students run by the Office of Economic Opportunity (OEO) in Washington, D.C. The project inspected and audited summer programs funded with federal dollars and operated by local anti-poverty agencies. Barry was assigned to travel to various cities to monitor how OEO funds were being spent. While in Washington he learned that VISTA was hiring law students and recent law school graduates to work in the inner cities or in rural poverty regions. He applied, was accepted into that program, and trained in Chicago.

Barry chose Cleveland as his destination because a friend who had just graduated from Yale Law School was employed by the Cleveland Legal Aid Society and described the exciting work he was doing in community economic development. In VISTA Barry earned $90 every two weeks. For the next fifteen months he lived in the Hough section of Cleveland, a predominately black ghetto that had seen racial rioting in July 1966. He rented space in an old mansion that had been converted into a rooming house. Sponsored by Cleveland's legal aid society, he was employed by a community neighborhood program funded by the OEO. His agency built low-income housing and a shopping center (a food supermarket plus a few shops, with public housing on the roof!), founded an injection mold and rubber parts factory that hired unemployed welfare mothers, and ran a maintenance company staffed by people who previously had been typecast as "hard-core unemployable."

While in Cleveland Barry also finally ended his relationship with Ruth, his on again-off again high school girlfriend. She moved to Los Angeles to begin her graduate studies in psychology at UCLA. He dated a woman who worked in his program until she departed for graduate school in Boston. Barry completed his initial thirteen-month tour with VISTA and then terminated his ties to that agency after the first draft lottery. His birth date of May 1, 1945 made him the oldest of us six guys and also the luckiest—at least in terms of the draft. Barry drew the number 330 in the lottery—high enough to virtually guarantee that he would never be drafted. (The highest number called to select inductees for that initial group would be 195.) He then re-enrolled in Yale Law School.

Yale Law School's administration, faculty, and students witnessed profound changes in matters of gender and race during the eighteen months that Barry was on leave. Yale enrolled more female and black students and also addressed their concerns. In the fall of 1968, one year before Yale College became coeducational, 25 women enrolled as first year law students (up from seven in Barry's class). A more aggressive affirmative action plan soon doubled the number of female applicants. Those women who enrolled campaigned successfully for a "Women and the Law" course, co-authored articles on feminist issues for the *Yale Law Journal*, lobbied for the repeal of Connecticut's statutory prohibition of abortion, and fought to end discrimination against women in law firms. In the spring of 1969, responding to demands submitted by the new Black Law Students Union (BLSU), the administration agreed to increase black student enrollment to 10 percent of each class, and also provide additional financial for minority students. The Admissions Office also instituted a new affirmative action policy to recruit and admit black applicants who were economically disadvantaged but who had demonstrated the potential to succeed in law school.

White radicals fully supported the agendas of the feminists and the BLSU and also lobbied for expanded clinical education to enable students to acquire the skills to combat racism and poverty. In addition, they proposed the creation of a new Law School Council to replace the faculty as the school's main legislative body. In March Dean Louis Pollak and the faculty rejected their plan. The activists then accepted a compromise brokered by Dean Pollak that provided for limited student input into the law school's governance.

When Barry returned to New Haven in January 1970 he found that during his absence Yale Law School had recruited more African American and female students, revamped its grading system, given students the option of taking required courses taught through lectures rather than by the Socratic Method, and even allowed them greater voice if not real power in the Law School's governance. These developments had generated much controversy on campus, and more excitement lay ahead in the spring term.

Activists planned a massive rally in New Haven in May 1970 in support of Black Panther chairman Bobby Seale, who was awaiting trial on kidnapping and murder charges. Kingman Brewster's notorious comment on the Seale case drew nationwide media coverage: "I personally . . .am appalled and ashamed that things should have come to such a pass that I am skeptical of the ability of black revolutionaries to achieve a fair trial anywhere in the United States." Though Yale had no direct involvement in the planning of the rally, Brewster took the initiative to reduce tensions in town. He opened the gates of Yale's campus to the hordes of demonstrators—at least 10,000— and provided them with food, shelter, and first aid. According to a *New York Times* news article, Brewster acted "partly through fear, partly through humanitarian sentiments." In fact, his strategy of accommodation helped to reduce the atmosphere of militancy, and the May Day weekend rally was relatively tranquil, marred by only a few violent incidents. It ended a day early.

As Brewster and the entire Yale community braced themselves for what appeared to be a tense and perhaps violent May Day weekend, Barry spoke to a dean about a potentially troublesome situation. The Law School had invited Supreme Court Justices Potter Stewart and Byron "Whizzer" White to speak on campus on the same day as the Black Panther rally. Barry went to see Jack Tate, the associate dean of law school admissions (who had granted Barry financial aid in the past) to inquire whether anyone had considered the possibility that militants might try to disrupt the lectures of Justices Stewart and White. Dean Tate realized that Barry was right, and shortly thereafter the speeches were cancelled.

A few days prior to the anticipated May Day weekend rally, the Yale community was stunned by the news of a fire of suspicious origin in the

International Law Library that destroyed about five hundred books (worth around $2,500) and also caused structural damage to the building. A bucket brigade of students (including Hillary Rodham) removed smoldering volumes. Students formed crews to clean up the stacks and protect the library's collection. Barry volunteered for the night patrol of the stacks, during which he wore his "squeakiest" shoes, in case whoever set the fire came back. According to his classmate Sid Stein, some students taped beautiful stained glass windows to protect them against stones that might be tossed at them by demonstrators (although none were actually thrown). Both Pollak and his newly appointed successor, Abraham Goldstein, viewed the fire as a pivotal turning point. The concluded: that the burning of the books "tamed the order of the firebrands, tamed the order of our homegrown student radicals." They concluded that the students "calmed down because it looked like things were getting out of hand." Though officials later determined the cause of the fire as "accidental," many continued to believe that it was the work of an arsonist.

Yale Law School, the entire university, and all of New Haven survived the Black Panther/May Day weekend with minimal trauma. But President Nixon's announcement of the U.S. invasion of Cambodia on April 30 soon led to renewed efforts by enraged antiwar radical students. When National Guard troops shot and killed four students at Kent State University, Yale students called for a student strike, to allow protesters to devote themselves to the antiwar crusade. Law students demanded that faculty and administrators cancel all final paper assignments and examinations and give students full credit for their spring semester courses. Dean Pollak and his newly appointed successor, Abraham Goldstein, worked out a compromise proposal. They did not cancel final examinations entirely, and permitted students to delay completing their final papers and tests. In doing so Yale Law School protected their future prospects for gaining bar certification.

During this crisis Barry attended a meeting of more than two hundred agitated students chaired by Hillary Rodham. He was impressed by how well she applied Roberts' Rules of Order to control the crowd (he recognized that she had a promising future). He got to know Hillary and dated one of her roommates. He also met another new student, William Clinton, though Barry did not get to know him very well.

The most intense period of discord and demonstrations at Yale Law School was over, but a year later some of the law students joined hundreds of undergraduates in support of a strike by the university's service and maintenance employees. Barry was sympathetic to the plight of the workers because of his labor as a food service employee during his freshman year. At dinnertime on April 30, 1971, a hundred Yale College freshmen expressed their solidarity with the workers by conducting a food fight in the Freshman Commons cafeteria. The next day about 150 of them marched three blocks from the Freshman Commons to the residence of President Brewster, carrying their lunch trays and chanting "Support Yale Workers." They then ate their food and departed after Brewster agreed to speak with a few of them. The demonstrators pledged to return for every meal until the strike was settled "quickly and with justice." During the strike Barry delivered a speech in which he supported the union demands. After that rally the crowd left much debris behind, mostly through carelessness or perhaps intentionally as part of the demonstration. Barry stayed afterwards to help clean up the site. ("I could not have been much of a radical," he says today.).The seven-week strike ended in mid-June with increased pay and union security for employees in a new three-year contract negotiated with Local 35 of the Federation of University Employees.

During 1971 student protests diminished at Yale Law School, as they did across the nation, and some of the militants even had second thoughts about their prior actions. In the spring of 1971 the BLSU held a party for Dean Pollak (who had returned to the faculty) to apologize to him for all the aggravation that black students had caused him when they entered the law school, and to recognize his efforts to address their grievances. Barry was one of only two white students invited to that event—perhaps because of his friendships with black classmates, or perhaps because they respected his service in VISTA.

During the summer of 1971 Barry did research and wrote legal briefs for a New Haven lawyer, becoming the first assistant that the sole practitioner hired. Barry was not a skilled typist, so his boss suggested that he drop off his handwritten drafts for typing by his young secretary, Cheryl Howard, a slim, black-haired beauty of Italian, Irish, and English descent. Born in Southington, Connecticut, she grew up in Wallingford and graduated from Lyman Hall High School there. When they met, Cheryl was nineteen years old and Barry was twenty-five. Cheryl recalls that initially she thought Barry was "good looking, very smart, and a genuinely nice guy." A few months later Barry asked her out, and they began steady dating.

During the fall of 1971—Barry's last term at Yale Law School—he and Sidney Stein lived in Yale's presidential mansion as "house-sitters" while Brewster was on sabbatical with his family in England. Barry was busy with his coursework, part time jobs, and interviews for positions with Manhattan law firms. All of his hard work paid off when he received an attractive offer to join the prestigious Manhattan firm Donovan, Leisure, Newton, and Irvine. (One of its founders, General "Wild Bill" Donovan, was the head of the Office of Strategic Services during World War II, which later became the Central Intelligence Agency.)

During the summer of 1971 Barry worked for Dean Goldstein, who helped him obtain a prize clerkship with a federal judge. President Nixon had recently appointed Arnold Bauman as a U.S. District Court judge in Manhattan. Bauman then called Goldstein to ask for nominees for a nine-month clerkship from the crop of midyear graduates. Goldstein mentioned the request to Sid Stein, who was then assisting Goldstein in the Dean's

Office. Sidney naturally recommended Barry. Goldstein agreed and Bauman offered Barry an interview and then the position. Barry then consulted with Kevin, who by then was clerking for a federal judge in New York. Kevin strongly encouraged Barry to accept the position if it were offered to him, even though it meant a one-year delay in starting his employment at Donovan Leisure. Barry followed his advice. Stein graduated in June 1972, one semester later than Barry, because of the extra time he spent as Dean Goldstein's assistant. His credentials were even more distinguished than Barry's, in that he was an editor of the *Yale Law Journal.* After his graduation he accepted a clerkship with Judge Stanley H. Fuld, Chief Judge of the New York Court of Appeals, the highest court in New York State.

Barry finished law school with a flourish, mixing hard work with good times. He and Cheryl socialized with several of his classmates, including Stein and Larry Lucchino (who later became president of the Boston Red Sox). They had a lot of fun together, going out to dinner and the movies, and also eating in at Brewster's residence. For a young woman who was just turning twenty, it must have been pretty cool to be hanging out with a young, handsome Yale law student.

Barry and Cheryl's relationship soon blossomed into a true romance. After Barry moved to Manhattan in January 1972 Cheryl began a regular weekend commute to his apartment on MacDougal Street in Greenwich Village. Sometimes Barry's younger brother Jimmy (then a Yale senior) would accompany her because he liked to drive her BMW. Cheryl recalls the heavy traffic and the struggle to get a good parking place in front of Barry's building. The choice spots (across the street from an Italian gun club) became legal after six, but they were generally blocked by a police barricade set up by a limousine driver whose passengers patronized the gun club. Cheryl made an effort to befriend the guy and he eventually consented to leave enough room for Cheryl's car as well. On weekends she and Barry would often take day trips with Kevin and his current girlfriend to historic sites and parks, like Bear Mountain in New York State and New Jersey's Great Swamp (not one of Cheryl's favorites). Cheryl has fond memories of meeting me and Susan at our apartment on Fourteenth Street. She thought that we were both "pretty cool," but she was more impressed with Susan, whom she remembers as "pretty, stylish, and sophisticated."

A Lawyer from Harvard

In his final term at Princeton Kevin was considering going to business school. His Fulbright grant to study in France would give him the opportunity to learn more about international economics and time to decide whether his talents and temperament were suited to the world of business. He and his fellow American grantees sailed to Europe on the SS *France* en route to their first stop in Paris, where they would spend six weeks in a

Fulbright program orientation, residing in the U.S. House in the Cité Universitaire. Kevin's roommate, Alfred Bloom, was a China scholar and prominent linguist who later became president of Swarthmore College.

Barry and Cheryl, early 1970s.

Kevin's home base for the academic year 1967-68 was the University of Nancy in northeastern France. His assignment was to do research on international economics, but for the first time since the eighth grade in State Street Junior High, the grades he earned would have little if any bearing on his future academic and career prospects. Furthermore, Kevin viewed the courses offered at Nancy as rather "childish" compared to the rigors of the Princeton curriculum. With a modest work load and little if any incentive to accomplish very much, Kevin was pleased to spend much of his time getting to know his new French classmates. With so many attractive women available he soon forgot his monkish existence at Princeton.

Spring 1968 was even more a time of turmoil and revolt in France than it was in the United States and Kevin found himself right in the thick of the action. Students at the University of Paris at Nanterre and at the Sorbonne in Paris were organizing street demonstrations and occupying university facilities in protest against several highly controversial educational and labor reforms instituted by Charles de Gaulle's government. The students' and workers' uprisings culminated in a two-week general strike involving eleven million workers. The disorders nearly caused the fall of de Gaulle's government.

Like the rest of the guys, (except Henry) Kevin was a liberal, not a radical. Yet his new friendships in Nancy turned him into one for a few weeks. He joined street rallies and participated in the more risky and potentially more dangerous takeovers of academic buildings. Unlike my situation in New York, Kevin resided on campus and was intimately involved with student militants at the University of Nancy. He was sympathetic to student demands for more equitable financial aid and more involvement in university governance and supported their charges that French universities were under funded and mismanaged.

Kevin joined in the Nancy student demonstrations partly for ideological reasons, but mostly he followed his peers because it was "the thing to do" and presented yet another opportunity to party with his friends. Kevin began to realize the consequences of the students' actions when police in Nancy dispersed crowds of demonstrators with water hoses and attacked protesters with leather-covered metal batons. He and many others fled after witnessing the officers beat up students, leaving many with bloody heads and bruised bodies. By the end of May the students' radical actions combined with revolutionary activity by workers had intensified class conflict and had brought France perilously close to the brink of civil war. Accordingly, Kevin withdrew from radical politics.

When Kevin sailed home in July he did not regret a thing—his year in France had been the most enjoyable time of his life. His good feelings soon came to an abrupt end, however, because he came home with infections that nearly proved fatal. He never learned how he acquired these illnesses—they may be partly attributable to his weakened resistance due to his partying and staying up all night during the protest marches and occupations of May. Shortly after his return he was admitted to Hackensack Hospital. A few days later he was quarantined for thirty-one days. He was so sick that the nurses had to check him every fifteen minutes to make sure that he was still breathing. His physician, Dr. Prager, diagnosed a severe case of mononucleosis with potential bacteria superinfection. Kevin's illness prevented him from attending our wedding on September 8, but by the following week he was well enough to travel to Cambridge to begin his first year at Harvard Law School. Kevin was treated by specialists during and after his recovery period in Cambridge. They concluded that he had contracted a variety of blood disorders, including hepatitis and a nasty staph infection, and treated him accordingly.

Kevin's decision to study law rather than business turned out to be a wise career choice, but ironically it hinged in large part on the negligence of a university professor in France. He enrolled at Harvard Law School because a professor from the University of Nancy failed to submit a letter of recommendation to Harvard Business School, which was required after the Fulbright year in France. Kevin needed to enroll somewhere to avoid the draft for one more year, and since his application to Harvard Law School was filed on time and was approved, Kevin wound up studying law rather than business.

When Kevin arrived in Cambridge in mid-September 1968 he was still weak from the infections he had contracted in France. Because of his illness he was assigned to a single room, and he remained under doctor's orders to have his blood tested frequently and to stay in bed as much as possible. After a few weeks he had recovered sufficiently to devote his usual degree of concentrated effort to his studies.

Kevin applied to Harvard Law School mainly because of its reputation as the leading law school in the United States Unlike Yale Law, which featured legal realism and a more socially progressive orientation, Harvard took a more traditional, conservative, and structural approach to the law, emphasizing legal precedents and principles. It did not take Kevin very long to realize that he was going to be happier at Harvard than he was at Princeton. Social class, religion, and gender seemed to matter less at Harvard than at Princeton. Although in 1968 a very high percentage of Kevin's classmates were graduates of Ivy League or other elite colleges, Harvard Law School was coeducational (although only about 9 percent were women), and more democratic in atmosphere than was Princeton. Moreover, Kevin quickly found the law to be a more interesting and intellectually challenging subject than his major and minor fields at Princeton—geology and economics. He also enjoyed the more urban environment of Cambridge and Boston over the small town setting of Princeton. Finally his social life was much more active, especially since his year of partying and his string of girlfriends in France had boosted his confidence with women.

The first-year curriculum at Harvard Law School in 1968 consisted of five subjects: torts, civil procedure, contracts, criminal law, and property. All were full-year courses with classes meeting one or more times a week. Most professors taught the material through the Socratic Method, randomly selecting students and asking them to answer their penetrating questions. Students were expected to be prepared to respond to a professor's query at any moment. There were no preliminary or midterm or mid-year exams; a student's entire record depended upon performance on the final exams held in June. One of Kevin's professors, Clark Byse, was the model for the crusty old professor in *The Paper Chase*. Kevin's true mentor and intellectual hero was Professor Benjamin Kaplan, a specialist in civil procedure. Kevin performed brilliantly on his final exams in the spring of 1969, and in midsummer he was notified that he was one of only twenty first-year students (out of a class of 550) to be selected as an editor of the *Harvard Law Review*.

The wave of student disorders and accompanying crackdowns by police flared up again at U.S. colleges in April 1969—most notably at Harvard and Cornell. It shocked many Boston Brahmins that Harvard College's chapter of SDS constituted not only one of the largest groups of radicals in the country, but also that it had the discipline and the nerve to challenge Harvard's administration over the university's complicity in the Vietnam War. One of SDS's first targets was the Harvard Reserve Officers Training Corps (ROTC) program, which had recruited 345 students; 40 percent were from the Law and Business schools. In the fall of 1968 their ranks included Kevin, who had signed up as a hedge against the draft and because the government was ending graduate student deferments. SDS occupied an auditorium where the Faculty of Arts and Sciences had scheduled a meeting to consider a resolution recommending the abolition of ROTC at Harvard. The incident ended peacefully, but the faculty divided over whether the protesters should be disciplined. In February 1969 the faculty rejected SDS's demand of an immediate end to ROTC on campus by a 7 to 1 margin. But by a 2 to 1 vote it approved a resolution to withhold regular college credit for ROTC courses and to deprive its instructors of faculty standing. ROTC would be reduced to an extracurricular activity; later a committee recommended that all ROTC programs be terminated within two years. During the early 1970s Harvard ended all ROTC programs, but it agreed to pay the costs for those Harvard students who wished to participate in the ROTC unit at the Massachusetts Institute of Technology.

The main event on Harvard's campus in the spring of 1969 was the SDS takeover and occupation of University Hall, the site of the office of the Dean of the Faculty of Arts and Sciences. On April 9 the radicals (most of whom were from white, upper-middle-class families) evicted the administrators. A crowd of supporters and opponents gathered nearby. President Nathan S. Pusey met with members of the university's governing Corporation Commission and other advisors. They weighed the example of the 1968 Columbia episode and especially the escalation of tensions that followed Grayson Kirk's decision to call in the NYPD to clear five buildings. Archibald Cox, a Harvard man and former U.S. Solicitor General under President Kennedy who had chaired an investigation of the Columbia disturbances, recommended that if the police were to be employed it must be early or not at all. Pusey decided to act. At five in the morning of April 11, two hundred state troopers and approximately the same number of local police removed the student activists from University Hall. SDS supporters chanted "Fascist Pigs!" as the officers dragged the occupiers out, clubbing some of them in the process. The working-class cops shouted, "Long-haired Commies!" Although Pusey's call for police bitterly divided the faculty, the crisis passed and the incident did not prove to be as damaging to Harvard as the Columbia episode was to that university.

Almost exactly a year earlier in Nancy, France, Kevin had had no compunction about marching in solidarity with fellow students, even joining the occupation of an academic building. But now at Harvard the circumstances were different. He explains: "Once back at Harvard, I had work to do, so the social aspect was of little interest to me. So I just let them riot on their own." Kevin was still antiwar, but he was not sympathetic with the tactics of SDS. The following year, police used tear gas to disperse crowds of students who were demonstrating in Harvard Square, close to the *Harvard Law Review*'s headquarters, where Kevin was an editor. The smoke drove Kevin out of his office, but that is as close as he got to participating in a riot. Later there were also a few smaller incidents, including student sit-ins, which concerned the law school's grading and other academic policies. Kevin was more active in those episodes, and more conservative.

Harvard's sponsorship of the Army ROTC had survived the first wave of student attacks, so Kevin was compelled to complete basic training at Fort Benning, Georgia in the summer of 1969. The military drills were rigorous and exhausting, especially since he was still feeling the aftereffects of his illness. He was training to be a Second Lieutenant in the Artillery, and he was anxious about his assignment as a forward observer, since that specialty had a very high casualty rate in combat. His tour of duty was shortened from eight to six weeks because at the end of the summer he was required to attend the *Harvard Law Review* orientation.

Kevin's second year in law school presented him with a new kind of academic challenge. He and his fellow *Harvard Law Review* editors were not expected to attend class. Instead, they were provided with detailed course outlines and notes for their courses, which included antitrust, Constitutional Law, and other tough subjects. Kevin worried about how his absences would affect his grades on his final exams—a workload of sixty hours a week on the *Law Review* made class attendance impossible. He did technical editing of all accepted articles and also researched and wrote one short case note and one long article. He was also required to attend ROTC classes and regularly scheduled weekend military exercises. Nevertheless he did well on his second-year tests and also landed an internship for the summer of 1970 at the prestigious Manhattan firm of Debevoise, Plimpton, Lyons, & Gates.

By his third and final year at Harvard Kevin was determined to avoid being sent to Vietnam as a Second Lieutenant Artillery officer. He applied for a position in the Army's General Counsel Office in the Pentagon in Washington. He was selected for that position, so now he no longer had to worry about serving in Vietnam. He completed his course work, which included a seminar on legal education with Derek Bok, just before Bok was appointed president of Harvard University. Kevin did not work as hard during that year because he assumed that after graduation he was headed to Washington for a term in the office of the General Counsel of the Army. Thus he did not enter the competitions for officer of the *Harvard Law Review* or for an elite clerkship in the U.S. Supreme Court.

Meanwhile, in January of 1971, during the winter intersession before his final semester in law school, Kevin had dental work in Hackensack that caused extensive bleeding from his gums. His dentist recommended further blood testing, and that spring hematologists in Cambridge referred him to two blood disorder specialists at the Chelsea Naval Depot. Those doctors gave Kevin a definitive diagnosis of hemophilia, which disqualified him from military service. The Army's General Counsel was rather irritated when he learned of Kevin's Honorable Discharge from the Army, because he had turned down other applicants for the position and would now have to complete another search.

Kevin received both his certificate of Honorable Discharge and his law degree in June 1971. Though relieved he was now free and clear of any military service, he deeply regretted that he had not competed to be an officer of the *Harvard Law Review*, and especially that he had not tried out for a clerkship with a U.S. Supreme Court Justice. Kevin had been on a star track but the U.S. Army had temporarily derailed him. Given his top performance at Harvard he might very well have secured one of those prized positions as law clerk for a Justice of the Supreme Court. Kevin still wonders about how his career might have evolved if he had been selected. Would being a clerk for a Supreme Court justice have profoundly changed the course of his life? Would he have received a stupendous offer that might have culminated in a plum multimillion dollar partnership at a Wall Street law firm? Or if he had still preferred an academic path, would he have wound up at Harvard or Yale rather than at Cornell? Would he have been any happier in either of those career scenarios?

In any event, Kevin planned to spend the summer of 1971 working on a research project for Benjamin Kaplan, his civil procedure professor and mentor. The day before graduation Kaplan told Kevin that even though he had not been a candidate for any clerkships he could have one anyway, in Manhattan, working for one of two federal judges. Kevin chose Murray Gurfein, whom Richard Nixon had recently appointed as a judge for the Southern District of New York, and clerked for him for a year, beginning in September 1971.

Kevin's stellar academic performance at Harvard Law matched his achievements at Princeton, but he was far happier as a law student in Cambridge. His continuing success and his preference for Cambridge contributed greatly to his sunnier disposition, but his improved social life was also a major factor. His year in France and especially his experiences with French women had boosted his confidence. His brilliant intellect, forceful (even aggressive) personality, competitive spirit, and impressive accomplishments all combined to give him a star quality. Although only about 9 percent of his classmates at Harvard Law were women, he had no trouble finding girlfriends. For most of his three years in Cambridge Kevin's constant companion was a brilliant young woman to whom he was clearly devoted. But by the time of their graduation they were content to go their separate ways. Over the next few years he lived in Greenwich Village and dated a woman who was a new associate in the law firm he joined after he completed his clerkship with Judge Gurfein.

Kevin believes that during his time there Harvard Law School provided an excellent legal education for those who were selected to be the editors of the *Harvard Law Review*. For the rest of the 530 students in each class who did not get that opportunity, it was not such a good place. Because of its size, the professors' application of the Socratic Method, and the pressure to perform on final exams, Harvard Law School could be an alienating institution. Kevin believes that Harvard's curriculum and law review experience gave him a legal education that was superior to that offered at Yale Law School, yet he concedes that Yale Law School's much smaller size and thus its more favorable faculty-to-student ratio made it a better place for the majority of its students.

A Doctor in the House

In September 1967 Richard began an intensive and grueling curriculum at the College of Medicine at the State University of New York (SUNY) Downstate Medical Center (Downstate). Downstate's heritage in Brooklyn goes back to 1858, when it was chartered by New York State as the Long Island College Hospital of the City of Brooklyn, and opened its doors in 1860. Its modern era began in April 1950 with the merger of the Long Island College of Medicine into the SUNY system. A few years later construction began on a complex of science and hospital buildings, residence halls, and student center on a new site. Several faculty members achieved national recognition, especially Dr. Clarence Dennis, chair of the Department of Surgery from 1951 to 1971. He built one of the first heart/lung machines and performed the second successful open heart operation in the United States (and the first in New York State). In 1964 Dr. Eli Friedman established the nation's first federally funded dialysis program at one of the institutions affiliated with Downstate—the University Hospital of Brooklyn. As a Downstate medical student Richard took a pharmacology course with Dr. Robert Furchgott, who was then doing the research in nitric oxide that earned him a Nobel Prize in 1998.

In the late 1960s Downstate was respected as a solid medical school with a terrific clinical program because of its affiliation with Kings County Hospital. It was not among the nation's elite medical colleges, lacking funding necessary to support the highest levels of faculty research, with a few exceptions noted above. But the connection with Kings County Hospital offered Downstate's students the opportunity to learn the fundamentals of medicine and proper patient care at one of the largest and busiest municipal hospitals in the country.

Downstate and Kings County Hospital were located in the East Flatbush neighborhood of Brooklyn, which was then in transition, as young and mostly minority black and Hispanic families were gradually replacing elderly middle-class Italians and Jews. Although the crime rate was rising in that vicinity (as it was throughout New York City), it was safe enough for Richard, who had experience in urban living from his years at Penn in Philadelphia. He knew which streets to visit for trips to a deli or a laundry, and he often took the subway to Manhattan to visit me and Susan and other friends.

During his first term at Downstate, Richard had the good fortune to meet a classmate, Peter Boorjian. Peter was looking for someone to occupy the second bedroom and share the rental fee for an apartment he had leased half a block from the campus. Rich and Peter turned out to be a good match as roommates and became close friends for their remaining three-and-a-half years at Downstate, even though they came from very different social backgrounds. Richard is a doctor's son and an Ivy Leaguer who was raised in a Jewish upper-middle class family. Peter is the child of Armenian immigrants, neither of whom made it past the eighth grade. Born in Hackensack Hospital in 1945 and raised in Rutherford and River Edge in Bergen County, he is a graduate of River Dell High School and Rutgers University.

Peter's parents (like Henry's mother and father) could not provide him with the guidance or the social and cultural advantages that Richard and the rest of us received from our families. But they did stress the value of an education, which enabled him to excel academically in high school while also gaining all-state wrestling honors. That helped him survive a highly competitive premedical program at Rutgers. Peter honored his father's desire that he place his education above his athletic career and chose to attend Rutgers over Lehigh University, even though Lehigh was a powerhouse in wrestling and had offered him an athletic scholarship. At first Peter was in awe of Richard, viewing him as very polished, sophisticated, intelligent, well educated, good looking, and athletic. He envisioned Rich as "flying loose and free" through his medical education. That was not the case, in that Richard's journey through four years at Downstate was hardly stress-free.

Over their first two years at Downstate Richard and Peter deepened their friendship through sports, social events, and even one special invitation that the Prager family extended to Peter. He enjoyed playing with Richard on a touch football team in games on Brooklyn Avenue. During one contest Peter ran into a chain link fence while chasing down a pass from Richard, which resulted in a bruised face and a nasty cut that required several stitches. Peter also joined in a few of our reunion touch football games at the Civic

Center in Hackensack over Thanksgiving and Christmas vacations. Shortly after the touch football mishap Richard's parents invited Peter to a Passover seder. He was at first quite anxious about attending, partly because of his black eye and bruised face, but also because he was not Jewish, had never attended a seder, and did not know what to expect. He appreciated how the Prager family warmly welcomed him to their home, put him at ease, and treated him with great kindness.

Many of Rich's classmates at Downstate were graduates of Brooklyn College or other city public institutions and were attending medical school on Regent scholarships. Rich called them the "tape recorder" guys, because they all sat in the first three rows so they could record all of the lectures for preparation for examinations. They had worked hard in college to gain admission and full scholarships to medical school, and were determined to succeed at Downstate. Rich knew that to be competitive with them he would have to match their efforts. Peter referred to them as "exponentially" beyond their classmates in their dedication to their coursework.

During their first three semesters Richard and Peter followed the traditional, classical medical school curriculum that had remained relatively unchanged in the United States over the previous half century. Professors lectured in a didactic and pedantic style on the basic scientific and medical principles, formulas, and facts. Given the protest culture of the `60s, especially student demands for curricular reforms at other universities, many Downstate medical students called on professors and administrators to revise the curriculum and the method of teaching. But when a few of their professors asked them for specific recommendations, the students did not know what to propose. Ultimately they responded with the standard complaints that they were sick and tired of classroom work and memorization. They wanted more contact with patients and more involvement with "the people." They wanted to learn more about how to become a physician, with less emphasis on learning chemical formulas—a short-sighted view, since to practice medicine properly they would have to know those formulas

Richard and some of his classmates at Downstate participated in antiwar protests. Like students all around the country, Richard was unsettled by the shootings of four students by National Guard troops at Kent State University in Ohio in early May 1970. Downstate and four other medical colleges in New York City suspended classes for a few days in protest. Richard and a few of his friends piled into his 1963 Valiant and drove to the nation's capital to participate in the antiwar rally held in Washington, D.C. on Saturday, May 9. They crashed in his sister Claire's apartment, sleeping on its living room floor. Rich and his fellow medical students from Downstate and other medical schools (most of whom were young, white, and male) manned first aid stations during the rally, during which 100,000 protesters gathered in 90-degree heat at the rear of the barricaded White House. The *New York Times* description of the crowd at the Ellipse near the Washington Monument compared the masses of youth with the scene at the Woodstock festival the previous summer. They heard Jane Fonda and other speakers demand the withdrawal of U.S. troops from Southeast Asia. Most of those present demonstrated peacefully, but there were a few violent confrontations between police and militants, who crashed through barricades, threw rocks, broke windows, and disrupted traffic.

Thanks to Claire's well-connected friends, Richard was able to meet privately on Capitol Hill with a few prominent legislators, including Representative William Widnall of New Jersey and Senator William Fulbright of Arkansas. Both were leading critics of the Vietnam War. Richard discussed his views and those of his peers with them, and they listened with concern. He remembers his participation in the antiwar event as a very special and broadening experience. As he explains: "I did not have the longest of hair and I knew what I wanted to be in life, but I did have quietly strong feelings."

The atmosphere at Downstate was intense and even cut-throat, and the professors were demanding and strict with their grading. Richard recalls: "The first year and a half you took Biochemistry and measured what was in urine; you memorized everything in Anatomy; had nightmares about the funny muscles in the body, and you had to regurgitate an amazing amount of information on your tests, so everyone studied." Rich experienced some compassionate treatment from Dr. Robert Furchgott, the pharmacology professor who later won a Nobel Prize. While discussing a Furchgott exam with a classmate just a few moments after he handed it in, Rich realized in a panic that he had not noticed the final page of the test. He immediately informed Dr. Furchgott about his error. Furchgott then asked if Rich knew what questions were on that sheet. Rich replied he did not, so he allowed him to complete the test. To this day Rich is grateful for that consideration.

Richard's primary goal at Downstate was to "make it through medical school" and that "dates and social opportunities were not a primary or secondary interest." So he and his roommate Peter spent most of their time in class or studying in their room or in the library, but occasionally they took a break in Manhattan for parties and mixers. Peter was impressed and even envious of Rich's social skills. But Richard was too focused on his medical training to indulge in a serious relationship, at least during his first two years at Downstate. Later in his medical school career he dated a friend of Susan's from Roslyn, Long Island, whom Susan had met as a teenager at Camp Che-Na-Wah in the Adirondacks. Their relationship lasted about a year, during which time the four of us enjoyed going to the movies, outings in Central Park, and trips to museums and concerts.

Rich and Peter began their training in clinical work towards the end of their second year, observing physicians at Kings County Hospital treat their patients. Rich's first year and a half had been very tense, but his spirits soared during the final months of his second year, when he began his rotations in specialized fields of patient care. He looked forward to going to the hospital every day, as he learned more about physical diagnosis and clinical medicine. His assigned tasks and time spent on duty were very demanding, but overall the work was easier than that required for the basic science subjects taught in the first three semesters.

Since Kings County was a major trauma center, Downstate's medical students benefited from an exceptionally extensive exposure to the treatment of a wide variety of injuries and acute illnesses. On some weekends it seemed as if Kings County Hospital's Emergency Room was in a war zone. One Friday evening, when Richard was a fourth-year student, he sprained his ankle playing basketball and went to the emergency room for a precautionary x-ray. When he arrived the place was packed with victims bleeding from knife and gunshot wounds. A staff member turned to Richard and said: "OK, while we're waiting to see you, could you sew up these lacerations?" Richard was happy to comply. An attending physician told Peter that on an average Friday night the number of gunshot and stabbing victims treated at the Kings County Emergency Room was comparable to the amount handled at the busiest field hospitals in Vietnam.

In Rich's final year the majority of his courses were electives. The Mayo Clinic in Rochester, Minnesota, offered resident scholarships for medical students, and he applied. Although he was turned down, he was eligible for funding for other programs at Mayo which would count toward his final year requirements at Downstate. Over three and a half months in the summer and fall of 1970 he thoroughly enjoyed investigating the unique style of medicine practiced at the Mayo Clinic. In his free time he bought a ten-speed mountain bike, trained with new friends for a hundred-mile bicycle race, and canoed on the back waters of the upper Mississippi River. The weather was gorgeous in Minnesota. Thus he was able to escape from the urban environment of Brooklyn, earn credits toward his M.D., and learn about a different approach to medicine—all the while enjoying the great outdoors in a scenic setting.

In his fourth and final year at Downstate Richard applied for internships in his preferred field of specialization—surgery. Richard's fascination with surgery goes back to science reports on the heart he wrote in eighth grade at State Street Junior High School. His fascination with surgical techniques grew as an undergraduate when he worked as an operating room technician at Hackensack Hospital. At Downstate, Rich had Dr. Dennis as an early role model. Yet despite Dennis's pioneering work in open heart surgery, during Richard's time at Downstate that specialty was still in its infancy. Richard observed some early heart procedures in an operating room amphitheater at Downstate, but he never scrubbed for a heart operation there.

Richard applied to eight highly rated programs in general surgery. He had interviews at Vanderbilt, the University of Michigan, Duke, Colorado University, Johns Hopkins, and UCLA. In September 1970, during his return trip to Brooklyn from the Mayo Clinic, he stopped off in Ann Arbor for a visit and squash matches with his cousin and an interview at Michigan's University Hospital.

Hospital internship and residency training programs conduct a "match day" each March, when candidates learn where they will receive their training. At Downstate the announcement of results was rather "sterile," in Richard's view. He walked into a lecture hall at Downstate and waited for a staff member to hold up an envelope with his name on it. Richard opened it and learned that his surgical training would be at the University Hospital of Michigan, in Ann Arbor. Michigan had an outstanding reputation and would prove to be an excellent place for him to begin his training as a surgeon.

In June 1971 Richard received his medical degree in a ceremony held at Brooklyn College. It was the first time that Rich had been on that campus. His proud parents attended. Prior to that special day Rich celebrated by visiting Coney Island. Shortly thereafter he and his roommate and fellow graduate Peter loaded their books, papers, and belongings into a truck driven by Peter's uncle. He helped them drop off the stuff at the Pragers' new apartment in the Whitehall on Prospect Avenue in Hackensack and the Boorjian residence in River Edge. Peter's uncle did not bother to pay the toll as they entered the Lincoln Tunnel, calling out to the guy in the booth: "Hey, we are all blue collar people and we don't have money to pay the toll."

Richard moved to Ann Arbor and began his internship in general surgery on July 1, 1971. His first year is a blur. Today he says: "I probably never slept, never went to the bathroom, and was probably petrified for a full twelve months." He rented an apartment five minutes from the University hospital, and was on call every other night. The regimen included a half year of general surgery, with rotations through a series of different surgical disciplines. These included abdominal and vascular surgery, neurosurgery, orthopedics, and urology, with special emphasis on how each pertained to general surgery. Five more years would pass before he was qualified to apply for a residency in thoracic (chest) surgery.

Medical interns and residents still were subject to the draft, but they had several options and could delay or even avoid service, depending on circumstances and the needs of the Pentagon. Richard had two options: the Public Health Service or one of the branches of the Armed Forces of the U.S. He declined an invitation to serve for two years in the Public Health Service on an Indian Reservation or a public health hospital. He then signed up for the Berry Plan, which permitted residents to extend their medical deferments until they completed their training in their specialty. As Rich progressed through his residency in thoracic surgery in the 1970s he was able to obtain further extensions. By then the Vietnam War had ended and the government was reassessing its need for physicians and surgeons. Thus because of reduced demand by the armed services for doctors and Richard's lengthy surgical residency, he was able to avoid the draft.

EPILOGUE: SIX GUYS TODAY

When Kevin celebrated his birthday in late October 1972 we were all twenty-seven years old. There was nothing particularly noteworthy about attaining that age—we had long since been old enough to drive a car, vote, or consume alcohol in New York and New Jersey. Our cohort was special in that we were in the vanguard of the first generation of baby boomers. We were all conceived during the final year of World War II and born during the days and weeks that followed victory over Germany and Japan. We were very lucky to grow up in an era and in a country that witnessed extraordinary economic growth, a significantly improved standard of living, and expanding opportunities—especially for white lower- and middle-class suburbanites. We were blessed with loving parents and good fortune during our childhood and adolescence and were well positioned for upward social mobility..

As young adults in the Sixties we navigated safely between the two poles of radicalism and conservatism, steering clear of the barricades and staying out of trouble. In politics and culture we leaned more to liberal reform than revolution, incorporating, reflecting, and sustaining our parents' faith in democracy and capitalism. We were all sympathetic (in varying degrees) to the civil rights movement. I campaigned for reform-minded politicians and conducted petition protests, and Barry Vasios worked to help displaced and unemployed people find housing and jobs, and he spoke at rallies in support of higher wages and better benefits for workers. Richard joined fellow medical students at the huge DC rally protesting the shooting of students at Kent State. He also voiced his opposition to the war to members of Congress. Henry was probably the most conservative of our group on political matters, but he traveled to Washington to pay his respects to John F. Kennedy as he passed by his coffin after the president was assassinated. We harbored doubts about the role of the United States in the Vietnam War, although like most of our peers our fear of the draft strongly influenced our views on that conflict. We loved our country, but we did not want to die in an unjust war. None of us seriously considered fleeing to Canada to avoid conscription into the military. Kevin and Barry Cohen enlisted in the Reserves; Henry, Richard and I obtained deferments; and Barry Vasios drew a high lottery number. We were cautious and rather conservative as we faced the temptations of the counterculture, except for our love of the new music of the era. We embraced the Beatles and Rolling Stones, the Motown sound, the protest songs of Joan Baez and Bob Dylan, and loved the Beach Boys, as they celebrated a California fantasy world of surfers, cool guys, fast cars, and cute girls.

We were not discouraged by the dismal conditions that we and the rest of our fellow citizens faced in the fall of 1972. We were fortified by the natural optimism of youth and by the self-confidence we had acquired from our prior accomplishments. As I commuted by subway from Union Square to

Riverdale to teach at Manhattan College, city streets were becoming dirtier and more dangerous. New York City's government teetered on the brink of bankruptcy. In early November Richard Nixon routed George McGovern in a landslide victory that gained him a second term as president, with only an inkling of the Watergate scandal that two years later would bring his administration to a startling and humiliating end. Shortly after that election the American economy began a long downward slide into "stagflation"—an unsettling combination of little or no growth in new jobs combined with a high rate of inflation. In foreign affairs Nixon was finally winding down the Vietnam War and would soon negotiate a peace treaty with all parties in Vietnam. But the result would be the first loss of a war by the United States as North Vietnam took control of all of Vietnam in 1975. The murder of Israeli athletes at the Munich Olympic Games in early September of 1972 gave us a shocking preview of international terrorism, which would escalate over the coming decades. The following year another Arab-Israeli war brought an oil shortage and the unprecedented sight of long lines of frustrated American motorists waiting to fill up their tanks at gas stations across the country.

We launched our careers during hard times, but better days lay ahead both for us and for Hackensack. The closing of the Arnold Constable department store on upper Main Street in February 1972 reflected the continuing slide of Hackensack's downtown shopping district. But the renovation of the building into offices for Bergen County's tax board, supervisor of elections, and other agencies also pointed toward the future expansion of governmental, legal services, and commercial offices I our town, even as a few more retailers closed their shops. However, it was not all doom and gloom on Main Street, because other stores were showing signs of life.

On the residential front, though the influx of Hispanics made Hackensack even more ethnically diverse, the town also continued to attract white middle-class families. Its public schools and overall quality of life remained strong enough to convince my brother and sister-in-law that it was a good place to raise their three daughters. At the upper end of the real estate market, affluent seniors, lured by spectacular views of the Manhattan skyline and the proximity to New York and suburban shopping malls, bought co-op and condominium apartments in the new luxury high-rise towers on Prospect and Overlook Avenues.

In 1972 Henry was already five years into a career that would span more than four decades as a scientist, business manager, and corporate executive in the consumer products and pharmaceutical industries. Along the way he survived five corporate mergers and divestitures, thriving by capitalizing on new opportunities and rising steadily to the upper echelon of management. His intelligence, work ethic, and especially his friendly, compassionate, and engaging personality and interpersonal skills made him a popular and valued colleague and endeared him to his supervisors. Yet he could never have risen as far as he did had he not also had complete command of a vast amount of technical information.

After brief employment at Avon Henry returned to his position as a research scientist at Shulton in 1972 He found himself in a new corporate environment, because the previous year American Cyanamid had acquired Shulton. He was promoted first to research group leader, responsible for a few chemists and laboratories, and then to section manager in product development for health and beauty aids. In the early '80s he became a director of fragrance development for upscale designer fragrances, including the Nina Ricci and Pierre Cardin brands. When Cyanamid sold off the fragrance division, Henry went back to Shulton. There he played a major role in the creation of Combat, an insect bait product that was designed to exterminate roaches. *Fortune* magazine ranked Combat as one of the top ten new consumer products for 1987, recognizing that it virtually eliminated the roach problem in millions of homes. In 1988 he made a major leap in Cyanamid's corporate hierarchy when he was appointed Division Director— reporting directly to Cyanamid's executive board. Henry was responsible for all consumer research and product development for well known global brands, including Old Spice, Breck, and Pine Sol.

When Cyanamid sold Shulton in 1991 Henry moved to Lederle Laboratories, a medical group and subsidiary of Cyanamid. In 1994 American Home Products took control of American Cyanamid in a hostile takeover. It then sold off many of its divisions to concentrate on pharmaceutical products, changing its name to Wyeth Corporation to reflect the company's new identity. During the late 1990s Henry became head of global operations for Wyeth Consumer Health Care, responsible for both domestic and international markets. Over the last five years of his career he concentrated on technical operations and product supply in Asia and Latin America. He contributed greatly to the growth of Wyeth's sales of its most popular over-the-counter drugs, including Centrum, Advil, and especially Caltrate in China. In both Latin America and Asia he worked with managers of local factories and third party suppliers of materials and manufacturers of Wyeth's brands of vitamins, dietary supplements, and over the counter drugs. After Pfizer acquired Wyeth in 2009 Henry was retained to focus on transition issues concerning operations in Asia. He retired in 2010 as Vice President of Technical Operations and Product Supply for the Intercontinental (Latin America and Asia) Region.

Henry reaped the rewards that came with his promotions. But his increasing responsibilities and travel took their toll on his marriage. Betty and Henry separated in 1995, but did not divorce. They still remain close today.

In 1972 Kevin completed his clerkship with federal Judge Murray Gurfein of the Southern District of New York and began full-time employment as an associate in the prestigious Manhattan law firm of Cleary, Gottlieb, Steen, & Hamilton. He rented an apartment in Greenwich Village. It did not take him long to realize he disliked living and working in such densely populated places, and the demands of his law firm assignments made him even more discontented. He was willing and eager to pursue an alternative career path in law. After two years with Cleary Gottlieb he accepted an invitation to join the faculty of Cornell Law School as an Assistant Professor, with a specialty in Civil Procedure. His relationship with Professor Benjamin Kaplan at Harvard Law School also began to pay major dividends, as he became the co-author with Kaplan and Richard Field of a bestselling casebook on Civil Procedure.

Over the following decades Kevin edited and authored numerous other casebooks, textbooks, collections of rules, plus dozens of scholarly articles. His teaching skills and his reputation as a legal scholar earned him promotions at Cornell to Associate Professor in 1977 and Professor of Law in 1980. He was further honored with endowed chairs—appointments as Flanagan Professor of Law (1989-2009) and Ziff Professor of Law (2009-present). The latter position was specially endowed for him by a former student—a first for Cornell Law School. In 1991 he taught one semester at Harvard Law School as the Henry J. Friendly Visiting Professor of Law. A Francophile since he was a teenager, in the mid-1990s he founded a Cornell Law School extension program in Paris, which offered courses in international law. In 2008, in recognition of his writings on civil procedure and international law and his many years of service to legal education in France, the government of France honored Kevin with membership in the French Legion of Honor. Not too shabby for a kid from Hackensack—even one who was our high school class valedictorian.

Kevin never regretted leaving the lucrative but pressure-packed world of Wall Street law for the pastoral setting of Ithaca and the laid-back academic lifestyle at Cornell. Kevin drove himself just as hard as a law professor as he would have labored as a partner in a "white-shoe" law firm. The crucial difference is that as a law professor and writer he became his own boss and thus controlled his own work schedule. Although his choice of an academic career probably cost him a small fortune in lifetime income, his salary at Cornell and royalties from his casebooks and textbooks enabled him and his family to live very well, and it doesn't hurt that the cost of living in upscale Cayuga Heights is considerably lower than that of Manhattan or suburban New York.

Kevin married Pamela Cummings in 1979. Their daughter Adrienne Shaine was born in 1986. After Kevin's divorce from Pam in 1994 they shared custody of Adrienne. In 2001 he married a Cornell Law School colleague, Emily Sherwin. The following year their daughter Jian Louise was born in China. Kevin and Emily adopted her in 2003. Adrienne majored in international relations at the Woodrow Wilson School of Princeton University and graduated Phi Beta Kappa with honors in 2009. Thus, in his mid-sixties, Kevin has a brilliant and accomplished adult daughter and an energetic and delightful pre-teenager who keeps her parents fully occupied.

By the end of 1972 Barry Cohen had been teaching in Park Ridge for two years and was still learning the tricks of the trade in the teaching profession. The following year he earned his Master's at Rutgers. In 1975 he completed his six years in the Army Reserves and was honorably discharged as a Specialist 5—equivalent to a Sergeant. During his thirty-two year career at Park Ridge High School he coached tennis for one season and was faculty advisor to the Student Council for many years. In recognition of his outstanding achievement as a teacher he was selected twice for inclusion in *Who's Who in American Teaching*, and was honored as Teacher of the Year at Park Ridge. After he retired from full time employment in 2002 he became a substitute teacher at the Dwight Englewood School in Englewood.

In December 1977 Barry married Debra Bell. They lived in an apartment in Belleville until the fall of 1980, when they purchased a house in New Milford. Debra ("Debbie") worked in a variety of jobs over the years, mainly in decorating or jewelry sales. Their daughter Amanda ("Mandy") was born in 1981. She graduated from the University of the Arts in Philadelphia in May 2004 and earned a Masters degree in art education in 2005. Currently employed as an art teacher in Bethlehem Township, New Jersey, she married Matt Esposito in December 2009.

In 2007 Barry and Debbie relocated to Yarmouth Port on Cape Cod. For the first few years they missed their life in New Jersey, but then they began enjoying what living on the Cape year-round has to offer. Barry is an active participant in the Academy for Life Long Learning at Cape Cod Community College, attending lectures and coordinating a sports class for seniors. In recent years Barry has struggled with health issues that have limited his mobility, but despite some disabilities he retains his optimistic and spirited outlook. He maintains his lifelong friendships with our group and several colleagues from his years at Park Ridge High School. He remains an avid sports fan. Though he still harbors some loyalty to New York teams, he also enjoys following the fortunes of the Red Sox, Patriots, Celtics and Bruins.

During my first decade at Manhattan College I taught introductory courses in U.S. history, developed upper level electives in American cultural and intellectual history and New York City history, and founded and served as Director of an American Studies program. I was promoted to Associate Professor in 1980 and Professor in 1988. In 1984 I was elected Chair of the History Department. I held that that position for seventeen years.

In the late 1970s I began to concentrate on a subject dear to my heart—the social and cultural history of American sports, with emphasis on its social class, ethnic, racial, and gender aspects. During the early 1980s I introduced an interdisciplinary upper division elective on sports and American society for the American Studies program. I later revised it for major credit in the History and Sociology departments and taught versions of that course in summer sessions at Newark Rutgers, the School of General Studies at Columbia, and Cornell. During the 1990s I served as a member of

Major League Baseball's Committee for Statistical and Historical Accuracy and was a consultant for Ken Burns's PBS documentary on baseball history. Over the past twenty years I have written and edited several reference works and monographs in American sports history, including *Baseball and Cricket: The Creation of American Team Sports, 1838-72;* volumes 3 and 4 of *Sports in North America: A Documentary History;* the *Encyclopedia of Ethnicity and Sports in the United States; Baseball in Blue and Gray: The National Pastime during the Civil War* and *Golf in America.*

In 1973 Susan and I bought a small house in Montclair. That year Susan began a five-year doctoral program in Educational Psychology at Yeshiva University in New York City. She earned her Ph.D. in 1978 and two years later was certified as a psychologist in New York and New Jersey. She opened a private practice in Montclair in 1981 and completed postdoctoral training at the Institute for Contemporary Psychotherapy and the Center for the Study of Anorexia and Bulimia in New York City. We moved to a larger and grander house in Glen Ridge in 1984.

Susan brilliantly combined her professional responsibilities with her family obligations. Over her twenty–six year career as a psychologist she became well known for her compassionate and effective treatment of her patients. She was a loving and devoted mother to our only child, Adam Lavitt Kirsch, who was born on August 19, 1981. Adam graduated from Glen Ridge High School in 1999 and earned a B.S. degree from Brown University in May 2003 and a Ph.D. in Mathematics and Computer Science from Harvard University in 2008. He married Ana DiRago in August 2011. He is currently a Software Engineer with Google and lives in Silicon Valley.

In the fall of 1972 Richard still had six years of postdoctoral training in general and thoracic surgery to complete at the University of Michigan. His first academic appointment was as an Assistant Professor of Surgery at Vanderbilt Medical Center in Nashville, starting in July of 1978 as an associate of Drs. Harvey Bender and John Hammon.

In the summer of 1983 he returned to Ann Arbor and joined the Section of Cardiac and Thoracic Surgery at St. Joseph Mercy Hospital. In July 1984 he renewed his affiliation with the University of Michigan's Section of Thoracic Surgery when he was appointed Clinical Associate Professor. Since his relocation to Ann Arbor he has also held administrative positions at St. Joseph Mercy Hospital as Associate Head, Department of General Surgery; and Head, Section of Cardiac & Thoracic Surgery, In July 1999 Richard was recruited "across town" to become the Head of the Division of Adult Cardiac Surgery at the University of Michigan. He resumed his academic career when was promoted to Professor in the Department of Surgery and was appointed a Director of the University of Michigan's Cardiovascular Center.

Richard is respected as a highly skilled surgeon who over the decades has kept up-to-date on innovations in heart procedures. He has also served with distinction as an educator, medical administrator, and clinical research scientist. His bibliography of academic publications lists over 70 scholarly medical articles and nine chapters in textbooks. He has made major contributions to the study of cardiovascular disease and to the evolution of new methods of open heart surgery. More important, whenever any of us experiences any serious medical problems (which happens more frequently these days) Rich is compassionate and willing to help us sort through our options. While we do not see him very often, we count on him for expert medical advice.

In his family life, Richard's first marriage ended in divorce after twelve years. He arranged his schedule so that his two children could live in his home for half of each week. His son, Jeremy David Prager, was born in 1976, and graduated from Duke University. He became the third generation of Prager men to become a doctor when he earned an M.D. from Washington University in St. Louis. He is as an Assistant Professor of Pediatric Otolaryngology at Denver's Children's Hospital and a faculty member at the University of Colorado. Jeremy married Amanda Reid, his high school sweetheart. They have two daughters: Rachel (born in 2006) and Olivia (born in 2008). Richard's daughter, Eliza McKay Prager, was born in 1978, graduated from Colorado College, and earned a graduate degree as an Occupational Therapy Doctor and a Master's in Clinical Study Design from Washington University. She is an occupational therapist in St. Louis.

In late 1999 Richard married Lauren Groves, an accomplished architect. Her three children and Richard's son and daughter grew up together in Ann Arbor. After Lauren and Richard married they and their five offspring bonded together as members of an extended family. Lauren's oldest child, Meghan, was born in 1978 and is a vice president in Health Care Finance at JP Morgan. She married William T. Armstrong. Their daughter Gwendolyn was born in 2010. Laurie's second daughter, Mary O'Keefe, born in 1980, is a physician and a resident at the University of Colorado. Her son T. J. O'Keefe was born in 1982 and is engaged to be married in the summer 2012. An architect with a Master's from Penn, he owns a design firm in Chicago.

Barry Vasios completed his nine-month clerkship in Manhattan in 1972 with federal Judge Arnold Bauman of the United States District Court for the Southern District of New York. He then joined the law firm of Donovan, Leisure, Newton, and Irvine as an Associate. After being admitted to the New York Bar in 1973, he concentrated in commercial and international litigation, handling cases involving antitrust, securities, contract, legal malpractice, reinsurance, trusts and estates, and environmental issues. After leaving Donovan, Leisure in 1975 he became an Associate at Breed, Abbott, and Morgan. In 1985 he became a partner with Gilbert, Segall, and Young, and in 2001 he became a partner in Holland and Knight LLP when it merged with Gilbert, Segall, and Young.

Now entering his fifth decade of practicing law in a highly competitive elite arena, Barry is highly respected as a first-rate litigator. Over the years Barry provided counsel on many cases that involved significant legal issues, including those in which he represented foreign clients and governments. As a young associate he worked on a case for Paul McCartney, freeing his royalties from an attachment order obtained by the former manager of the Beatles. On the international front he successfully represented the Republic of Lebanon in defeating an attempt to attach its assets in New York; and the Government of Dubai, which was sued in the Southern District of New York on claims that certain creditors were unfairly treated in bankruptcy proceedings in Dubai. He represented the Finnish government-owned liquor monopoly in litigation in New York. He also represented Rolls-Royce PLC as a secured creditor in the bankruptcy cases of Eastern Airlines and Trans World Airlines. Overall he has represented many foreign clients, especially Finnish and other European companies who conduct business in the United States. He also has represented large international law firms in commercial disputes and malpractice claims.

Barry's record of achievement earned him recognition in *The Best Lawyers in America*, Guide in Commercial Litigation, 2005-2011; New York *Super Lawyers* magazine, 2006-2008, 2010; and Corporate Counsel Edition, *Super Lawyers* magazine. He has also been a guest lecturer at the New York City Bar Association and has spoken in many sessions of Kevin's civil procedure courses at Cornell Law School.

After her marriage to Barry at the Yale Chapel in 1973, Cheryl enrolled in Hunter College to complete her college education, earning her B.A. in 1977. (She had begun her undergraduate work at Quinnipiac College, but had to drop out after her father died. She then took courses at Southern Connecticut State College while she dated Barry.) In 1980 she gave birth to their first child, Alison, in April, earned a degree from Brooklyn Law School in June, and passed the New York State Bar Examination in July. Their younger daughter, Carrie, was born in 1985. Cheryl also earned professional certifications as a financial advisor and real estate agent and has taught in public and private schools in New York City.

Alison graduated from Cornell University's College of Arts and Sciences in 2002, married John Flannery in 2010, and is now a teacher in a private school in Brooklyn. Carrie graduated from Yale in 2007, earned a Master's of Fine Arts in Fiction Writing from Columbia in 2010, and now is the San Francisco Bureau Chief for the online food magazine, "Serious Eats."

Shortly after Susan and I were married we began hosting annual reunions of the six guys and their spouses or girlfriends on New Year's Eve. After we moved to Montclair in 1973 we continued the tradition for nearly twenty-five years, gathering either on New Year's Eve or New Year's Day in Manhattan or New Jersey. After Richard left for Ann Arbor in 1971 and Kevin moved to Ithaca in 1974 they could only join us on a few occasions. The remaining four couples became the core group. When we turned forty in 1985 we met over a rainy weekend in August for a joint birthday party at Henry's rental beach house on Long Beach Island on the Jersey Shore. In 1994 all six guys attended a New Year's Eve event (at that point Richard and Kevin were divorced). The separation of Henry and Betty in 1995 effectively ended the New Year's Eve tradition.

In June 1992 I initiated an annual group pilgrimage to Ithaca to visit Cornell, reconnect with Kevin, and get acquainted with his daughter Adrienne. After 2001 our trips enabled us to get to know Emily and the fun-loving Jian. In Ithaca we renew our childhood competitiveness, but now with a reversal of fortunes. Barry Vasios, the best athlete of our group in youth, no longer participates in games that are more strenuous than bowling, and Henry, never a stand-out athlete, is the perennial champion in golf. Over the last few summers I have taught a sports history course at Cornell, so I have enjoyed spending time with Kevin's family for two months each year. Ithaca is also a favorite destination for Barry Vasios. His older daughter Alison is an alumnae of Cornell, and once a semester he delivers guest lectures in Kevin's Civil Procedure course at Cornell Law School. So Ithaca has replaced Hackensack as the guys' favored playground. We spend way too much time talking about the good old days in school, Boy Scouts, sports, and our college and graduate school days. We are aging—(not so gracefully). There is no turning back the clock. You can't live in the past all the time; but sometimes remembering our back pages helps us "get by with a little help from our friends."

Four of us with our wives and children at our fortieth birthday celebration at a house Henry and Betty rented on the Jersey shore, mid-August 1985. We retained an aura of youth. Our wives radiated beauty, and our kids were adorable. My son Adam is at the bottom center. Barry Vasios is sitting behind him holding Carrie. Left to right: Susan and George, Betty and Henry, Cheryl (with Alison in front), Barry Cohen and Debbie (with daughter Mandy in front).

After Richard moved to Ann Arbor and Kevin went to Ithaca it was a rare occasion when all six guys attended the New Year's Eve reunion. This is the group in 1994, a few years after the divorces of Richard and Kevin. Susan and I are front and center. From left to right are Barry Cohen, Debbie, Cheyl and Barry, Kevin, Henry, Betty, and Richard.

Our second Ithaca getaway weekend, June 1994. From left, front row: Kevin, Barry Vasios, George; back row, Richard, Henry, Barry Cohen.

CPSIA information can be obtained at www.ICGtesting.com
Printed in the USA
BVOW04s1215130914

366646BV00007B/56/P